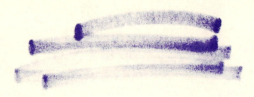

FROM GOOD GODDESS TO VESTAL VIRGINS

FROM GOOD GODDESS TO VESTAL VIRGINS

Sex and category in Roman religion

Ariadne Staples

London and New York

First published 1998
by Routledge
11 New Fetter Lane, London EC4P 4EE

Simultaneously published in the USA and Canada
by Routledge
29 West 35th Street, New York, NY 10001

© 1998 Ariadne Staples

Typeset in Garamond by
Poole Typesetting (Wessex) Limited
Bournemouth, Dorset

Printed and bound in Great Britain by
MPG Books Ltd, Bodmin, Cornwall

British Library Cataloguing in Publication Data
A catalogue record for this book is available from the British Library

Library of Congress Cataloguing in Publication Data
Staples, Ariadne
From Good Goddess to Vestal Virgins : Sex and Category in Roman
Religion / Ariadne Staples.
p.   cm.
Includes bibliographical references and index.
1. Women and religion – Rome.   2. Rome – Religion.
3.   Women – Rome.   4.   Rome – Social life and customs.   I.   Title.
BL815.W6S73   1998
292.07′082–dc21   98–7381

ISBN 0–415–13233–9

To the memory of my father
and to my mother
with my love

CONTENTS

CONTENTS

PREFACE

This book is a revised version of my doctoral dissertation. I should like to begin by thanking the Cambridge Commonwealth Trust, whose generous grant made it all possible.

Over the years many people have read various versions of different chapters, and given generously of their time and expertise. This book is immeasurably better for their insights. It is impossible to thank them individually but I would like to record here my debt to them all. Some however have gone so far beyond the call of duty or even of friendship that I cannot let this opportunity pass by without mentioning them with special gratitude.

John Crook steered me through the intricacies of Roman Law, a subject with which I had very little acquaintance when I first went to him for help. Under his guidance I realized that the law was both fascinating and fun. His enthusiasm for his subject proved so infectious that I decided to make law my life's work. I should also like to thank him for his unwavering belief that this study should be published. It was that belief, and his insistence that I get on with the job no matter what, that kept me at the task of revision when the added burden of a Yale law school curriculum made it at times almost intolerable.

I should also like to thank Mary Beard, who was a dedicated and conscientious dissertation supervisor. It was while I was being supervised by Keith Hopkins for a term that, encouraged by him, I started reading works of anthropology; this would have been a very different book if I hadn't. Joyce Reynolds spent far more hours than she should have reading various versions of different chapters and her meticulous comments saved me from many an error. Richard Saller and John Scheid both took time during their brief visits to Cambridge to read my drafts and talk to me about them.

I thank Jack Holtsmark for his friendship and encouragement while I was living in Iowa City. He actually read the entire dissertation and took the time to give me careful written and verbal comments. Jim Whitman is still waiting patiently for two class papers that I owe him from my first year in law school. He has always been a sympathetic listener to a harried student's tales of woe about a book that never seems to get finished. To all of them I say thank you. But my greatest debt, I think, is to Jeremy Tanner. His friendship and support through good times and bad, and his steady conviction that I could do it, gave me the courage I needed to pull it all together.

I hope they all enjoy this book despite its numerous shortcomings which are my responsibility entirely.

New Haven
January 1997

INTRODUCTION

The last couple of decades have seen a remarkable evolution in the study of women in antiquity. Forty years ago Charles Seltman could write with a straight face, '"Women." There is no need to attempt a definition. We are always with them and they with us' (Seltman 1956: 15). Or more astonishing yet, 'Woman has always been able to maintain her right to unpredictability, and this, which is really part of her charm, has supplied her with a perpetual strategic advantage over the predictable ways and thoughts of her males' (*ibid.*: 20). A few years later Balsdon in a monograph devoted to *Roman Women: Their History and Habits*, wrote that 'the history of early Rome was written by men . . . [who] . . . appreciated the fact that women as a sex were obviously of no great historical importance' (Balsdon 1962: 25). For many years Balsdon's was the definitive work on Roman women.

The change in the historiographical landscape today is startling. There is a prolific and constantly expanding literature on women in antiquity.[1] The study of women is now of fundamental importance to the study of cultural history. Scholarship on ancient women has developed in two directions. First there has been a surge of interest in precisely those areas of human existence in which women's roles have always been pivotal and acknowledged as such: family, marriage, child rearing and so forth. At the same time, legal scholars have focused attention on women's legal status and the ways in which it changed and developed over time. Second, scholars have tried to identify ways in which women were culturally constructed and defined. This is an ongoing attempt to understand not only what it meant to be a woman in the ancient world (the subjective experience of women), but also how women were perceived both by themselves and by men (the objective experience).

1

This book is a study in the latter tradition. It is a book about women's participation in Roman religion, but it is not a book about Roman religion as women experienced it. I do not tell a story about fertility rites or all-female festivals or virgin priestesses, although they all figure prominently in the tale. It is rather about how religion constructed and defined women; how Roman cults and rituals both created and reflected a society's perception of its female members.

The question that may be considered the starting point of my enquiry is why Roman women were never allowed a constitutional role – not even the basic right to vote. Roman women of the late Republican period (roughly the period I concern myself with in this book) were, from a late twentieth-century perspective, something of a paradox.[2] Freed from the tedious chores of domesticity by (often very great) personal wealth,[3] Roman women enjoyed a remarkable degree of social and financial independence despite the heavily male dominated society in which they lived. Many were, to judge from the representations of women such as Cornelia (mother of the Gracchi), Servilia (mother of Brutus), Sempronia (who participated in Catiline's conspiracy), or Hortensia (daughter of the orator, Hortensius), accomplished, highly educated, politically competent, and indeed sometimes possessed of considerable political influence as well.[4] Guy Fau, for example, traces the 'emancipation' of the Roman woman, showing what enormous strides women made socially, economically and juridically (Fau 1978). But despite their extraordinary achievements and accomplishments women never did achieve any degree of political authority in their own right. Nor did they ever pose a real threat to the political dominance of men. Some scholars would challenge this observation. Nicholas Purcell argues, for example, that Roman women were more powerful politically than they have been given credit for (Purcell 1986). But he fails to make the critical distinction between the informal influence women wielded through their relationships and connections with men, and the legitimate constitutional authority vested in men. Similarly Richard Bauman has described in careful detail how women not only played a part in but even influenced the political process (Bauman 1992). Both accounts are valuable in demonstrating that Roman women were politically sophisticated and eminently capable of effective political action. This accords perfectly with the theme of 'emancipation'. But it begs a huge question. Why, if women were manifestly capable of participating in the political process, did they never succeed in acquiring a legitimate constitutional role? Why was their political involvement always either a 'politics of protest' as Bauman calls it, or a politics of individual influence? Bauman gives plenty of examples of women organizing themselves in order to wring concessions out of the political system. The protest against the Oppian Law is one such example; another is Hortensia's protest before the triumvirs against the unfair taxation of women (*ibid.*: 31 and 81). But if women were capable of this kind of organization – and there is no reason to doubt that they were – why was there never any attempt at a 'struggle of the sexes' along the lines of the 'struggle of the orders'? It is a fact – something rare in the study of women in antiquity – that Roman citizen women never had the vote. While women for one reason or another, individually or in groups, were undoubtedly politically powerful, this is no substitute for legitimate political authority. Why did these women never seek such authority? The question becomes even more compelling when we are faced with evidence that despite women's political incapacity men feared that they could, and would (unless kept firmly in their place), usurp power and undermine the very structure of male dominated society. Men perceived the public, collective action of women as a threat to the stability of the male establishment.[5]

Despite this fear there was one area where the public, collective action of women was not merely tolerated, but was actively encouraged. *Religious ritual provided the single public space where women played a significant formal role.*[6] It is only in the domain defined and demarcated by ritual that we find 'ordinary' women acting formally, collectively and publicly sometimes alongside men, sometimes apart. Moreover, women's public religious activity, far from being perceived as threatening, was sanctioned by the male establishment, even deemed vital for the well-being of the polity. In Rome, where religion and politics formed virtually a single cultural institution, women's complete exclusion from one aspect of it and prominence in the other is noteworthy. Can the prominence of women in religion help provide an answer to the puzzle of their absence in politics? What can Roman religion – cults, rituals, festivals – tell us about Roman women? And how can we be sure that the image that a study of religion yields is not distorted?

The answer to the last question is of course that we can never be sure. But if the image of Roman women as seen from the perspective of religion is consistent with images seen from other social and cultural perspectives, law say, or satire, or myth, the image acquires a degree of plausibility. To understand this notion by means of a metaphor, consider Monet's studies of the cathedral at Rouen.[7] Monet produced thirty studies of the cathedral at Rouen. Each one is different, building on the artist's experience, reflecting different light and shade from the different time of day. It is the same cathedral, but each representation is different; each study constitutes just one view of the cathedral. But each study contributes to the others and through them all, individually and collectively, we begin to appreciate Monet's experience of the cathedral. A study of Roman women from the perspective of Roman religion is one view of the cathedral.

Roman religion, however, is not alone in its attempt to define and construct Roman women. There are other views of the cathedral: Roman law, for example, or Roman myth or Roman lyric poetry or Roman satire. What unites these different views into a kind of coherence is the concept of 'Romanness'. So I begin with the fundamental assumption that Roman culture, in the broadest possible sense of that term, is a system. Each aspect of that system operated in a different way but generated meaning within the same bounds and constraints that affect all the other aspects of the system. Thus Roman women as constructed by their religion, for example, are recognizable as the Roman women constructed by, say, Roman law. Each is a different view of the cathedral.

That notion of a system must, for the moment, be taken as an article of faith. It is not susceptible of independent proof, at least not in a book of this scope. One way to test the hypothesis, however, is to approach the same question from a variety of perspectives to see if we are left with a reasonably coherent outline or with irreconcilably different representations. If the picture of Roman women drawn from religion is unrecognizable from the picture drawn by law or myth or politics even, then the idea of Roman culture as a system becomes hard to defend. If not, the idea is not only defensible but is very helpful in filling out the inevitable gaps created by the very nature of ancient historical evidence. Thus Roman law can provide clues to puzzles encountered in Roman myth, Roman myth clues to puzzles encountered in Roman religion and so forth.

My contention that Roman women played a central role in religion goes against the grain of the current orthodoxy which would accord such prominence only to priestesses such as the Vestal

Virgins, the *flaminica Dialis*, or the *Regina Sacrorum*.[8] The ordinary Roman woman, according to this argument, was almost entirely excluded from active roles in the religious community.

The orthodox argument begins like this: Roman women, as far as their religious roles were concerned, were of two kinds. There were, on the one hand, the ordinary women who played very little part in religion and there were priestesses, who were exceptions to this rule. It was only the priestesses, female religious functionaries, that were important to the civic religion. However, the religious functions of these women were so specific, carefully defined and removed from the common experience of ordinary Roman women, that they cannot be subsumed under the category of women for purposes of analysis. Therefore women as a sex had no religious importance.

This argument is seriously flawed. The religious roles of female priestesses were indeed very different from that of the average woman. But then so were the roles of their male counterparts very different from that of the average man. The *flamen Dialis* and the *Rex Sacrorum*, for example, had ritual duties and obligations that set them conspicuously apart from other men.[9] For that matter the specifically religious duties of the pontiffs or the augurs or any of the other numerous male religious functionaries were also quite different from those of any other male. But nobody would conclude from this that men in general did not have meaningful roles to play in religion or that their roles were marginal.

The orthodox argument then becomes circular. If women played a marginal role in religion, then the cults that they participated in must necessarily be marginal. '[Women] were so thoroughly excluded from Roman religion that they frequented suburban sanctuaries and the temples of foreign gods, and . . . threw themselves into all sorts of deviant religious practice and thought' (Scheid 1992a: 377). The temples of 'foreign gods' thus frequented by women included those of Mater Matuta, Venus Verticordia, Fortuna Muliebris and Bona Dea, for the rites of these deities were performed by women. These constituted the 'fringe' of Roman religion. 'Women participated in the ceremonies of imported cults, those governed (in Roman eyes at any rate) by the Greek rite. . . . [I]n some cults . . . they mingled with slaves and others from the fringes of Roman society' (*ibid.*: 397). This is an incautious definition of the religious fringe. One of the oldest and most revered foci of Roman worship, the cult of Hercules Invictus at the *Ara Maxima*, was by Republican times in charge of public slaves.[10] Its

rites were conducted according to Greek custom – *Graeco ritu* –
with head uncovered.[11] But most significantly, this rite was strictly
forbidden to women. The cult of Hercules at the *Ara Maxima* was
exclusively a male cult. Men such as Sulla and Crassus were known
to have participated – and participated spectacularly – in the rites,
both sacrificing, according to custom, a tithe of their enormous
wealth by feasting the Roman populace at the altar.[12] In charge of
public slaves, its perceived Greek origins manifestly affirmed in
ritual practice, this cult, together with the elite Roman men who
participated in it, ought, within the terms of the orthodox argument, to be consigned to the fringes of Roman religion – surely an
absurd proposition.

While no one has suggested that the cult of the *Ara Maxima* was
marginal to the civic religion, the cult of Bona Dea is an accepted
example of marginality. But we need to think again. The
December rites of Bona Dea, nocturnal, secret, forbidden to men,
might at first glance appear to exemplify marginality. Nevertheless
this rite was conducted annually not in 'a suburban sanctuary' but
in the house of a magistrate with *imperium*, a consul's house – as
in 63 BC in Cicero's – or a praetor's house – as in 62 BC in Caesar's.
Moreover, the ceremony was conducted by the Vestal Virgins, who
belonged to the ranks of the priestesses who are widely acknowledged to have played a central role in the civic religion. Cicero
described this rite as being *pro populo* or *pro saluti populi*. It is
difficult to reconcile such a description with marginality.

In effect then, the orthodox theory boils down to an argument
that women's cults were *ipso facto* marginal. This is profoundly
unsatisfactory for it renders the bulk of our evidence on women's
religious activities residual. Women participated in rites that were
indisputably important to the civic system. For example, on 1
March, the beginning of the old Roman year, married women,
matronae, performed rites to Mars Gradivus.[13] This was the same
deity who presided over the *Salii*, male priests chosen from the
elite, who with ritual dance and song paraded through the streets
of Rome with the *ancilia*, or the sacred shields, one of which was
the pledge of Roman power believed to have been given to Numa
by Jupiter himself. One of the occasions when the procession of
the *Salii* took place was on 1 March.[14] It is very difficult to justify
an argument that would have the role of the *Salii* central to the
civic religion, and the role of the *matronae*, in rites to the same
god on the same day, marginal.

Women's ritual activities extended beyond their regular duties at annual festivals. They were sometimes called upon to perform ritually at times of crisis in the state. Most of our evidence for this is in connection with rites for the expiation of prodigies. These rites varied in form, which appear to have depended on the recommendations of the religious functionaries involved – *haruspices*, *decemvirs*, more rarely *pontifices*. Sometimes they were performed by magistrates alone, sometimes by men, sometimes by women divided into the sexual categories of *matronae* and virgins, sometimes by two or more of these groups acting together.[15] These rituals were often public, with the participants processing through the streets or from temple to temple. There is absolutely no evidence to suggest that women's roles on such occasions were considered less important than men's. We are not justified in seeing them as marginal.

Nevertheless, although women did participate in the rituals and festivals of the civic religion, they were absent at the political interface of religion. Scheid is right when he says that religious power was wielded only by men. Where religion impinged on public policy women had no voice.

> Public sacerdotal responsibilities were always exercised by men. Important public liturgies were presided over by magistrates, sometimes assisted by priests chosen from among the people of Rome. Priests and magistrates shared the responsibilities of the res publica and formulated and interpreted sacred law. Only they were authorised to announce the will of the gods, determined by consulting auspices or the Sibylline Books. Together with the Senate, the magistrates examined any religious problems that arose and in consultation with the priests prescribed remedies. . . . Since the public religion was limited to these prescribed activities, religious power was almost entirely in the hands of these men.
>
> (Scheid 1992a: 378)

This is scarcely surprising for, as we know, women had no political authority, and in Rome priesthoods and magistracies often went hand in hand. Indeed Scheid's words are a modern echo of Cicero:

> Among the many divinely inspired expedients of government established by our ancestors, there is none more striking than

that whereby they expressed their intention that the worship of the gods and the vital interests of the state should be entrusted to the direction of the same individuals.

(Cic., *Dom.*, 1.1)[16]

If women had no religious authority to make and impose decisions, it is logical to infer that women's religious roles were sanctioned by men.[17] Why were women allowed – assigned? – public roles in religion? One function of this book is to explore this question. The book is structured as a selective study of cults and rituals in which women played an important part. Each chapter has as its primary focus a single cult or – in chapter 2 – two thematically related cults. To an extent the choice of cults has been arbitrary, but they are all ones in which the dominant female role is defined by a male role which is sometimes overt, sometimes covert but always present if understated. It is in fact the male role in each of these cults that is critical to an understanding of the role that the women play. The cults I have chosen to examine are those of Bona Dea, Ceres, Flora, Venus and Vesta. I have examined only those aspects of the cults that are concerned with gender and sexuality.

Finally, I must briefly return to the idea of a system – this time my thesis is that Roman religion is itself a system, a complex network of meaningfully related cults and rituals. Polytheistic religions, including Roman religion, have by and large been treated as a congeries of separate cults and ritual practices. As Alan Wardman puts it,

> [I]t is difficult for those who are used to monotheism or a theistic philosophy to detect any sign of order within this multitude of deities and divine powers. It seems at first sight to be no more than an anarchy of tradition and novelties.
>
> (Wardman 1982: 3)

The assumption underlying my analysis, however, is that Roman religion was more than an arbitrary collection of cults, each fulfilling a function independent of the others. Rather I proceed on the assumption that the different cults confer meaning on each other, and are related according to the various ways in which such meanings are generated. Again this thesis is not susceptible of independent proof. Rather I hope that the richness of meaning generated by it will provide its justification.

Part I

THE CULT OF
BONA DEA

INTRODUCTION TO
CHAPTER 1

Roman religion ritualizes the dichotomy between male and female in complex ways. The cult of Bona Dea is a striking example of this complexity. On a superficial level Bona Dea appears to have been defined by sexual exclusiveness. The best known feature of her cult was a festival which permitted only participation by women, from which men were excluded on pain of sacrilege. Indeed men might not even know the ritual details of the cult, much less witness them. Sexual exclusiveness in itself is not unusual in ancient religions and is often presented as a commonplace ritual feature of one cult or another. But the literary sources for the cult of Bona Dea insist upon this exclusiveness with a stridency so unwonted as to seem suspicious. And indeed there is evidence that men did play some role in the cult. We have evidence of votive offerings made to the goddess by men, and a cryptic remark by Ovid suggests that men might have had some formal sacral role to play.

Most of the rhetoric of sexual exclusiveness focuses on the festival celebrated in early December by women only. It stems mainly from Cicero and carries a distinct political tinge to it. But Cicero does not exaggerate the importance of the feature of sexual exclusiveness to this festival. The cult presents men and women as distinct ritual categories. The ritual details of the cult – at least the ones we know about – all appear to be variations on the theme of male avoidance. These details parallel in their elaborateness the exaggerated rhetoric of exclusiveness, and like that rhetoric invite scepticism by their very elaborateness. In this chapter I analyse the myth and ritual of the cult and argue that while men were physically barred from the December festival, the ritual details were meant to invoke their symbolic presence. The thesis of this chapter is that the December festival of the Bona Dea is not just about

11

women as is commonly supposed (see e.g., Versnel 1993) but about the relationship between men and women.

The cult of Bona Dea established a boundary between male and female. But the boundary was not a barrier. The physical exclusion of men was not meant to symbolise a total absence of the male from the cult. On the contrary the ritual features as well as the aetiological myths performed the more complex task of exploring the nature of male–female relationships. The aetiological myths connected Bona Dea with Hercules Invictus and his cult at the *Ara Maxima*, and with Faunus, both of whom were objects of sacrifice in the civic religion. The two myths represented the two extremes of male–female relationships. On the one hand, the story of Bona Dea and Faunus, which was explicitly intended to account for the goddess' abhorrence of men, dealt with the theme of incest – a form of sexual intercourse that was manifestly and unequivocally unlawful. On the other, the story of Bona Dea and Hercules explored the lawful way in which male and female could come together – marriage. These contradictory themes of union through marriage and sexual avoidance were also reflected in the ritual details of the cult. Thus despite the rhetoric of the cult, which appears to suggest that the boundary that the ritual established between male and female was a solid and uncrossable barrier, the myth and ritual itself explored ways in which that boundary might be negotiated.

Fire and water; wine and milk; violence; these are some of the symbolic devices that were used to ritualize the segregation of the sexes and to negotiate the boundaries that separated them. These elements are not peculiar to the cult of Bona Dea but occur in other cults that concern themselves with the themes of gender and boundary. Some of these cults, Ceres, Liber and Libera, Flora, Venus and Vesta, I examine in later chapters. In this first chapter I discuss the symbolic elements only as they are presented in the cult of Bona Dea. But I wish to draw attention to them, and to the manner in which they are presented, for while the symbols remain constant, the symbolism is complex and multi-faceted. The cult of Bona Dea by no means exhausts the complexity of the way in which sexual categorization occurred in Roman ritual or the ways in which it was presented. But because the cult was explicit in its demarcation of boundaries, and the resulting creation of categories, it is a good place to begin to understand that complexity.

1

THE CULT OF BONA DEA

What sacrifice is so ancient as that which we received from our kings, and which is coeval with our city? Or what so secret as that which fences itself against the eye not only of the inquisitive, but even of the idle, and to which access is debarred, not merely from wickedness but even from inadvertency? A sacrifice, too, which none in all history violated before Publius Clodius, none ever approached, none made light of; a sacrifice from the sight of which no man but sank with horror; a sacrifice performed by Vestal Virgins on behalf of the Roman people, performed in the house of a magistrate, and with the most elaborate ceremonial, in honour of a goddess whose very name men are not permitted to know.

(Cic., *Har. Resp.*, 17)

Cicero is describing here the rites of Bona Dea, a festival celebrated each December, exclusively by women, in the house of a Roman magistrate. In 62 BC the ceremony was being conducted in the house of Caesar, who was a praetor that year. P. Clodius Pulcher, apparently intent on seducing Caesar's wife, Pompeia, disguised himself as a flute-girl and gained access to the rites.[1] Hence Cicero's fulminations. How seriously should we take Cicero's attack? Did Clodius commit a serious act of profanation and was Cicero's fury more than self-serving hyperbole? Was the cult of Bona Dea a central part of the civic religion? The fact is that if not for the Clodius affair we would in all likelihood have had very little knowledge, if not about the goddess herself, certainly about her festival. Our evidence comes from Cicero and later writers who based their accounts on his.[2] But Cicero's motives are, to say the least, suspect. As Brouwer observes, it was only when he himself had fallen foul of Clodius that he took the moral high ground over

13

Clodius' infiltration of the rites. Before that, soon after the incident itself, he displays a marked reluctance to support a senatorial motion for a trial of Clodius for *incestum*.[3] After he had become a target of Clodius' enmity, however, his moral indignation knew no bounds. His brilliantly vituperative rhetoric captured the imagination of later writers and we have an exceptionally large volume of material on the incident. None of it, however, tells us much more than we already know from Cicero's own works. This has led some modern scholars to conclude that Bona Dea was a minor, relatively unimportant deity. Dumézil, for example, writes:

> Did this group of savage divinities [i.e. Faunus, Silvanus, the Lares] include in ancient times, a feminine element? Fauna is hardly more than a name, which takes on substance only in legends where, as wife, daughter, or sister of Faunus, she passed into fiction, and into the Hellenized novel. Under the name of Bona Dea, she was the object of an annual ceremonial in December which was official but secret – strictly limited to women – highly coloured, but Greek. She was no more than a 'Damia', probably imported from Tarentum, and perhaps through a mistranslation when that city was conquered in 272.
>
> (Dumézil 1970: 350. My parentheses)

Brouwer's is to date the most comprehensive study of the Bona Dea (Brouwer 1989). He argues that the literary evidence as derived from Cicero has given us an exaggerated view of the importance, not of the cult as a whole, but of the festival in December and its particular rites (*ibid.*: 260 *et seq.*). The epigraphical material reveals a somewhat different type of cult with some elements apparently contradicting the evidence of the December ritual. The most significant of these differences is that while the December ritual explicitly and very rigorously excluded men, the epigraphical evidence shows that men did, in fact, worship this goddess.[4]

Bona Dea was a goddess of many parts, as are most deities in polytheistic systems. The fact that her cult took different forms on different occasions is not in itself surprising or unusual in any way. Nor does evidence that men dedicated votive offerings to her diminish the significance of the December festival which was celebrated by women alone. That is, not unless we believe that women's rituals were *ipso facto* of little importance. The December festival was undoubtedly a part of the civic religion. Whatever the political motives behind the fracas occasioned by Clodius' escapade, the fact is that Clodius did stand trial for *incestum*.

Nevertheless the all-female festival does raise interesting questions. Particularly since, as we shall see, the mythology of Bona Dea seems designed to explain the goddess' avoidance of men. Also, the rhetoric of male avoidance in descriptions of the festival is exceptionally strident. Even if allowance be made for the fact that most of it harks back to Cicero and the Clodius affair, the cult of Bona Dea does seem to protest its abhorrence of males a little too much. Sexual segregation in cult and ritual is not unusual in Roman religion and most of the time it is presented as just another ritual feature. There is generally no attempt made to explain or defend the exclusion of one sex or the other from a particular rite. The striking exceptions are the cult of Bona Dea and the cult of Hercules Invictus at the *Ara Maxima*, which excluded all women from its rites. Significantly, as we shall see, at least one account of the founding of the *Ara Maxima* explains the exclusion of women by means of a story featuring Bona Dea.

As far as the rites at the *Ara Maxima* were concerned the exclusion of women was merely a ritual detail. Women simply did not participate in the rites.[5] And though I have nowhere found it explicitly stated, it is, I think, safe to assume that women were also excluded from the public banquets that followed sacrifices at the *Ara Maxima*, even when the sheer numbers of people involved would have meant that the participants in the feast spilled out of the precincts of the shrine onto the public streets.[6] Gellius cannot explain why men were not allowed to swear by Castor, but finds nothing strange in the fact that women could not swear by Hercules. After all, he says, they abstained from all sacrifice to that god.[7] But there do not seem to have been any elaborate ritual mechanisms for keeping women out such as the cult of Bona Dea had for keeping out men.[8] The myths that are connected with the rites at the *Ara Maxima* are however another matter altogether. Here, the exclusion of women is given a degree of prominence that makes it appear one of the most important, if not *the* most important feature of the cult. Moreover, except for one variant which links the exclusion of women to the goddess Carmenta,[9] it is Bona Dea, who is made to occupy the opposite end of the male/female axis which the myths create.

The ritual separation of male and female is frequently expressed in terms of the opposition of fire and water. Fire and water together symbolize life itself: *hae duae res (sc. aqua et ignis) humanam vitam continent* – 'These two elements constitute human life'.[10]

Aqua et igni tam interdici solet damnatus, quam accipiunt nuptae, videlicet quia hae duae res humanam vitam maxime continent. Itaque funus prosecuti redeuntes ignem super gradiebantur aqua aspersi; quod purgationis genus vocabant suffitionem.

Water and fire are both denied to condemned men and accepted by brides. The reason is probably because these two substances contain the very stuff of human life. Therefore, those returning from a funeral sprinkle themselves with water and step over fire. They call this *suffitio*, a kind of purification.[11]

Death is equivalent to the denial of fire and water. Hence the reason why mourners after a funeral seek symbolic contact with the two elements. The *Digest* states that there were just two modes of capital punishment: exile and death. Exile – *exilium* – was not simple banishment; it signified the loss of Roman citizenship and was expressed in terms of the denial of fire and water. Simple banishment – *relegatio* – was not accompanied by the denial of fire and water, did not entail the loss of citizenship and was therefore not a form of capital punishment.

Individually, fire and water represented the male and female principles respectively. In the *Roman Questions* Plutarch asked 'why did the bride touch fire and water?'[12] And he answered, 'fire without moisture is without nourishment and dry, while water without heat is barren and inactive: and so male and female apart from each other are ineffectual but their coming together in marriage produces the perfect communal life'. Varro defines the ritual separation of male and female in terms of fire and water explicitly in terms of sexuality and procreation:

The conditions for procreation are two: fire and water. Thus these are used at the threshold in weddings, because there is union here. And fire is male, which the semen is in the other case, and water is the female because the embryo develops from her moisture, and the force that brings their binding (*vinctio*) is Venus.

(Varro, *Ling.*, 5.61)

The perception of the dichotomy of male and female in terms of fire and water was diffused throughout what I have called the cultural system. The social rituals of marriages and funerals embodied the symbolism as did legal ritual and indeed legal discourse. There are other references[13] but one is particularly striking, because it is so obviously untrue on the level of experience that it can only reflect a very strong ritual belief. Macrobius refers to a passage in Aristotle, where the philosopher maintains that women rarely become drunk, but old men often do. Aristotle gives no reason for this. The reason that is vouchsafed in Macrobius is that women's bodies are full of moisture. This is evinced by the smoothness and sheen of a woman's skin, but above all by her repeated purgings which rid her body of superfluous moisture. This enables a woman to imbibe with relative impunity because the wine becomes diluted by the abundance of moisture in her body and its force is diminished. Old men on the other hand are extremely dry creatures and wine takes a powerful hold on them.[14]

Most important in terms of the present argument is the fact that the opposition of male and female in Roman religion, as it was ritualized in the cults of the *Ara Maxima* and of Bona Dea, is expressed in the aetiological myths connected with these cults in terms of the opposition of fire and water. The symbol of fire, in fact, plays a very important role, as I shall show in the first two sections that follow, in the myth of the founding of the *Ara Maxima* as well as in the explanation for the exclusion of women from its rites.

HERCULES AND CACUS

The story of Hercules and Cacus provides a framework for an analysis of the story of Hercules and Bona Dea. It reveals important attributes of Hercules which are treated differently in the story of Hercules and Bona Dea. The very same attributes, which in the Cacus story align Hercules on the side of strength against cunning, light against darkness, and life against death, in the Bona Dea story align him on the side of male against female.

To begin with, I shall focus on two versions of the story of Hercules and Cacus – Virgil's and Ovid's.[15] The story constituted the aetiological myth of the founding of the *Ara Maxima*, which, it is important to note, was still an important place of sacrifice at the time these accounts were written. The narrative details are, in both Virgil and Ovid, almost identical. In both cases the action takes place in remote antiquity – long before the founding of the City of Rome, before even the arrival of Aeneas in Italy, during the reign of the Arcadian king, Evander. This very early setting of the myth is of critical importance; I shall return to it later in this chapter. For now the relevant details are that Hercules arrives in Italy, having completed the tenth of the twelve labours imposed on him by Eurystheus – the theft of the cattle of Geryon.[16] He comes bringing the cattle with him. Cacus is described by both poets as a fire-breathing figure of monstrous proportions, who lived in a cave on the Aventine hill, emerging at will to ravage the surrounding countryside. The inhabitants of the area lived in mortal terror of him.[17] With great cunning, he steals some of Hercules' beasts (in Virgil eight, in Ovid two) by dragging them backwards into his cave, thus obscuring the evidence of their footprints. Hercules discovers the whereabouts of his cattle only when he hears them lowing. Infuriated by the theft, he rushes to recover them by force and a terrible battle ensues in which the fires of Cacus are pitted against the superhuman strength of Hercules, but in vain. Cacus is slain and Hercules not only recovers his cattle, but becomes the liberator of the surrounding land from the monster's reign of terror. To commemorate the incident, he sets up an altar, the *Ara Maxima*, at which the Romans henceforth sacrifice to him.[18]

The parallelism between Hercules and Cacus is striking and forms an important element in the story. To begin with, they both possess enormous size and physical strength. True, this is not explicitly stated of Hercules in either Virgil's version or Ovid's, but by the time of Augustus when both poems were written, it is reasonable to assume that the poets and their public perceived Hercules as he was perceived in the Greek context, where his outstanding attribute was his great physical size and strength. By stressing Cacus' physical power both writers seem to wish to point out a parallel between the monster and Hercules. Another parallel feature is the theft of the cattle. Cacus steals Hercules' cattle, but they were stolen cattle in the first place. The myth, however, seems to make a distinction between the two thefts, for Hercules' is ignored while Cacus' is seen as a crime in keeping with his habitually obnoxious behaviour.[19] A further point of similarity is that both are the sons of gods – Hercules of Jupiter, Cacus of Vulcan. This stress on the parallel features shared by Hercules and Cacus is neither accidental nor idiosyncratic. Its function is to throw into sharper focus the battle that takes place between them, which in both versions is the point and main substance of the story.

But if the similarity between the two is important, even more so is the difference. A conflict implies antagonism and the points of antagonism between Hercules and Cacus are seen by Virgil, at least, as points of opposition. Virgil tells the tale in a way that invests this opposition with the significance of a cultic feature.

The physical focus of the conflict is Cacus' cave. This is where he hides the cattle and himself when Hercules seeks to destroy him. He shuts himself in by barricading the entrance with rock. The cave however is not merely a place of refuge for Cacus, nor is it simply the setting for the scene of the fight. It is an important element in the myth and is directly associated with the monster, sharing many of his attributes and thereby helping to define his function. The cave is Cacus and Cacus is the cave. Virgil's description of the cave was meant to evoke in the readers' mind the classical notion of the underworld. The lack of sunlight was the most important and the most terrifying feature of the underworld in Graeco-Roman thought.[20] Virgil deliberately exploits this idea in his description of Cacus' cave.

> hinc spelunca fuit, vasto summota recessu,
> semihominis Caci facies quam dira tenebat,
> *solis inacessam radiis*;

Here was once a cave, receding to unfathomed depth, *never visited by the sun's rays*, where dwelt the awful shape of half human Cacus;[21]

Even more evocative is the simile used to describe the effect of Hercules hurling a huge rock through the roof of the cave:

> at specus et Caci detecta apparuit ingens
> regia et umbrosae penitus patuere cavernae,
> non secus ac si qua penitus vi terra dehiscens
> infernas reseret sedes et regna recludat
> pallida, dis invisa, superque immane barathrum
> cernatur, trepidant immiso lumine Manes.

But the den of Cacus and his huge palace stood revealed, and, deep below, the darkling cave lay open: even as though beneath some force, the earth, gaping open deep below, should unlock the infernal abodes and disclose the pallid realms abhorred of the gods, and from above the vast abyss be descried, and the ghosts tremble at the inrushing light.[22]

By comparing the effect of Hercules breaching the roof of the cave to the effect of sunlight should it penetrate the underworld, Virgil makes a clear statement of association between the cave and the underworld.

So far the equation is clear: cave = underworld. But Cacus too, as I have already suggested, is part of the equation, which must then be rendered cave = underworld = Cacus. Consider now the different treatment by the two poets of the axis along which the fight takes place. In Virgil the fight between Hercules and Cacus takes place on the vertical axis, in Ovid on the horizontal. In Ovid, we find Cacus blocking the entrance to his cave with crags, a barrier so strong that 'twice five yoke of oxen could scarcely move it'.[23] But Hercules, with his powerful shoulders that once bore the weight of the world, can and does shift the mass, thereby succeeding in reaching and destroying Cacus.[24] Thus the action takes place on the horizontal axis. Ovid gives no indication that Cacus or his cave, which Hercules breaches from the front, is to be compared with the underworld, or indeed, is to be invested with any symbolic significance at all. It is simply a cave. Not so in Virgil, whose cave is meant to signify much more than a monster's lair. In Ovid, Cacus blocks up the entrance to the cave with rocks – enormous pieces of rock, perhaps, but still just rock. In Virgil, the barrier is a single rock suspended in iron, a contrivance of Cacus' father, Vulcan.[25] Against this barrier Hercules' mightiest efforts fail. Therefore the physical strength of Hercules which Virgil's readers knew was ultimately going to prevail against Cacus, proves to be no match for Vulcan's divine cunning, and so Hercules is defeated on the horizontal axis. In making Hercules thus try and fail on the horizontal axis, Virgil skilfully directs the reader's attention to the manner in which Hercules does breach Cacus' fortress – from above, i.e. along the vertical axis, by hurling a rock through the roof of the cave, and breaching it from above. In the poetic discourse the opposition between Hercules and Cacus is seen in terms of the opposing concepts of the 'above' and the 'below', Hercules representing the 'above' and Cacus the 'below'. This opposition, I suggest, reinforces the association of Cacus with the underworld and at the same time, confers on Hercules associations of the world above – the world which contains sunlight. The defeat of Cacus is poetically expressed by the description of sunlight pouring into the cave from above and destroying the darkness of the cave.

This fundamental opposition between Hercules and Cacus is very important. The parallel features of the two protagonists in this drama are the more readily discernible, but are important only in so far as they throw into clearer focus the opposition. Take for example the feature of physical power. Hercules' weapon in this conflict is indeed his strength. But Cacus, while possessing physical strength, also possesses and uses against Hercules a quality which I shall call devious cunning. Both poets stress this factor in Cacus' character. For example, the dragging of the cattle backwards into the cave so that the evidence of the footprints might be obscured, is so consistently described in all the extant literary versions of the myth, that we may regard it as an accepted feature of the story rather than a poetic interpretation.[26] Indeed this device of Cacus succeeded in fooling Hercules, who was only alerted to the theft – Virgil – and to the whereabouts of the missing cattle – Ovid – when he heard them lowing. Virgil takes this generally accepted feature of Cacus' character – i.e. devious cunning – and uses it to project an opposition between Hercules and Cacus that will eventually define Hercules' cultic position after he is accepted as a god. It is Cacus' devious cunning represented by the divinely constructed barrier with which Cacus barricades himself in the cave, which causes Hercules to fail along the horizontal axis.[27] Hercules' strength is no match for this cunning device. Frustrated, he rages to and fro, then spurred on by fury he takes up a mighty crag and hurls it onto the cave from above. Thus Virgil moves the conflict onto the vertical plane, projecting the important opposition between the above and the below. Significantly the factor that pushes the conflict onto a different plane and thereby focuses the spotlight, as it were, onto the opposition is the quality of cunning that is peculiar to Cacus.

If Cacus' cunning caused Hercules to fail on the horizontal axis, what helped him succeed on the vertical? There are two other attributes of the antagonists that must be considered, this time attributes which are at the same time parallel and dichotomous. Apart from his strength and cunning, but complementing them, is Cacus' ability to belch forth fire at will. 'At will' are the operative words here. Cacus – both poets make this clear – is able to control his fire-breathing. This puts the attribute on a par with devious cunning. Both are controllable attributes which may be measured and manipulated at will. Not so in the case of Hercules. Hercules' second attribute is his anger, his uncontrollable fury when he discovers the theft of his cattle and is frustrated in his attempts to recover them. The language Virgil chooses to describe Hercules' anger is highly significant. He seems to be deliberately equating Hercules' wrath with Cacus' fire-breathing. For example the adjectives *furens* (*animis*) and *fervidus* (*ira*) connote fire and heat.[28] In the line, *hic vero Alcidae furiis exarserat atro/felle dolor*,[29] *exarserat* is in poetic terms equal to fire-breathing. So on one symbolic level Hercules and Cacus appear to share the same attribute. But the fact that in Cacus it is controllable, while in Hercules it is not, renders it dichotomous rather than parallel. Again the device of a real opposition is rendered more effective by an apparent similarity.

Turning now to the conflict itself, it appears that in Ovid's version, Cacus uses fire (*flamma*) as a weapon.[30] But once he is defeated by Hercules, the flame turns to smoke mixed with blood.[31] The metaphor, here, is quite straightforward. The dying flame gives out smoke, and since one that dies is mortal – apropos, one recalls that Virgil calls Cacus *semihomo*[32] – the smoke is mixed with blood. In Virgil, however, as I shall show, the metaphor is richer and more complex. Virgil takes it further, and uses it to give greater emphasis to the fundamental dichotomy that is already apparent between Hercules and Cacus.

When Cacus' cave is breached from above in Virgil's story, the primary effect is to let the sunlight into this frightful place that had been 'inaccessible to the rays of the sun'. Cacus, being a fire-breathing monster, naturally – or so one would think – reacts to this situation by belching out those fires which Ovid portrays merely as a weapon. Virgil's interpretation of the story differs subtly. Here, Cacus belches out not *flamma*, as in Ovid, nor *ignis*, which Virgil has already told us was his wont[33] but *fumus*, smoke.[34] But *fumus* is not a weapon, in the sense of something with which to harm the enemy, but a cunning device intended to deceive. By filling the cave with dense smoke (*ingentem fumum*), Cacus restores it to its former state of blackness and inaccessibility to light and sight (*caligine caeca*)[35]. Fire (*ignis*) is mingled with the smoke, but the primary feature is the smoke, and the primary intention is to recreate the illusion of the underworld. Virgil describes this phenomenon as follows:

> ille autem, neque enim fuga iam super ulla pericli,
> faucibus ingentem fumum, mirabile dictu,
> evomit involuitque domum caligine caeca,

> prospectum eripiens oculis, glomeratque sub antro
> fumiferam noctem commixtu igne tenebris.

He, the while, for now no other escape from peril was left, belches from his throat dense smoke, wondrous to tell! and veils the dwelling in blinding gloom, blotting all view from the eyes, and rolling up in the cave's depth smoke-laden night, its blackness mingled with flame.[36]

The opposition is plain. The cunning of Cacus with all its associations of darkness and the underworld is opposed to the strength of Hercules with its associations of light and the world above. Hercules' light – identified here with sunlight – is a darkness-destroying light, just as Cacus' fire is a darkness-creating fire. And while Hercules' strength, by itself, could not overcome Cacus' cunning, his strength combined with light vanquished Cacus' cunning combined with darkness. The dichotomy is now complete, its logic intact. Darkness, obfuscation, and the world below are opposed to bright light, clear vision and the world above. But which world above? In the classical vision, which the Romans shared, there were two: the earthly abode of mortals and the heavenly abode of immortals. Where did Hercules belong? In the chronology of this myth Hercules is still a mortal. But I suggest that Virgil is looking forward to his eventual apotheosis and defining its terms. The following image,

> desuper Alcides telis premit, omniaque arma
> advocat et ramis vastisque molaribus instat.

Alcides hurls missiles from above, calling all weapons to his aid, and rams upon him boughs and giant millstones[37]

is a poetically projected image of Hercules hurling missiles onto his foe from above. But it might also have conjured up a corresponding image of Jupiter hurling thunderbolts. It is a reasonable assumption that this would have been part of the cultural perceptions of Virgil's public. And on the strength of that assumption I suggest that Hercules was here perceived as belonging to the world of the immortals, although technically he was still a man.

It was not Hercules' strength that finally triumphed over Cacus; it was his passion, violent and uncontrollable. It was a passion that was rewarded because Evander, in gratitude for the destruction of Cacus, who had terrorized his people for so long, instituted a cult in Hercules' honour to commemorate the incident.[38] One of the most ancient and honoured foci of Roman sacrifice, the *Ara Maxima* and its cult, was perceived to have been instituted long before the founding of the city itself. In fact some of its ritual features recalled the 'Greek' origin of the cult.[39] The violence, represented here by the fury of Hercules, which in the last resort caused the founding of this cult, was also responsible for one of its most important features – the exclusion of all women from its rites. This is where the Bona Dea enters the story.

HERCULES AND BONA DEA

The fact that all women were strictly excluded from any participation in the rites at the *Ara Maxima* was sufficiently noteworthy even in antiquity, to warrant more than one attempt at aetiological myth making.[40] One of these myths is particularly important in terms of this study. There are two existing references to the story – one in Propertius and the other in Macrobius.[41] The story, briefly, is as follows. Hercules is overcome with a terrible thirst after his epic battle with Cacus. Wandering about in search of water, he comes upon a grove of women celebrating the rites of Bona Dea. He begs the women for water, but is refused because, as it is politely explained to him, it is unlawful for a man to taste of that water. Enraged by the refusal he takes the water by force – note here too the notion of violence, to which I shall return later in the discussion – but in order to punish the women for their inhospitable behaviour he banishes them from his newly established rites for all eternity. A frivolous little story perhaps, but it holds out an opportunity to make some sense of a ritual restriction that might otherwise be cast on the heap of historical imponderables.

Up until the telling of the founding of the *Ara Maxima* Propertius' story tallies broadly with other extant literary versions of the myth.[42] Propertius, however, takes the story further. Alcides, he relates, was tortured by thirst, but 'teeming earth supplied no water' – *terraque non ullas feta ministrat aquas*.[43] *Feta terra*: rich, fertile, teeming, pregnant and therefore female earth. The reader's initial impression is that of sharp contrast, antagonism almost, between the hot dry Hercules and the teeming earth with all its connotations of moisture. Thus the reader is confronted instantly and simultaneously with two sets of contrasts: male and female; dry heat and moisture. Having established this opposition, Propertius proceeds to reinforce it on the cultic level. Hercules comes across a grove,

femineae loca clausa deae fontesque piandos,
impune et nullis sacra retecta viris.

The secret place of the Goddess of Women, with holy foun-
tains and rites ne'er revealed to men save to their cost.[44]

Propertius chooses to emphasize three 'facts' about the grove: it
was sacred to the goddess of women, its rites were forbidden to
men, and it contained water. All three are important for the significance of the story, which reaches its climax with the exclusion of
women from the already established cult of the *Ara Maxima*.

We now have on one side an exclusively male cult – that of the
Ara Maxima, and on the other, an exclusively female cult – that of
Bona Dea. Both were important cults in the civic religion, but there
is nothing in the ritual features of either – as far as we can tell – to
connect it with the other, except this opposition defined by exclusiveness of gender. It is interesting and highly significant, therefore,
that the aetiology of these two particular cults links them mythically, for they were by no means the only cults in Rome to contain
elements of sexual exclusiveness. The problem lies in seeing how
and why the link was significant and how it contributed to the
meaning generated by the cults.

It is clear that the cults of Bona Dea and Hercules Invictus at the
Ara Maxima were linked by the notion of an opposition of male
and female. The terms of the opposition are however neither
absolute nor inflexible. The opposition of male and female is, as
I have already suggested, paralleled by the opposition of fire and
water. The motif of fire played an important part in the myth of
Hercules and Cacus, as told by Virgil and Ovid. There, we saw an
opposition between the light-giving fire of Hercules and the
darkness-creating fire of Cacus. The quality of Hercules' fire here
in Propertius' tale is however very different. What is emphasized
here is the heat and dryness of fire expressed in terms of Hercules'
great thirst. In the lines

nec tulit iratam ianua clausa sitim
at postquam exhausto iam flumine vicerat aestum

nor could the closed gate endure the fury of his thirst. But
after he had quenched his burning and drained the stream
to naught[45]

the words *sitim* and *aestum*, each placed at the end of consecutive
lines, have the identical value. *Aestus* connotes a burning heat,

which Propertius has compounded with the notion of dryness.[46]
Aestus also – and this is important – contains connotations of
passion. It is, for example, a word often used to denote a roiling
sea.[47] Moreover, in these particular lines, *aestum* reflects not only
sitim but the adjective used to describe it – *iratam*. This is evocative of Hercules' rage when confronted with Cacus' cunning. While
the qualities of fire and passion are therefore common to both
stories, they are given a different emphasis in Propertius.

In Propertius the symbolism of fire and water is used to express
the ritual opposition between male and female.[48] Propertius'
Hercules is subtly different from Virgil's. Although in this nexus of
myths Hercules is regarded as mortal, Virgil is very obviously
looking forward to his subsequent apotheosis. In Virgil's version it
is the divine qualities of Hercules that are emphasized. Not so in
Propertius; he makes a point of portraying Hercules as mortal. In
fact it is possible to go one step further and say that Propertius
makes an effort to portray Hercules as non-immortal, by underscor-
ing his mortal qualities. Tortured by thirst, for example, Hercules
rushes up to the door of the shrine and speaks words 'less than
those of a god' (*iacit . . . verba minora deo*[49]). When begging for
water he refers to himself as *vir*, man, and the word is also
contained in the reply of the priestess. This emphasis on the fact
that Hercules in this myth must be seen as a man operates also on
a metaphorical level. To appreciate this it is necessary to see how
the concept of fieriness functions in the myth. The Cacus myth will
again be useful as a point of comparison. In keeping with his
perceived divinity, the fiery nature of Hercules triumphed once and
for all over Cacus. Cacus' destruction is permanent, as is signified
by the establishment of the *Ara Maxima*, the altar at which the
Romans have sacrificed 'forever more'. The notion of eternity is
apparent here, in keeping with the notion of Hercules' divinity. The
Cacus incident is closed, and the world has become a different
place. The monster is dead, he can no longer tyrannize the land
that is destined to become the site of Rome. The *status quo* has
changed. All that remains is to commemorate this changed state of
things, a state which is going to endure, indeed Virgil could say has
endured, forever.

In the Bona Dea myth, by contrast, Hercules' fieriness is represented by thirst. This is critically important. For thirst is not something that can be destroyed for ever as Hercules destroys Cacus. It
is constantly renewed and is in constant need of quenching.

Therefore we have here the notion of a cycle, of repetition, in keeping with the notion of Hercules' mortality. In Propertius Hercules is man not god. As for the *status quo*, Hercules' violent act in breaking down the doors of the shrine and drinking the water does not alter it; it simply reinforces it, for in forbidding women his rites at the *Ara Maxima*, Hercules pushes the male and female elements further apart and strengthens the opposition. But Bona Dea, unlike Cacus, is not destroyed, and her continuing presence creates a tension, a perpetual dynamic opposition between herself and Hercules, between men and women.

Precisely for this reason, the opposition between male and female is neither absolute, nor inflexible. In the poem, the climax of the action is in fact the collapsing of the poles when Hercules forcibly enters the sacred grove and drinks the water. It is helpful to interpret this as a metonymy for sexual intercourse. Note also the notion of violence. The cause of the collapse of the poles or the mediating factor is violence. But violence, in this instance, is not portrayed as an inbred characteristic of Hercules as it was in Virgil's story of Hercules and Cacus. It is something outside him, something inevitable, the only factor that could bring together the polar opposites of male and female. Hercules does not simply rush up to the door and break it down, which is what he did, or tried to do, with Cacus. He first pleads with the priestess. The structure of that pleading is significant for it reveals an attempt to bridge the gap between male and female, to pull the poles together.[50] He begins by asserting his masculinity: first, he invokes his extraordinary physical strength – he carried the globe of the earth on his back – and then his skill in hunting and warfare, both peculiarly male attributes. When that fails he invokes his visit to the underworld, which is very significant, because it demonstrates the power of being able to cross uncrossable boundaries. It is all in vain. Finally, he attempts to identify with the female, thus denying an opposition between male and female.

> I also have performed servile tasks, clad in Sidonian cloak, and wrought the day's tale of wool with Libyan distaff. My hairy chest was girt by a soft breast band, and though my hands were calloused I proved a fitting girl (*apta puella*).
>
> (Prop., 4.9.47–50)

This is a reference to the time when he served Omphale, Queen of Lydia.[51] That story too deals with an inversion of sexual roles, for while Hercules spun, dressed as a girl, Omphale dressed herself up in his lionskin and club.[52] But the opposition will not be denied. For what Hercules is trying to do is effect a social inversion of the sexes. Though 'his chest was girt with a soft breastband', it remained hairy – *hirsutum* – and his rough hands, though performing a woman's task, were those of a man.

The priestess' reply is not easy to interpret. She reminds Hercules that the great seer Tiresias was punished – with blindness – for accidentally catching sight of Athene at her bath.[53] The problem here is one of connotation. If the priestess' words are taken at face value and we limit the poetic view to the story of Tiresias and Athene, the point she makes becomes fairly straightforward, even banal, a simple threat: Tiresias went blind by invading the sphere of a goddess that was forbidden to men, so Hercules had better watch out or something of the same sort might happen to him. We could leave it at that. But I suggest that if we do so we would be missing a very important point. As a mythical figure Tiresias was known as much for his sexual inversion as for his blindness. And I suggest that this was what the name of Tiresias was supposed to conjure up. The point that the priestess makes then, is that the ritual divide between male and female is such that not even a biological sexual inversion can bridge the gap. The essential difference between the sexes, as manifested in cult and ritual, appears to have gone beyond social conventions, and also beyond biological differences. The boundary between life and death may be crossed on occasion with impunity, as Hercules had done, but nothing can lawfully cross this boundary. Male and female must remain polar opposites.

Nevertheless the poles do converge. In spite of the priestess' injunctions, Hercules forces his way into the sacred precinct and drinks the forbidden water. Moreover, he does it with apparent impunity. Again, as in the Cacus myth, he achieves his purpose by violence. But in this instance, as I have suggested, violence has a different meaning and significance. In several myths that deal with the issue of relations between men and women, violence is a recognizable theme. Bona Dea herself features in one. According to this story, her father Faunus sought to seduce the goddess. She rejected his advances and in a vain effort to force her to submit, he beat her with branches of myrtle.[54] The feature of beating must, I suggest, be understood in terms of ritually conceptualized violence. The myth of the Sabine women is another such story, and one that in the literary tradition, at any rate, was an important part of the civic ideology and self-perception of the Roman state.[55] In order to provide wives for the citizens of his new state Romulus resorted to force. He invited the neighbouring Sabines to Rome, ostensibly to help celebrate the rites of the Consualia, and at a crucial moment in the proceedings, when the attention of their guests was diverted by the ceremony, the Romans carried away the unmarried women by force in order to marry them. Thus the earliest legend that dealt with marriage in the context of the Roman state focused on violence. The point is always made in the various versions of the story that the Romans could not get wives by peaceable means, so that again, as in the Hercules–Bona Dea myth, violence becomes a necessary factor. St Augustine, whose very antipathy to the pagan religion can at times give valuable insight as to how it worked, records the belief that without violence a woman cannot cease to be a virgin.[56] The cultic perception that violence was the mediating factor between male and female is reflected in the social ritual of the wedding. The bride was torn from her mother's arms by her bridegroom with a mock violence.[57] Even the carrying of the bride over the threshold might have been regarded as a representation of an act of violence.[58] Hercules' violence at the fountain of the Bona Dea must be understood in the light of this complex of myth and ritual.

It is important to be aware that violence in such a context had no destructive connotations as it did in the myth of Cacus. In all the examples I have cited violence achieved a desirable end. The rape of the Sabine women resulted in peaceful union between the Roman and the Sabine nations. Marriage was not only vital for the ordering of society and for its continuation, but was particularly important for the Roman male. For it was only by lawful marriage – *iustum matrimonium* – that he could have children that were legally his own. Macrobius' story of Faunus and Bona Dea has especially interesting implications. In this case violence does not have the desired effect. Despite the beating, Bona Dea does not succumb to her father's incestuous desires. She is finally seduced by stealth when Faunus changes himself into a snake for the purpose. Thus violence, which appears to be important in the mythical discourse about sexual relations, and which has been made a feature of the ritual designed to bring the sexes together, operates only when those relations are perceived as lawful, as in marriage. In the case of Faunus, the failure of violence must be seen as a ritual expression of the implacably unlawful nature of sexual intercourse between father and daughter.

The myth of Hercules and Bona Dea also appears to suggest that the convergence was temporary. Male and female are polar opposites that are forcibly drawn together, but are then pushed apart again. Or to put it another way, sexual intercourse might bring the sexes together, but only temporarily. The boundary that separates them is always ultimately reasserted. The result of Hercules violating the rites of Bona Dea was, in effect, the reinforcement of the opposition by his excluding women from his own newly founded cult. And so we have, within a single ritual framework – for both these cults were important components of the state-sponsored religion – two mutually exclusive categories – male and female. But it is a self-conscious exclusion. We are not left with two entirely separate cults. The cults of the *Ara Maxima* and Bona Dea give each other context and meaning within a crowded and – to the uninitiated – confusing polytheistic system.

THE WOMEN'S GODDESS

The consensus of modern scholarly opinion on the December ritual of Bona Dea is that it was conducted by well-born matrons. Such women were not, however, the only participants although they did undoubtedly play a prominent part in the rites. The festival was held in the house of a magistrate and the women of his family clearly had a leading role to play. In 62 BC when Clodius was discovered in the house during the ceremony, it was Aurelia, Caesar's mother, who took charge of the situation. She ordered the ceremonies to be suspended and Clodius evicted.[59] While Cicero does state that the rites were celebrated by women of the elite – *nobilissimae feminae*[60] – other writers indicate that they were not the only women present. There certainly were slave girls at the festival for it was one of these that discovered Clodius' deception.[61] The third book of Ovid's *Ars Amatoria* concerns courtesans, including freedwomen; these women frequented the temple of the goddess, and it is reasonable to assume participated in the festival.[62] Moreover, Juvenal writes of *ancillae lenonum* being present.[63] The festival of Bona Dea was more likely than not celebrated by all members of the female sex, regardless of distinctions of status. Just as all women were excluded from the rites of Hercules, all women participated in the rites of the Bona Dea. However, although the cult incorporated the different sexual categories of women – matrons and prostitutes, including slaves – it was not blind to those distinctions. Propertius' choice of language in describing Bona Dea's worshippers invites such an interpretation of the festival.

Nowhere in his poem does Propertius mention the Bona Dea by this name. Instead, he calls her the Women's Goddess, *Feminea Dea*. Her worshippers are referred to throughout the poem as *puellae*. Could Propertius not have been writing about the Bona Dea at all, but of an entirely different goddess? The question might never have received a satisfactory answer if not for the passage in Macrobius, which clearly refers to the Bona Dea and which contains a myth similar but not identical to the one in Propertius, which is made to account for the banning of women from the rites of the *Ara Maxima*.[64] Propertius and Macrobius are undoubtedly referring to the same tradition. Moreover Macrobius, whose purpose is the identification of the Bona Dea with Maia, refers to her also as *dea feminarum*, the goddess of women.

What can we infer from Propertius' use of *puellae* to designate the goddess' devotees? Does it add anything to our knowledge of the way in which the cult was perceived? The goddess was called *feminea dea*; why not call the women *feminae*? I suggest that a word like *femina*, a blanket term which essentially meant 'female' without regard to sexuality or sexual categorization would have been too weak in this context. *Puella*, and this is important, appears both to define and to transcend female sexual categorization. The word has been used to denote 'daughter', with its connotations of youth and unmarried status;[65] 'wife' i.e. *matrona*;[66] more importantly, 'mistress', which could refer either to a *matrona*[67] or to a concubine; and finally even 'prostitutes' in the context of a brothel.[68] The only category which it cannot be made to include is one that was less important in Roman cult, that is old women. But Propertius does not overlook even this group. The priestess is an old woman, an *anus*.[69] Thus the use of the word *puella* is very suggestive. Not only does it emphasize the male–female polarity, but it projects the concept of the female in terms of sexual status rather than in terms of simple gender. It also implies that in this instance the concept of sexual categorization does not apply. *Puellae* has the effect of embracing all female categories at once. The boundaries that the Bona Dea draws are between male and female, not between the various categories of the female.

31

'A RITE SO ANCIENT . . . '

Propertius explicitly links in time the myths of Hercules–Cacus and Hercules–Bona Dea. Hercules' fateful thirst was caused by his battle with Cacus. Both Cacus and the laws governing the rites of Bona Dea are in a sense overcome by Hercules. And the *Ara Maxima* is made to represent both these victories. It was founded either by Hercules himself to celebrate the recovery of the cattle, or, in another version, by Evander to celebrate the deliverance of the region from Cacus' reign of terror.[70] One of the earliest of its ritual features was the exclusion of all women from the altar. Indeed this fact is so fundamental to perceptions of the cult that there is another myth to account for the phenomenon.[71]

This chronological context of the founding of the *Ara Maxima* was not merely a poetic embellishment. The great age of the altar, the fact that it was founded before the city itself, was one of its defining characteristics. It was arguably the earliest shrine of the civic religion. Propertius' account of the Hercules–Bona Dea story reminded his readers that Bona Dea's cult, which was also believed to be very ancient, actually existed before the *Ara Maxima* was founded. In this section I argue that this chronological structure had profound implications for the way that the beginnings of Roman religion itself were perceived.

Bayet observes that one reason that the popular tradition of Hercules' sojourn in Italy is particularly important is that the story can be connected very precisely to specific topographical evidence (Bayet 1926: 127). Considering the cult from the perspective of the writers of the period of the late Republic and early Principate, we might add that the cult was also precisely related to a specific chronological perception. Hercules' arrival in Italy was an important chronological marker. For the Romans it marked, as it were, pre-Roman Rome in terms of time as well as space. From a purely topographical perspective, Hercules' adventures took place in 'Rome'. Cacus was killed on the Aventine, and it was at the foot of that same hill, in a place that was to become the *Forum Boarium*, that the *Ara Maxima* was founded.[72] In addition, all these events were perceived to have occurred in dim and distant antiquity, before Romulus had founded the city, or indeed Aeneas arrived in Italy. The story is always placed within this chronological context. From a religious point of view, it all happened before the foundations of Roman religion were laid first by Romulus, and then, more importantly, by

Numa.[73] The *Ara Maxima* existed in Republican times, and was regarded as an ancient and venerable Roman shrine, but it was also a tangible link back in time to a period before Rome was Rome.[74]

What was it from a religious point of view that defined this period? How was it different from the time that Rome was unequivocally Rome? And how, if at all, did this pre-Rome, or perhaps more accurately proto-Rome, help to define Rome? The enigmatic deity, Faunus, sometimes described as the father or brother of Bona Dea is a defining feature of this mythical period. Faunus was a mysterious and ambivalent figure in the Roman mythic ideology. He is difficult to interpret. The literary descriptions of him give an initial impression of confusion. Was he man or god? For Dionysius of Halicarnassus he was king of the native inhabitants when Evander arrived in Italy. He was a prudent and energetic king who welcomed Evander with kindness and gave him as much land as he desired.[75] For Virgil, Faunus was the father of Latinus, but he was also a prophetic deity who appeared to supplicants in dreams during the rite of incubation.[76] The theme of prophecy and incubation is found in Ovid too, where Numa, by the process of incubation, learns from Faunus that a current famine might be alleviated by the institution of the rite of the Fordicidia.[77] Was he singular or plural? In the examples cited he was certainly a single figure but Cicero talks of *faunorum voces*.[78] Was he beneficent or maleficent? In all the examples above Faunus was a beneficent deity whose help could be relied on in times of crisis, the good host of Evander, the wise father of Latinus, the kindly prophet. But Faunus was also the incestuous father of Bona Dea, who plied her with wine, beat her with rods of myrtle and changed himself into a serpent in order to satisfy his incestuous lust.[79] In a tale very different from the aetiological myth of the Fordicidia, where Faunus comes voluntarily to Numa in a dream, Ovid tells how Faunus – and Picus, who was associated with Faunus in this story[80] had to be made drunk with wine and forced to divulge the secret – of expiating Jupiter's thunderbolts. They struggled to escape Numa's shackles but failed and were forced to speak.[81] Plutarch, in his version of this story, makes Picus and Faunus change shape in their vain effort to evade Numa's grasp.

> When captured they dropped their own forms and assumed many different shapes, presenting hideous and dreadful appearances. But when they perceived that they were fast

caught and could not escape, they foretold to Numa many things that would come to pass.

(Plut., Num., 15.4)

Finally, Ovid connects Faunus and Hercules in what at first glance appears to be a trivial little story. Faunus conceives a desire for Omphale when he spies her one day out walking with Hercules. Hercules and Omphale sleep apart that night for they plan to celebrate the rites of Bacchus in the morning. But they exchange clothes, he dressing himself in her gauzy garments while she dons his lionskin. When the lovers are asleep Faunus creeps up on them hoping to seduce Omphale, but is confused by the garments, attempts to seduce Hercules instead, and comes to grief. Faced with this jumble of evidence one cannot but sympathize with the character of Cotta in Cicero's *De Natura Deorum*: 'As for the utterances of a faun, I never heard one, but if you say you have I will take your word for it, although what on earth a faun may be I do not know.'[82]

This, however is precisely the point: we do not know what Faunus was. The significance of Faunus was that it was impossible to pin him down. He was every thing at once – beneficent and maleficent, singular and plural, man and god. To interpret the evidence as confused is to miss the point. If the various accounts are accepted as a single body of evidence, patterns of perception become discernible. For one thing every account unequivocally projects Faunus back into a vague, amorphous past. Although he did receive cult in Rome in historical times[83] he belonged in a mythical past.[84] Ovid described that age thus:

> Their life was like that of beasts, unprofitably spent; artless as yet and raw was the common herd. Leaves did they use for houses, herbs for corn: water scooped up in two hollows of the hand to them was nectar. No bull panted under the weight of the bent ploughshare: no land was under the dominion of the husbandman: there was as yet no use for horses, every man carried his own weight: the sheep went clothed in its own wool. Under the open sky they lived and went about naked, inured to heavy showers and rainy winds.
>
> (Ov., Fast., 2.292–300)[85]

The ritual complement to Ovid's description was that Faunus belonged to and represented an age which lacked the twin concepts of boundary and categorization. This is the second pattern contained in the evidence. In general terms this is how the multi-faceted nature of Faunus is most usefully interpreted. More specifically, the stories of Faunus and Bona Dea, Hercules and Omphale, and Plutarch's version of the story of Faunus and Numa all form part of this same pattern. In the rapid change of shape, Picus and Faunus represent the ability to slide unceremoniously across boundaries, as if the concept itself did not exist. In the story of Hercules and Omphale, Faunus is made to betray sexual confusion: he could not tell male from female; again as though the concept of a boundary between the sexes did not exist. With Bona Dea, he attempts to cross a sexual boundary that can never be crossed, in any circumstances whatsoever: the sexual distance that must be maintained between father and daughter.[86] This, the inability to discern boundaries, represented the significance of Faunus within the Roman religious system. The function of that inability was to define by contrast the religion that was acknowledged as Roman, the religion that had as its basis – as I hope this book will demonstrate – the concepts of boundary and categorization.

The significance of Hercules, and especially of his cult at the *Ara Maxima*, was that he was perceived as having laid the foundation of the religion that was considered Roman. The related concepts of boundary and categorization were first articulated by the establishment of the exclusively male rite at the *Ara Maxima* in conscious opposition to the exclusively female rite of Bona Dea. This also marked, in Roman perception as expressed in myth making at any rate, the beginning of the notion of a religious system. The importance of the two cults of Hercules and Bona Dea was that they were defined in terms of each other; they complemented each other; they were linked by a relationship of meaning. It was this that marked out the religion defined as Roman from the one represented by Faunus. However chaotic a polytheistic system such as the Roman might appear to us, to the Romans it was an ordered, meaningfully structured system. The Roman conception of religious chaos was symbolized by Faunus.

The *Ara Maxima* existed in historical times,[87] providing a tangible link between the religious past and present. In this sense it might well be regarded as the earliest Roman shrine. Significantly it was also, in terms of its aetiology, the first expression of the concept of exclusively male ritual space. Note that according to the logic of Rome's myths, female ritual space was not a Roman creation. Bona Dea with her female rites was already part of the enchanted landscape into which Hercules intruded, and which he ended up by dominating. None the less that female space needed to be incorporated into the new system, for it was that which defined and complemented the newly created male space. Together they constituted the germ of the new Roman system. Cicero, in his harangues against Clodius, was certainly not exaggerating the importance of the cult of Bona Dea to the civic religion. It is arguable that he did not go far enough when he described the cult as one which 'we received from our kings and is coeval with our city'.[88] The perceived antiquity of Bona Dea's cult, with the particular meanings that antiquity was invested with, clearly constituted a large part of its significance.

BONA DEA AND THE MYSTERIES OF MITHRAS

We come now to the problem of status. Were the male and female cultic spaces perceived to have an equal status, or in the patriarchal society of the time was the female cultic space marginal to a central masculine space? This is the current orthodoxy on Roman religion.[89] In this section I shall argue that in Rome, male and female cultic space were equally important to the civic system. It is time to rethink the notion that Roman religion placed a negative value on the female and a positive value on the male.

The mysteries of Mithras, like the cult of Hercules, were, to the best of our knowledge, forbidden to women.[90] But in contrast to the cult at the *Ara Maxima* the cult of Mithras occupied a space marginal to the public cults of Rome. This was an ancient mystery religion of uncertain oriental origin[91] which did not reach its classic western form until the 1st century BC to the 1st century AD.[92] It was especially popular among the Roman legions, which were also undoubtedly responsible for the wide dissemination of the cult throughout the Roman empire. According to Plutarch, Mithras was introduced to Rome by the Cilician pirates conquered by Pompey.[93] But it is unlikely that the initiates were at this stage anything more than a tiny sect operating on the fringes of society, and with no effect on the dominant ideology of the day. Cumont in 1913 writes of the mysteries in the time of the Republic, 'L'action de ses sectateurs sur la masse de la population était à peu près aussi nulle que celle de sociétés bouddhiques dans l'Europe moderne.'[94] The mysteries were therefore not part of the religious system which included the cult of Bona Dea and Hercules Invictus. But they provide a useful analytical tool with which to evaluate the relative importance of male and female cultic space.

The mysteries of Mithras, like the cult of Hercules, did not admit women to its rites. But the dynamics of this exclusion were quite different from those operating in the cult of Hercules Invictus. The nature of this difference is instructive. I am not suggesting an opposition here in the structuralist sense; merely the contrast between two very different views of the world. What I hope will emerge from this analysis is not so much a positive as a negative hypothesis; not so much what Bona Dea was as what she was not. This in turn will, I hope, be helpful in understanding the status of her cult in the civic religion.

The cult of Mithras was based on a deliberate rejection of the realities of the world as they were perceived to exist.[95] Instead, the initiate entered into a deliberately constructed cosmic entity, governed by a carefully constructed cosmology. Central to that cosmology was the rejection of the female. It is important to note that unlike the male cultic space created by Hercules, which had to exist within a wider cultic universe, the Mithraic cosmos was complete: it *was* the universe. Beyond its boundaries existed nothing. The rejection of women was therefore total. In the mysteries of Mithras women had no status because they simply did not exist. Even their exclusive function of child-bearing was denied in both the myth and the ritual by an appeal to the fantasy of sexless generation. Mithras was born from a rock.

In his discussion of the significance of grade names in the mysteries, Gordon argues that the only way to make them meaningful to the initiates was to make an appeal to the commonly held associations of ideas which each of the names evoked. Thus although rejecting the outside world, the mysteries needed to use it as a point of reference to make the nature of the rejection intelligible to its initiates. In other words, the terms of the denial of elements in the outside world admitted the existence of those elements, albeit outside the cult. Thus the systematic rejection of women at each level in the progress of the initiate may be interpreted as a recognition of women's status in the 'non-existent' world beyond the cult. The rejection of women occurred on every level, mundane, mythic and cultic. It occurred on an empirical level: women had no part in the ritual. The myth of Mithras' birth also excluded women on a mythic level. But most significant was their exclusion at a cultic level. It was not simply women that were excluded but the female principle itself. The central myth of the cult, that Mithras was born not of woman but of a rock, can very instructively be compared to the myth of Hercules and the Bona Dea. In the cult of Hercules too, women were excluded, so that female members of the population had no place therein, just as in the cult of Mithras. But the aetiological myth recognized the necessity for the female principle and the necessary cultic space was provided, albeit at a safe distance. Exclusion of women from a cult was in itself nothing very much out of the ordinary. But exclusion of the female principle from a cultic system – which is what the Mithraic mysteries did – was a different proposition altogether and needed to be legitimated repeatedly. This, I suggest, is why the theme of female rejection occurs at every level in the initiatory process in the cult of Mithras as well as in the myth.

I suggest that if the mysteries of Mithras were inordinately preoccupied with legitimating the denial of any status to the female principle it could only be because of the important status conferred on the female in the cultic system that the mysteries had rejected, which was the traditional civic ideology. The cult of the Bona Dea, as I argued, occupied its own well defined space within the civic system where the cult of Hercules also existed. Whatever may have been the actual process of the formation or invention of these cults in an antiquity so remote that it has not been recoverable by historical investigation, analysis, or indeed imagination, the common perception of that formation, in the myth of Hercules and Bona Dea at any rate, was that sexual exclusiveness was a feature imposed initially by women. Far from being pushed by the male into a marginal position, the female occupied centre stage to begin with, and it is the male that was refused entry. Indeed if we were to carry the logic of this aetiological position to its extreme, we would arrive at a scenario where the male cultic space is the marginal one.

But carrying logic to its extreme in this instance will seriously undermine the plausibility of this analysis. Nowhere in the ancient sources do we find the slightest hint that the cult of Hercules at the *Ara Maxima*, much less male cultic space, occupied a marginal position in the cultic universe. And yet, the evidence of the aetiological myths, especially with respect to chronology, appears to support a case for the hypothesis. Both in the case of Bona Dea and of Hercules, a fact that is stressed repeatedly is the antiquity of the cult. The *Ara Maxima*, as we saw, derived a large part of its cultic importance from its perceived antiquity.[96] But the cult of Bona Dea was even older. It was believed to have been in existence when Hercules arrived on the scene. Both our sources for the Hercules–Bona Dea myth imply that the cult was well established before Hercules' arrival.[97] According to the mythological account Hercules was refused entry to the women's rites first, and his exclusion of them from his was done in retaliation. So according to the logic of the myth, at any rate, not only did women exist within the cultic universe, but they were there first, and what is more they made the rules. This is almost an inversion of the Mithraic scenario. However, cultic practice does not appear to have reflected the mythic logic, and nowhere is the cult of the Bona Dea accorded a status superior to that of Hercules. Myth and cult appear to have been in conflict on this issue although the conflict would, I suspect, be more of an issue to the modern analyst than to the ancient. No such conflict is apparent in the sources, nor are the logical consequences of the myth as I have delineated them ever discussed.

If there is no evidence that male cultic space occupied a marginal position, the same can be said for female cultic space. The cult of the Bona Dea was unquestionably perceived to have been of great importance to the welfare of the Roman state. Cicero repeatedly refers to the ceremony as being performed *pro populo* or *pro salute populi Romani*.[98] Moreover, the furious row that Clodius caused can only partly be put down to political exploitation of the event. The rites had certainly been polluted. We are told that the *pontifices* pronounced them polluted in response to a question by the senate.[99] We cannot ignore the possibility that this could have been a politically expedient decision, and that they would just as easily have decided otherwise if that had been politically more desirable. However, it appears that the pontiffs' decision was in this instance merely an endorsement of one taken much earlier. The Vestal Virgins had almost immediately repeated the ceremony,[100] which would imply that it was they who had taken the decision that the rite was polluted and had acted on it. Thus the college of pontiffs was merely endorsing a decision already made. They had no room to manoeuvre politically and their decision appears to have been a mere formality, an expression of conventional religious wisdom that they had to present formally to the senate so that it could proceed to take action in the matter. Furthermore I suggest that the level of the fuss generated by the event could only have been sustained if Clodius' crime had been perceived as heinous. Nowhere is it suggested that it all could have been dismissed as a youthful escapade. The gravity of his conduct was never disputed. Indeed Clodius was forced to go to improbable lengths to 'prove' his innocence. The elaborate fiction that he had not even been in Rome at the time of the incident[101] was not meant, I suggest, simply to convince the jury, who had been heavily bribed and were guaranteed in any case to acquit him,[102] but also to influence the general perception of the incident. This was no marginal rite that had been violated, but one which occupied an important niche in the civic system.

OPERTANEA SACRA

The cult of Bona Dea is a study in paradox. Nowhere is this more evident than in the secret December rites that Clodius made notorious. 'One of the characteristic devices of the non-traditional religions of the Graeco-Roman world was secrecy,' writes Richard Gordon, in his opening remarks in an article on the mysteries of Mithras. 'Secrecy contrasted with the public character of the dominant civic cults intimately associated with the cultural and political power of the elite' (Gordon 1988: 45). Of the Adonia, Marcel Detienne writes, 'the Adonia, an exotic festival tolerated by the Athenian city on the periphery of the official cults and public ceremonies were a private affair'. One mark of this marginal status of the Adonia was the fact that it took place not in a sanctuary or other public place, but in the house of a private individual (Detienne 1977: 65). In 186 BC when the consul Postumius was investigating the exposure of the secret rites of Bacchus in Rome, one of the more sinister developments of the cult was seen to be the fact that what had started out as a daytime ceremony had been changed by the Campanian priestess into a nocturnal one.[103] Nocturnal ceremonies conducted by women were a source of potential danger to the well ordered state and Cicero would have none in his ideal state, with one exception: *nocturna mulierum sacrificia ne sunto praeter olla, quae pro populo rite fient* – 'Let there be no nocturnal sacrifices by women, with one exception: that which is performed for the welfare of the people'.[104] *Sacrificia pro populo* referred to the rites of Bona Dea.[105]

Secret, nocturnal, conducted by women in a private house, yet far from being a threat to the state, the festival ensured its well-being. What is to be made of this enigmatic cult? I turn now to the rituals connected with the cult – specifically the rituals connected with the December festival. Bona Dea had a temple on the Aventine built by the senate and dedicated by a Vestal Virgin.[106] Ovid describes it as a temple which 'abhors the eyes of males'.[107] This is the only reference to a temple for the goddess that we have for this period.[108] Ovid's dramatic description has, reasonably enough, been taken to mean that men were excluded from the temple.[109] Yet Ovid himself, this time in the *Ars Amatoria*, appears to suggest that this exclusion may not have been all-encompassing. 'The Good Goddess repels from the temple the eyes of men *except such as she bids come there herself*.'[110] Who were these men who were allowed into the temple? Dedicatory inscriptions to Bona Dea found in Rome indicate that both men and women worshipped her.[111] Moreover she was believed to possess powers of healing, and in this capacity was identified with the Greek Medea by some ancient exegetists.[112] It is a reasonable surmise that men as well as women benefited from the healing arts of her priestesses and visited the temple to avail themselves of it. Bona Dea was also a prophetic deity[113] and here again men might well have had recourse to her talents. But none of this satisfactorily explains Ovid's claim: *fuget a templum oculos Bona Diva virorum,/praeterquam siquos illa venire iubet.*[114] This seems to suggest some sort of male official of the cult rather than an ordinary worshipper. But we have no way of knowing for sure, and not enough evidence even to make an informed guess. However Ovid's testimony is important in that it allows us to say with confidence that the exclusion of males was not as strict as we have been led to think by the large quantity of writing in contemporary and later ages of the Clodius affair. I am not suggesting that the general claim, from Cicero down to the Christian apologists, that the rites Clodius violated were strictly confined to women was in any way adventitious. But I am suggesting that the insistence on that aspect of the cult may have clouded our perception of the overall picture. It is entirely possible that selected males may have had a role to play in some of her rites, although not in the December festival.

Our knowledge of what actually went on in the temple of Bona Dea and the ritual that was conducted in conjunction with the temple on the Kalends of May is very slender indeed.[115] But thanks to Clodius we have a slightly better idea of what took place early in December. The most striking feature of this rite was that it did not take place in the temple of the goddess but in a private house – the house of a consul or a praetor for the year in question.[116] We have references to two separate occasions on which the rites were conducted. In 63 BC the festival was held in Cicero's house[117] and in the following year in Caesar's,[118] when they were consul and praetor respectively. This poses a very interesting problem: here was a cult perceived to have been strictly confined to women; it was sacrilege for a man to even know what went on; yet the performance of its rituals was mediated by male status. What is more, this status was politically defined. It was not confined to a member of a particular class, for example, the senatorial class. If that had been the case, it would have been harder to argue for male mediation for the venue of the rites, for women too were defined by class, even if that definition was derived from their relationship with men.[119] But political status unequivocally excluded women. At the same time it anchored a cult, full of avowedly dangerous elements, firmly in the nexus of state-sponsored rituals. A deliberate choice was made to hold the rites in a private house, for the Bona Dea did possess at least one temple in Rome. The reason for holding them in the house of a magistrate, I suggest, was to provide a symbolic if not physical presence of men at the rite.

The symbolic presence of men in the rites of the Bona Dea was not limited to the venue of the festival. The wife of the magistrate in question appeared to play a leading part in the business of the evening although it is impossible to know what exactly her duties entailed, or how far her authority extended over the activities involved. The Vestal Virgins were present, and it appears that it was they who actually performed the rites.[120] In 62 BC when a man – Clodius – was discovered in the house, it was not the Vestals but Aurelia, Caesar's mother, presumably taking the initiative from her disgraced daughter-in-law, who ordered that the rites be stopped immediately.[121] The Vestal Virgins later repeated them. During the rites celebrated the previous year, when flames leaping out of a dead fire signalled a prodigy, it was interpreted as a divine message for the presiding matron for that year, Cicero's wife, Terentia. It was a signal from the goddess that the course of action Cicero was contemplating – i.e. summary execution of the Catilinarian conspirators – had divine endorsement, and it was his wife who was sent to tell him so.[122]

The self-conscious and ostentatious way in which the exclusion of males from the house was effected also served to emphasize their 'presence' within it. For one thing the men – and a wealthy Roman household contained a sizeable number of them – had to find alternative accommodation for the night. This could hardly have been effected unobtrusively.[123] Second, all traces of previous male presence had to be masked. Even pictures of males, we are told, had to be covered up – not removed, but covered up.[124] Those draped objects, present throughout the proceedings, could not have failed to serve as reminders of what lurked beneath the drapery – symbolic representations of men. Not only that, but in the house of a senior magistrate, portraits and busts of men would have included those of distinguished ancestors, and would thus have largely been representative of those who had held positions of power in the state. Absent males, dead and alive, representing the continuous power of the Roman state, dominated with a symbolic presence a rite ostensibly restricted to females.[125]

What exactly did these women do all night? Cicero writes of elaborate ceremonial (*Sacrificium. . . . fit incredibili caerimonia*).[126] Juvenal paints a lurid picture of a drunken orgy.[127] Clodius disguised himself as a female musician in order to infiltrate the ceremony of 62 BC.[128] There may well have been music, even dancing, but Versnel's hypothesis that the festival of Bona Dea provided a ritual setting for the licentious behaviour of women is not supported by the evidence.[129] Such a hypothesis could only have been based on Juvenal's description, for nowhere else do we find a suggestion of debauchery in connection with the rites. But quite apart from the literary context – the infamous sixth satire – which in itself would be sufficient to challenge an uncritical acceptance of its contents as historical evidence, Juvenal makes it quite clear that what he is describing is not the prescribed practice of the rites but a deplorable lapse from the strict standards of the past. 'O would that our ancient practices, or at least our public rites were not polluted by scenes like these.'[130]

> Who ever sneered at the gods in the days of old? Who would have dared to laugh at the earthenware bowls or black pots of Numa, or the brittle plates made out of Vatican clay? But nowadays at what altar will you not find a Clodius?
>
> (Juv., 6.342–345)

The solemnity of the rites cannot be doubted. When Clodius was discovered, the women with great presence of mind evicted him and repeated the rites. This is not in keeping with a picture of a drunken orgy. In 63 BC the goddesses' will was signalled by a flame shooting out of a dead fire. I suggest that the fact that the fire had gone out may be taken to imply that the rites were at an end, when, if Juvenal's description were to be taken seriously, the women would have been worn out by debauchery. Yet the sign was noted, interpreted and promptly reported. In the time of the late Republic and early Principate at least, the rites of Bona Dea were a serious business, meticulously performed to ensure the well-being of the Roman people.

The rites of Bona Dea were not merely part of the civic religion, they were a part thereof *par excellence*. When Roman writers referred to a rite performed *pro populo* or *pro salute populi* they were invariably referring to the rites of Bona Dea.[131] How these rites were believed to ensure the safety of the people is not clear to a modern historian. It is a question never posed by our sources, not even by curious Greeks like Plutarch. My own thesis, which will be elaborated during the course of this book, is that the concept of boundary in general and sexually defined boundary in particular, was closely linked with the notion of the welfare of the state. It was expressed in its most extreme form in the priesthood of the Vestals as I shall argue in the final chapter. For the moment we need to look more closely at how the notion of boundary operated in the rite of the Bona Dea by examining more of the ritual features of the cult.

WINE, MILK AND HONEY

Two details of the ritual that took place in December are particularly important in terms of this analysis. One is the exclusion of myrtle from the house where the festival was to be celebrated, the other is the use of wine at the festival. Plutarch surmised that the reason that myrtle was excluded from Bona Dea's rites was because it was a plant sacred to Venus and Bona Dea was a chaste goddess.[132] Both myrtle and wine were used by Faunus in the story, in a vain attempt to force his daughter to yield to his incestuous advances.[133] As a result, myrtle was excluded from the rites altogether, and wine was brought in a honey pot (*mellarium*) and called milk.[134] The significance of the exclusion of myrtle will be more conveniently discussed in chapter 3, where I examine aspects of the cult of Venus. Here I shall examine the significance of wine in Bona Dea's festival.

Again the most useful approach to the problem is through an examination of another rite – the Parilia, which was celebrated on 21 April. Our main source for the Parilia is Ovid, who claims to have participated in the festival, and describes it in gratifying detail.[135] It appears to have been principally a rite for shepherds, designed to purify the sheep and ensure both their preservation from harm and their fertility during the coming year. Both ancient and modern commentators appear to agree on this point.[136] But that wasn't all it was. The Parilia was also regarded as a celebration of the birthday of Rome, although the festival itself, like those of Hercules at the *Ara Maxima* and Bona Dea, was perceived to have existed before Rome was actually founded.[137] The Parilia was a festival admirably suited to accommodate the multivalent significations that cults were endowed with, and which helped maintain their vibrancy and meaning as social, political and economic structures evolved.[138] Already in the time of Ovid, the rite had acquired many layers of meaning, as Ovid's eager attempt to interpret them shows. 'The multitude of explanations creates a doubt and thwarts me at the outset,' he complains, then devotes twenty-two lines to a dizzy succession of baffling interpretations.[139] The evidence we have for the ritual practices of the Parilia serves only to mystify if considered simply in the context of this single rite. However, when put into the wider context of Roman cult practice it is possible to formulate a plausible hypothesis as to their meaning and function. In terms of this analysis, the rites of Bona Dea and the Parilia will give each other meaning. It is important to bear in mind, however, that there is no discernible structural parallelism of the sort that was demonstrated between the rites of Hercules and Bona Dea. Here it is rather a case of two separate rites within a common polytheistic religion, embedded in the same cultural matrix, using a ritual mechanism in a similar way. The ritual mechanism in this case is the use of wine and milk in the Parilia and the wine that is called milk in the rites of Bona Dea. Neither of these two features makes much sense when the cults are considered separately. But they do make quite a lot of sense when the two cults are compared. For this reason the following discussion will be a bit disjointed. I shall start with a discussion of the Parilia, switch to the rites of the Bona Dea, then return to the Parilia before summing up the argument.

This is not going to be a comprehensive analysis of the rites of the Parilia – only an examination of one particular aspect of them which will help shed some light on a feature of the cult of the Bona

Dea. The most striking feature of Ovid's description of the Parilia is fire. Indeed it is the fires of the Parilia that Ovid tries to explain in his exegetical exercise. The fire appears to have a twofold function: purificatory and generative, concepts which indeed appear closely interrelated in other areas of religious ideology.[140] First of all the sheep are purified with fire in which sulphur is burned together with special ritual fumigants supplied by the Vestal Virgins.[141] The purification is followed by a prayer. The structure of this prayer as set forth by Ovid reveals the close connection between purificatory and generative power in the rite. The prayer for expiation of all involuntary infractions of ritual injunctions, whether committed by sheep – e.g., browsing on graves – or shepherd, is smoothly transposed into a prayer for bountiful offspring for the sheep and prosperity for the shepherd. And the fire is the single signifier for both aspects.

That fire is used to purify is a commonplace in many religions in different cultures. Its generative aspects are not so intuitively discernible. But in Rome, as we saw, fire was a symbol both of the male principle and also of the generative power of the male. This symbolism is also present in the rites of the Parilia where fire is used to signify the generative or procreative power of the male, not just of the ram but of the shepherd as well. The shepherd having uttered his prayer – four times – washes his hands in dew, drinks wine and milk mixed together, then leaps over the fires set three in a row. From a reading of Ovid it is impossible even to guess at the meaning of this but Tibullus provides a clue.

> And drenched in wine the shepherd will chaunt the feast of Pales the shepherds holiday. Ye wolves, be ye then far from the fold. Full of drink he will fire the light straw heaps in the appointed way, and leap across the sacred flames. Then shall his dame bear offspring, and the child take hold of his father's ears to snatch a kiss; nor shall the grandsire find it irksome to watch by his little grandson's side, nor, for all his years, to lisp in prattle with the child.
>
> (Tib., 2.5.87–94)

The shepherd leaps across the flames, according to Tibullus, in order that his wife – *matrona* – may bear offspring. 'Lustful be the ram', prays Ovid, 'and may his mate conceive and bear, and many a lamb be in my fold.'[142] If I've read Tibullus correctly (and it does seem quite straightforward) the same prayer could, with equal validity, have been said for the shepherd himself on this occasion. The generative power of the fire touched man and beast alike.

This is a most remarkable rite. It was usually women who, until very recently, were concerned with fertility, and there are many aspects of Roman religion which address the problem of female fertility. The 'fertility goddess' worshipped by women is a common-place in popular notions of pagan religion in general. But in the Parilia it is the fertility of the male that appears to have been at issue. What is meant here by 'fertility' is no more than lustfulness, yet it is striking that the capacity of the female to bear offspring was perceived to depend on the fertility of her mate. Nowhere is mention made of women participating in this rite. But it is highly improbable that they were not present in some capacity. The Parilia was very much a multi-faceted ritual. It was both public and private, rural and urban: 21 April was a merry day in Rome and there must have been celebrations everywhere.[143] But the most prominent ritual role was played by men.

The sex of the deity Pales who was the object of sacrifice at the Parilia was a matter for controversy in ancient times and most modern scholars have believed that she was one of those deities whose sex was unknown – those addressed by the formula *sive deus sive dea* in formulary prayers.[144] Dumézil however has argued convincingly that Pales was a goddess (Dumézil 1970: 380 *et seq.*). A feature of the rite gives further support to Dumézil's hypothesis. Tibullus speaks of the shepherd at the Parilia as drenched in wine (*madidus baccho*) and drunk (*potus*).[145] Ovid describes him drinking wine mixed with milk before leaping through the flames.[146] But the liquid offering made to Pales was simply milk. Where milk and wine occur together in ritual they seem to correspond to the male–female dichotomy inherent in the cults of which the rituals were a part. But to demonstrate this convincingly it is necessary to look at the rites of Bona Dea.

Wine was brought into the rites of Bona Dea but it was called milk and its container was called a honey-pot. It was also kept covered. The ancient aetiology for this was that Faunus had tried to make his daughter drunk with wine, hoping thereby to seduce her. Another explanation was that the cult of Bona Dea was a very old one, and in the old days libations to the gods were made with milk not wine.[147] But whatever it might have been called, what was brought in to the rite was wine not milk. Moreover myrtle had the same function in the myth as wine did and it was unambiguously excluded from the rite. Wine was not.

In the ideology of the early Romans wine and women apparently did not mix. 'In Rome', writes Pliny, 'women were not allowed to drink wine.'[148] The reason for this prohibition is very problematic. Pliny seems to suggest that the reason was an economic one – the theme of the passage is that wine, in the early days of Rome that Pliny was talking about, was a scarce and precious commodity and had to be carefully husbanded. Yet it appears from examples of women who were punished for drinking wine and from other sources, that the basis for the prohibition was ideological rather than economic. It appears that the prohibition against drinking wine was particularly important in the case of *matronae*. In their case drinking wine was tantamount to adultery. They were punished in the same way for both 'crimes'. A law attributed to Romulus states that for wives the penalty for the crimes of adultery and drinking wine was death.[149] Egnatius Maetennus, says Pliny, beat his wife to death for drinking wine, and Romulus acquitted him on the charge of murder.[150] Valerius Maximus, following the same tradition, though his character is called Egnatius Metellus, writes that when the man killed his wife 'everyone considered this an excellent example of one who had justly paid the penalty for violating the laws of sobriety'.[151] Cato, describing the powers of husband over wife, mentions two serious marital offences for which wives could be severely punished by their husbands: committing adultery and drinking wine.[152] Moreover men needed to be vigilant to be sure that their women folk were not secretly imbibing. It was the custom for women to kiss their male kinsfolk on the mouth, and after they were married they did the same to their husband's kinsfolk. The ancient commentators felt that an explanation was needed for this curious custom. It was done, according to both Pliny and Cato, for the purpose of detecting whether the women had been drinking or not. If they had, the odour of the wine would betray them to their relations.[153]

But merely to label this prohibition ideological is to beg the question. What we have here is not simply a distaste for the sight of a tipsy woman, such as Ovid expresses in the *Ars Amatoria* when he warns his female readers to drink moderately at parties because a drunken woman is an ugly sight.[154] It is not simply a fear that an inebriated woman would be more likely to commit adultery, although Valerius Maximus does suggest that as the reason. It is not intoxication that is at issue here, but the idea that wine was somehow completely outside the domain of the female. Wine represented maleness, a preserve on which women were not allowed to encroach. For a woman, especially a wife, to drink wine was equivalent to committing adultery. It represented in ideological terms an unmediated union of the sexes, an unlawful crossing of the boundary between male and female. This, I suggest, is what wine represents in the story of Faunus and his daughter. The sexual separation between father and daughter is such that no ritual mediation can make a union between them licit. To make her drunk with wine was to give her the same status as a wife who had stolen wine, i.e. an adulterous wife. But incest went beyond adultery, and so even by making his daughter drunk Faunus could not compel her to submit to his advances.

From an ideological perspective wine represented the masculine pole of a male–female axis. I shall return to this theme when I discuss the significance of Liber in the cult of Ceres, Liber and Libera in the next chapter. But in the context of the present discussion we can finally make sense of the presence of wine in the rites of the Bona Dea. Wine was another instance, on a ritual level, of the symbolic presence of males at the rite. Like the pictures of males, the wine was covered up, and it was accorded further ambiguity by being called milk and being contained in a honey-pot.

Milk was believed to have been the libation of choice in older, simpler days. And this has been suggested as a reason why the wine in the rite of the Bona Dea was called milk.[155] But to explain this feature it is not enough to explain just one facet of it. The wine, the milk and the honey must be understood as it has been presented – as a composite whole. By now it will be possible to intuit the significance of milk in the rite: it must symbolize the female principle. It does. But not, however, only by virtue of the obvious fact that milk is produced exclusively by the female of the species. That, of course, is the basis of the ideological beliefs about the significance of milk, but those beliefs go further than that. Milk was considered to be the female's equivalent of semen, continuing to fashion the infant in body and mind after it was born. Gellius, quoting the philosopher Favorinus, writes,

> Just as the power and nature of the seed are able to form likenesses of body and mind, so the qualities and properties of milk have the same effect. . . . This is observed not only in human beings but in beasts also.

> (Gell., *N.A.*, 12.1.14–15)[156]

Moreover the quality of milk was believed to vary from individual to individual, affecting the mental and physical characteristics of the nursling. So if an infant was nursed by a woman of evil character its own character would be affected, regardless of the nature of its parents. In this respect milk and semen had a symmetrical relationship. The idea of milk affecting the characteristics of the nursling occurred in poetry too. In the seventh book of the Aeneid, Camilla, who was so fleet of foot that 'she might have flown o'er the topmost blades of unmown corn, nor in her course bruised the tender ears', was suckled by a mare.[157] In a more practical context Soranus, when prescribing the qualities to look for when employing a wet nurse, also warned that the nature of the nursling became similar to that of the nurse.[158] Milk thus becomes a powerful symbol not just of the female but of the female's procreative power. Male and female were both present at the rites of Bona Dea. But the male presence was veiled while the female presence was exaggerated. The ritual feature of the wine that was covered up and called milk epitomized the respective roles of both male and female in the rite.

Returning to the Parilia from the perspective of the preceding argument the significance of wine and milk at that ritual becomes comprehensible. It is possible that women had no ritual role to play at the Parilia; we know of none. Nevertheless, as the passage quoted from Tibullus makes clear, the enhancement of the shepherd's virility by participation in the rite affected the fertility of his wife. By drinking the mixture of wine and milk before leaping over the flames the shepherd ritually acknowledged that fact and established a symbolic if not a physical involvement of women at the rite. Moreover the offering made to Pales was not this mixture of milk and wine, but pure milk.[159] In the context of the Parilia this must be seen as an acknowledgement of the female nature of the deity, lending support to Dumézil's position that Pales was, in Rome at least, if not elsewhere in Italy, unambiguously a goddess.[160] In the Parilia and the rites of Bona Dea then, the ritual functions of milk and wine were exploited in similar ways.

Similar, but not identical. The Bona Dea presents us with one more feature that must be taken into consideration. The wine that was called milk came in a 'honey-pot'. A honey-pot would ordinarily be expected to contain honey. This one contained wine–'milk'. It is not honey, but it is bounded and contained by the notion of honey. Why honey? Marcel Detienne's admirable analysis of

Virgil's account in the fourth *Georgic* of the myth of Aristaeus the bee-keeper, whose bees desert him when he attempts to seduce Eurydice, offers a persuasive account of the mythological perspective on honey (Detienne 1981b). Bees, Detienne argues, exemplify in the mythological context, the idea of strict chastity within marriage. They were believed to single out for attack those guilty of illicit sexual relationships. So strong was the bees' abhorrence for sexual incontinence that a bee-keeper was obliged to observe exemplary marital fidelity. 'The bee-keeper must approach his bees as a good husband does his lawful wife, that is, in a state of purity, without being polluted by sexual relations with other women' (*ibid.*: 99).[161] Aristaeus' bees desert him, Detienne argues, because of his lapse from this ideal. A remark of Pliny's neatly connects Detienne's discussion with mine. According to Pliny, Aristaeus was the first to mix honey and wine together.[162] A mixture of honey and wine was one of the traditional offerings made to Ceres, who was perceived as being concerned especially with sexual intercourse within marriage.[163]

The way in which the concepts of wine, milk and honey operated within the rite of Bona Dea extended into the ritual sphere the same ideological patterns that I traced in her mythology. The overt polarization of the sexes is evoked in the wine that is disguised as milk, as opposed to the Parilia where, although the notion of dual sexuality is present, there was no apparent polarity and the wine and milk were mixed and drunk together. Honey which contained and bounded the wine–'milk' represented the lawful way in which the poles could be made to collapse – marriage. Finally, the fact that the offering was in reality wine rather than milk, represented the symbolic participation of males in a rite ostensibly confined to women.

In summary, the cult of Bona Dea established the nature of the boundary between male and female. Male and female were polar opposites whose converging had to be ritually mediated. At the same time there was an acknowledgement that the opposed elements existed within a common context and were interdependent. Finally it seemed to suggest a way in which society might be served by such an interdependent existence. It was indeed a rite *pro populo*.

Part II

THE CULTS OF CERES AND FLORA

INTRODUCTION TO
CHAPTER 2

Misogyny was pervasive in Roman ideology. The work of the satirists, particularly Juvenal's sixth satire, is perhaps the best known vehicle of misogynistic discourse. But the belief that women by their very nature constituted a threat not only to individual men, but to society in general found wide expression across the cultural spectrum. In myth and cult, in legal discourse and institutions, even in conventions of dress, we can discern the belief that women's behaviour needed to be strictly regulated.

All women were subjects of misogynistic discourse. But wives – *matronae* – more than any other category bore the brunt of the invective against women. It took Juvenal nearly seven hundred lines of relentless invective to describe the living hell that matrimony was for a man. However the real threat from wives was the threat to the state itself. Despite the political and legal incapacities imposed upon them, women, especially married women, were perceived to possess the power to undermine male political authority and destroy the very foundation of society. Women were perceived to possess this power by their capacity for collective action. The early history of Rome is full of examples of women collaborating to influence the course of events. Most often their actions resulted in averting danger to the state or in otherwise benefiting it in some way. But sometimes women banded together to wring concessions from men, to influence the legislative or executive process in their favour and to the detriment of male authority. There is therefore an ambivalence in the attitude towards women which undermines somewhat the robustness of the invective against them. Even Juvenal grudgingly acknowledges that women were once virtuous. It is hardly a compliment. Women were virtuous only because life in early Rome was arduous and they had no time to be anything else. But the ambivalence is there in Juvenal and elsewhere. Women and especially wives were a necessary evil.

Ambivalence towards women is also a constant theme in the myths of the founding of Rome and her political and legal institutions. Women played central roles in the myths that commemorated the three critical events of Rome's earliest history: the founding of the city itself; the establishment of its social order and political continuity; and the establishment of the Republic. In all three events the figure of the *matrona* is centrally important. The ambivalence in the attitude towards wives is played out in these stories. Wives were indispensable for the preservation of the fledgling state and its political continuity. But the earliest wives, the Sabine women, were foreigners, outsiders, not Roman. This 'foreigness' of the wife is reflected in the legal position of the *matrona* within her husband's *gens*. It is important to be aware that the *matrona* was a Roman creation. Not all wives were *matronae*. The *matrona* was the product of a peculiarly Roman form of marriage. Wives were therefore in a sense a 'foreign' intrusion into a man's *domus*. This too was a source of ambivalence. A chaste and industrious wife could prosper a man's house and family. But an unchaste wife could destroy it. The story of Lucretia demonstrates how the potential for either outcome could inhere in the same woman.

Cult used the device of sexual categorization to isolate wives. The cults of Ceres and Flora were the focus for the categorization of wives into a ritually distinct group. This group was complemented and defined by the ritual category of prostitutes. The two cults of Ceres, who was concerned with wives, and Flora, at whose festival prostitutes played a prominent role, were structured in contrast to each other. The Floralia was a vivid, exuberant festival; the *sacrum anniversarium Cereris* a sober, somewhat forbidding affair. Critical to the display of the contrasting attitude towards wife and prostitute was the role of men in each cult. The cult of Ceres established a degree of formality and distance between men and their wives, while at the festival of the Floralia men participated on equal terms with the women.

2

CERES AND FLORA

If we could get on without a wife, Romans, we would all avoid that annoyance; but since nature has ordained that we can neither live very comfortably with them nor at all without them, we must take thought for our lasting well-being rather than for the pleasure of the moment.

(Gell., *N.A.*, 1.6.2)

These words were not meant to be ironical. They are quoted in all seriousness by Aulus Gellius from a speech 'On Marriage' delivered to the people by an 'earnest and eloquent man' (*gravis ac disertus vir*), Q. Metellus Numidicus, when he was censor in 102 BC.[1] Since the speech was intended to encourage Roman citizens to marry, Gellius wonders if Metellus was wise to have admitted 'the annoyance and constant inconveniences of the married state'. But he concludes that Metellus could have done no less. Being a

blameless man with a reputation for dignity and a sense of honour, . . . it did not become him to say anything which was not accepted as true by himself and by all men, especially when speaking on a subject which was a matter of everyday knowledge and formed a part of the common and habitual experience of life.

(*ibid.*, 3–6)

Misogyny was a pervasive force in Roman ideology. Metellus' speech as Gellius interprets it was neither an isolated nor an exceptional example of Roman attitudes to wives. The diatribes of the satirists, on the themes of the insatiable lusts, the unbridled licence, the bottomless greed and wild extravagance of women, are its most obvious manifestation.[2] Women were a threat to the stability of society. But somewhat paradoxically women were also perceived as weak-willed and simple-minded, incapable of managing their own affairs, and in need of male protection and supervision.[3] Such attitudes and the political and legal incapacity that necessarily accompanied them applied to all women. Wives, however, appear to have been a particular subject of misogynistic discourse. In particular, the attitude to wives appears to have been marked by anxiety and ambivalence.

The cult of Bona Dea offered a glimpse of how male ambivalence towards women was incorporated into the dynamics of myth and ritual. At different levels it established and undermined, affirmed and denied the dichotomy of male and female. Female space was simultaneously forbidden to and dominated by males. But the cult of Bona Dea, as we shall see, represented only one dimension of what was a complex ideological discourse on the nature of gender relationships.

Roman religion categorized females in terms of their sexuality or, more accurately, in terms of the stages of their sexual relationship with men. From a general perspective women who were, or were potentially sexually active constituted a separate ritual group to women who were not. The former category was again divided into two opposed groups – wives and prostitutes. This chapter will be concerned with the display of this division in myth and ritual. Women who were not sexually active were also further categorized into two groups – virgins and old women, that is, women before and after the sexually active stage. This group was much less important in ritual and was never explicitly polarized as were wives and prostitutes. Although young children of both sexes participated in the ritual life of the family and the city, virgins did not form an element of cult in the way that matrons and prostitutes did.[4] Though the Vestal Virgins did represent in some ways the status of virginity, their case was a special one.[5] The references to old women in cult are also extremely rare.

This chapter will be divided into three sections. The first will show that it was the married woman who was perceived as the greatest threat to the male dominated system; the second will examine Roman myths dealing with wives, and show how they reveal a deep ambivalence in male attitudes to married women; and the third will show how this ambivalence was reflected in ritual practice.

UNEASY MISOGYNY

No woman escaped the stab of the satirists' pen. Neither social class nor sexual status insulated women from satirical invective. The most formidable example of invective against women, Juvenal's massive sixth satire, nearly seven hundred lines of vicious, misogynistic, vituperation is directed chiefly at the married woman – *uxor*. The satire, addressed to a young man about to be married, is on the theme of the suicidal folly of marriage. There was to be no respite from the horrors of matrimony for the unlucky husband. However the satirist does grudgingly admit that once upon a time women actually were virtuous. True, this was in the dim and distant past, either in the legendary age of Saturn, or in the early years of the Republic, before Rome was corrupted by long years of peace and excessive wealth. Virtue was forced on women in those days, says Juvenal, because life was hard and they had neither time nor opportunity for corruption. A sting in the tail perhaps, but none the less it was a hint of ambivalence, a respite from hatred however begrudging, in a monument to misogyny. The virtuous wife was pushed so far back in time that she was inaccessible, but she existed as an ideal, if only that. Juvenal provided only a glimpse of such an ideological respite from the relentless attacks of misogyny. Elsewhere the ambivalence of the discourse about women is more clearly articulated.

Livy, writing much earlier of the repeal of the Oppian law in 195 BC, attributed to Cato and Valerius – consul and tribune respectively for that year – a debate on the dangers posed by married women – *matronae* – to the state.[6] The rhetoric of misogyny is very similar to that found in satire but the issues that are being dealt with are quite different. The Oppian law was a piece of sumptuary legislation which had been passed almost a generation previously when Rome was reeling from the defeat at Cannae. The apparent purpose of the law was to curb female extravagance. Two tribunes, Valerius and Fundanius, were now proposing a repeal of the law, since the state was enjoying a period of prosperity and there was no longer any need for legislative control on consumption. But as there was opposition to this proposal, the *matronae*, who wanted the law repealed, had in a body lobbied the voters making their way to the forum to vote on the bill. It was the appalling and unprecedented sight of *matronae* in the public streets talking to men who were not their husbands, that prompted Cato's attack on women.

Juvenal's poem was concerned with women as individuals, who posed a threat to men only in their private capacity as husbands. Livy's passage offers a different perspective. Cato's resentment and anxiety were directed at a particular category of women, the *matronae*.[7] But it was not the *matronae* themselves that he feared; it was the fact that they had organized themselves into a lobby and were attempting to influence the legislative process. The *matronae*, by their capacity for collective action, posed a threat not merely to individual males but to the very foundation of the social and political structure. Legislative power belonged to a domain that was exclusively male. But Cato's words suggest a fundamental insecurity about men's dominance of that domain; women were capable of encroaching on it and men had to guard their territory vigilantly. Consider the following excerpts from the speech:

> I thought it a fairy tale and a piece of fiction that on a certain island the men were destroyed root and branch by a conspiracy of women; but from no class is there not the greatest danger if you permit them meetings and gatherings and secret consultations.
>
> (Livy, 34.2.3–4)

> Our ancestors permitted no woman to conduct even personal business without a guardian to intervene in her behalf; they wished them to be under the control of fathers, brothers, husbands; we – Heaven help us! – allow them now even to interfere in public affairs, yes, and to visit the forum and our formal and informal sessions (*iam etiam rem publicam capessere eas patimur et foro quoque et contionibus et comitiis immisceri*). What else are they doing now on the streets and at the corners except urging the bill of the tribunes and the repeal of the law?
>
> (*ibid.*, 2.11)

> If you suffer them to seize these bonds one by one and wrench themselves free and finally to be placed on a parity with their husbands do you think that you will be able to endure them? The moment they begin to be your equals they will be your superiors.
>
> (*ibid.*, 3.2)[8]

Cato feared political domination by women. Such a threat could come from one category of women only – the *matronae*. This notion that *matronae* were capable of collective political action was not peculiar to Cato. Roman myth abounds in similar tales and there are plenty of examples from historical times, as Valerius points out in reply to Cato. Through Cato and Valerius Livy was expressing a common theme in Roman attitudes towards women. *Matronae* were a double source of anxiety; they were a threat to husbands as well as to the old established – male dominated – traditions of the state.

But though the threat from *matronae* was political, it was expressed in terms of women's sexuality and by means of sexual innuendo.

> Give loose rein to their uncontrollable nature and to this untamed creature (*indomitio animali*) and expect that they will themselves set bounds to their licence (*licentia*). . . . it is complete liberty, or rather if you wish to speak the truth, complete licence that they desire.
>
> (*ibid.*, 2.13–14)

Whatever the nature of the threat from women, whether it was directed at individual husbands or the hallowed institutions of the state itself, whether it came from individual women or from organized groups of them, it was always seen to stem from their sexuality. Women were seen, moreover, as being incapable of curbing their dangerously wild natures on their own initiative. If men were to avoid the consequences of untamed female sexuality, they had to do the taming themselves, ideally domestically where each man kept strict control over his own wife, or if that failed, by law. The consequences of failing to control women would be social and political turmoil.[9]

Cato's diatribe, like Juvenal's, was not all unrelieved gloom. Here too we can discern an ambivalence towards women. Cato also admits the existence of the virtuous woman, but like Juvenal puts her out of contemporary reach. Female virtue existed in the old days because those grand old Romans – *maiores nostri* – knew how to control their women. Subsequent wealth and ease had caused the degeneration of both men and women. This state of affairs was deplorable in men but dangerous in women. Thus, although my examples were taken from two very different literary genres, with very different social agendas, the rhetoric of misogyny is quite similar. More particularly the ambivalence in the attitude towards women was expressed by Cato in a manner very much like that of the sixth satire. It is arguable that both Livy and Juvenal drew on a wider tradition of misogynistic discourse that obtained in Roman society.

Livy however went further than Juvenal. He shifted the focus of male ambivalence towards women from the past onto the present. Valerius replying to Cato's warning is made to use examples from the past to redeem contemporary women. The phenomenon of *matronae* organizing themselves to act in ways which had political repercussions was not unprecedented in the history of Rome. Valerius cites four examples: the Sabine women; the women led by the mother of Coriolanus who went to him in a body and persuaded him to withdraw his Volscian army and desist from a threatened attack on Rome; the women who ransomed the city from the Gauls with their own jewellery; and the women who in a body escorted the image of Cybele into Rome. These were all actions taken by women in times of the gravest national crises and each time the outcome had preserved and strengthened the state. But their importance in this particular debate was to give immediacy to the ambivalence that Cato would have relegated to the past. Forcing the comparison between women from the semi-mythical past and those lobbying for the repeal of the Oppian law effectively mitigated the force of the misogynistic attack and blurred the stark outlines of the female threat as Cato had laid it out.

WIFE AND PROSTITUTE IN MYTH

A similar ambivalence informs the stories which constituted Rome's self-representation, and in which women featured in important ways. In this section I shall examine the myths of Romulus' birth, the Sabine women and Lucretia, from the perspective of attitudes towards women in general and wives in particular.

The myth of the birth of Romulus reveals much about the way the Romans separated women into sexual categories and about the ways those categories were defined in relation to men. The story concerns three sexually defined categories of women – virgins, wives and prostitutes. Romulus' mother was a virgin; the Vestal, Rhea Silvia. The most prominent part in the story was given to a prostitute, Romulus' nurse and foster mother, Acca Larentia, who was also an object of cult in Rome. The figure of the *matrona* is conspicuous by its absence. Of female sexual categories the *matrona* was arguably the most important since, as I shall show, it was only by a *matrona* that a male Roman citizen could have children that were legally his own. The absence of the *matrona* from the foundation myth is therefore significant, as is the usurpation of her position by the prostitute.

The story is well known, and I shall here delineate only those features that are of particular interest to this discussion. The Vestal Virgin, Rhea Silvia – Ilia in some versions – gave birth to twin boys, Romulus and Remus. The babies were exposed by order of their mother's wicked uncle, the king, but were saved and suckled by a wolf. Later they were found by the shepherd Faustulus, who took them home to be nursed and reared by his wife, Acca Larentia, who was a prostitute, and therefore called Lupa – she-wolf – a name commonly given to prostitutes.[10]

In historical times the Vestal Virgins were strictly bound by an obligation to observe the most uncompromising chastity.[11] The very survival of the state depended on their unequivocal sexual purity. Theoretically a Vestal could not hope to conceal a lapse from this rigid ideal, because the gods themselves would reveal it by means of prodigies. The offending Vestal and her lover would be sought out and punished; she by being buried alive, he by being flogged to death. Significantly, the fate of a potential child is never mentioned; presumably because it was not thought possible that the woman's transgression could be hidden long enough for her to bear a child. Nevertheless, Romulus' mother was a Vestal Virgin. The myth circumvented this difficulty in all sorts of ways.[12] The most widely accepted tradition was that Mars was the father of the twins and that he had seduced their mother in a dream.[13] By this device the story kept the Vestal's virtue unblemished. She was not made to suffer the traditional punishment, and her pregnancy, far from presaging disaster, resulted in the birth of the founder of the Roman state.[14]

Romulus' birth, as it was interpreted by ancient writers, was paradoxical, indeed impossible, and hence wondrous. The rest of the myth of Romulus, from his being suckled by a wolf, to his mysterious disappearance and subsequent apotheosis, was in keeping with the miraculous nature of his birth.[15] But his mother is given no further share in the story. She simply fades out of the picture. She is in fact the only significant character in the myth of the birth of the twins that plays no further part in their story.[16] It is tempting from a modern perspective to compare Rhea Silvia with the Virgin Mary, whose performance of a similar feat turned her into an object of veneration in her own right, a symbol of chaste and blessed womanhood, set apart by the miracle from the rest of her sex. But where Christianity flaunted the concept of the virgin mother, the Romans, having expended much imaginative energy setting it up, proceeded from that point on to ignore it.

The explanation, I suggest, is that a Vestal Virgin who was a mother was in ritual terms an anomaly. She could not be placed conveniently in any ritual category. She was neither virgin nor wife. This was why she did not feature either in the subsequent adventures of her sons or in Roman cult. Roman religion, as I hope this book will demonstrate, was not constructed to incorporate the sexually anomalous within its ritual boundaries.

The mythological tradition was not content, however, simply to ignore the Vestal mother. It replaced her. The tradition here records two versions of the story, which are related but different. In one, the twins were suckled by a wolf – *lupa* – an animal believed to be sacred to Mars.[17] Mars was believed to have been the Vestal's lover and the twins' father. So by an association of ideas the normal function of a mother, suckling her infant, was in this instance carried out by the father.[18] The biological role of the mother is thereby devalued, and the notion of paternity exaggerated at the expense of the notion of maternity. It is important to note also that the paternity thus established is an artificial or constructed paternity, opposed to the natural maternal function of the mother. This is important. I shall argue shortly that it was analogous to the legal institution of *patria potestas*, which was also a method of constructing paternity.

The second tradition about the fate of Romulus and Remus after they were separated from their mother, appears to be an alternative to the first. It was almost as widely recorded as the story of the wolf and is, in fact, closely linked with it. According to this tradition the twins were suckled not by a wolf at all, but by a prostitute. The word *lupa* meaning both she-wolf and prostitute, serves to link the traditions. The prostitute was the wife of Faustulus, the shepherd who found the twins by the water's edge. Her name was Acca Larentia, but they called her Lupa because she slept around.[19] While 'Lupa', by connecting the two traditions, also evokes Mars the father, in this case that evocation is weaker, for Romulus – and Remus – are here provided with a 'mother'. From the wider perspective of myth and ritual together, the 'mother' effectively usurps the position of the mother, for it was Acca Larentia who was offered cult and not Rhea Silvia.

The myth and cult of Acca Larentia repay close attention. The ancient exegetists have recorded somewhat different traditions about her, but though the stories vary in narrative detail they contain evidence of a base of common assumptions about her.[20] One was that she performed a great service for the Roman people and was for this reason accorded a public religious festival. Testimony comes from Cicero. Writing to Brutus after Caesar's murder, Cicero says that he, Brutus, like Acca Larentia, ought to be granted public sacrifice and a place on the ritual calendar.[21] A reference so casually made is indicative of a widely held cultural perception.

The great service that Cicero was referring to was Acca Larentia's bequest of a large fortune, to the Roman citizens in some versions of the story, to her foster child, Romulus, in others. More interesting, though, is the way in which she came by this fortune. Acca Larentia was a public prostitute – *corpus in vulgus dabat*.[22] According to Gellius she earned her money by her trade[23] but the more widely held tradition was that she acquired it in the following fashion. The guardian of the temple of Hercules alleviated his boredom one day by playing at dice with the god; he threw the dice with one hand for himself, with the other for Hercules. The wager was for a good meal and a night spent with a woman. Hercules won, and the guardian provided him with a fine meal and the celebrated courtesan Acca Larentia, who was locked up in the temple for the night. The next morning she announced that the god had promised her that she would be paid for her services to him by the first man she met on her way home. That man turned out to be Tarutilus, an old man in some versions, a youth in others, who was enormously rich. She lived with him and when he died she inherited his wealth, which she in her turn left to the Roman people. Thus the two stories about Acca Larentia, though superficially unrelated, have common features. In both stories she was a prostitute. In each she performed a service for the state. In one story she nurtured its founder, in the other she enriched its citizens.

Except for one version, recorded by Macrobius, that all this took place during the reign of Ancus,[24] tradition managed to connect her with Romulus in one way or another. In some versions Acca Larentia was Romulus' nurse, in others she was a courtesan, who left her money to Romulus. Plutarch suggested that there were two separate women by the name of Acca Larentia. One was Romulus' nurse whose festival was celebrated in April, the other the courtesan whose festival was celebrated in December. But there is no other evidence for an April festival dedicated to Acca Larentia. Even Plutarch, however, connected the two traditions by recording of the death of the courtesan, that she disappeared at the same place where Romulus' nurse was buried. Afterwards, he says, they discovered her will in which she had left her large fortune to the Roman people.[25] The only version of the story which contains a device to make her Romulus' mother instead of only his nurse is one by Masurius Sabinus quoted by Gellius. Here she was originally Romulus' nurse. But when one of her own twelve sons died Romulus gave himself to her as a son. These twelve sons of Acca including Romulus, were, according to Sabinus, the original Arval Brethren.[26]

Amid the complexities of the various versions, the three salient features are that Acca Larentia was a prostitute, that she was Romulus' nurse, and that her services to the Roman people were so great that she was paid divine honours. A note in the *Fasti Praenestini* recording the festival of the Larentalia on 23 December reads as follows:

> The Parentalia are held in honour of Acca Larentia. Some say that she was the nurse of Romulus and Remus, others that she was a courtesan, the mistress of Hercules. She received public funeral rites because she had left to the Roman people a large sum of money which she had received under the will of her lover Tarutilus.
>
> (CIL 1, p. 319. Trans. Scullard 1981: 210)

Varro provides an interesting detail about the Larentalia. He says that the sixth day after the Saturnalia is called the day of the Parentalia of Larentina [*sic*] after Acca Larentia. Roman priests – *sacerdotes nostri* – performed ancestor-worship – *parentant* – on that day at her tomb in the Velabrum.[27] Gellius identifies at least one of the priests as the *flamen Quirinalis*.

It is significant that this festival was a *parentatio*. A *parentatio* was a private ritual performed by families at the tombs of dead ancestors.[28] On the ides of February the calendars record a ritual called the Parentalia. This was one of three consecutive rituals, extending from the 13th to the 22nd, which commemorated family relationships spanning both the living and the dead, although the emphasis was definitely on dutiful observance of rites to commemorate the dead.[29] Ovid describes the simple offerings made by families at the tombs of their dead relatives at the Parentalia.[30] The Larentalia was celebrated like the Parentalia, except that it was a public ritual performed by state priests, while the Parentalia was a private family ceremony. It was an apt rite for the 'mother' of Romulus, Rome's founder. The *flamen Quirinalis* was one of the officiants at the Larentalia. Quirinus was the deified Romulus. Acca Larentia, 'mother' of Romulus and benefactress of the state, was honoured by the civic religion as though she were the mother of the state itself.

What was the reason for this elaborate creation of myth and cult? Why when Romulus had a mother, did myth take such pains to provide him with a 'mother'? What was the point of Acca Larentia? She appears to have been quite extraneous to the story of the founder and the founding of the state. The story of her encounter with Hercules has no obvious or necessary connection with Romulus. Ritually however, she does appear to derive her importance from her connection with him. The comparatively large number of references to her in the ancient writers, suggest that she captured the imagination over a considerable period of time, and that her cult was an important one. Gellius, for example, says that she was frequently mentioned in the early annals.[31]

It is helpful to put the problem in the context of ritual sexual categories. The relationship of Romulus, Rhea Silvia and Acca Larentia reflects the tensions inherent in the sexual categorization of the female. Of Romulus' 'mothers', one was a Vestal Virgin, the other a prostitute. Conspicuously absent from the whole story of the birth of Romulus, as I have already observed, is the figure of the *matrona*, the legally married Roman woman. The reasons for this, and for Acca Larentia's prominence in myth and ritual, are complex. A brief and schematic outline must suffice here. I shall develop the theory in the course of the chapter.

The ancient writers attributed to Romulus not merely the physical founding of the city but also the ideology of Romanness. A defining attribute of a male Roman citizen was *patria potestas*, a man's legal authority over his legitimate children. A man possessed *patria potestas* only over children born to him in *iustum matrimonium*, by a wife with whom he had *conubium*, i.e. a *matrona*. Children born in *iustum matrimonium* derived their legal status from their father, all other children from their mother. *Iustum matrimonium* was an artifact of Roman law, a Roman invention. This was expressed in myth in the story of the Sabine women. They were the first *matronae*. Romulus was not a product of *iustum matrimonium*. The founder of Rome was not himself unequivocally Roman. This, I shall argue, accounts for the fact of Acca Larentia. If *matrona* and virgin are both ritually disqualified, the *matrona* because she didn't yet exist and the virgin because a virgin mother was a ritual anomaly, a prostitute, in terms of ritual categories of the female, becomes the only possible 'mother' for Romulus.

The importance of Acca Larentia in cult is a function of the contrasting attitudes towards wives and prostitutes. It is an interesting fact that to the best of our knowledge, there was no matronal parallel to the cult figure of Acca Larentia. A prostitute was made the object of public sacrifice, but never, as far as we know, a *matrona*. It is important to note that Acca Larentia was never more than a prostitute. She was not a goddess and nowhere is it suggested that she was apotheosised like Romulus, for example, or Hercules.[32] On the other hand the fact that she was a prostitute is emphasized in the aetiological myth of the cult – the wealth she bequeathed to the Roman people was obtained by prostitution. Was it merely coincidental that a prostitute was offered cult while a *matrona* was not, or is it indicative of a fundamental difference in attitudes towards the categories of 'wife' and 'prostitute'? That there was such a difference is in itself unremarkable. But contrary to our intuitive expectations, the evidence from myth and ritual suggests that it was the *matrona*, not the prostitute that was perceived as 'foreign', as 'the outsider', as 'threatening'. It was the *matrona* not the prostitute that ritual kept at a formal distance from men. Moreover the distance between men and *matronae* was deliberately contrasted with the easy familiarity that ritual allowed to exist between men and prostitutes.

Before looking at the myth, it will be helpful to glance briefly, by way of an introductory aside, at the way in which Roman vestimentary codes revealed an ideology of sexual categorization similar to that discernible in religion. In Rome, especially during the Republic, dress was used as a visual marker of status. The *toga* worn by men was an unmistakable badge of a free born male Roman citizen. *Togatus* as an epithet was meant to denote Roman as opposed to non-Roman.[33] In fact, if a Roman discarded the *toga* for a different form of dress, even temporarily, he became a legitimate target for criticism.[34] But the *toga* was not simply a mark of Romanness. It and the tunic worn underneath, were used as subtle ways of distinguishing status among men. The *toga virilis*, for example, the plain white *toga*, was worn by all males after they had officially attained adult status.[35] The *toga praetexta*, with the broad purple border along the bottom edge, was worn by magistrates (Wilson 1938: 37). While the *toga* thus was a marker of political status, the tunic displayed social status as well. A purple stripe ran down each shoulder of the tunic. By its width the wearer's *ordo* could be determined. A broad stripe, the *latus clavus*, proclaimed a man of senatorial rank, while a narrower stripe was worn by members of the *equites*.[36] Candidates for public office wore a brilliant white *toga* – the *toga candida* – without the tunic underneath.[37] But a Roman male's dress was not restricted to the *toga*. A man's dress was almost as varied as his duties and obligations as a citizen. As a soldier he would adopt a distinct form of attire which varied according to his military rank (Wilson 1938: 100 *et seq.*). On assumption of priestly duties he sometimes had to dress, or, as in the case of the *Luperci*, undress appropriately.[38] In fact the *Luperci* are an excellent example of the varied duties and responsibilities that went with being a male member of the Roman elite, and how easily and unselfconsciously a man could move between them. In 44 BC for instance, Mark Antony was consul as well as *Lupercus*. Surely there could not have been more startling a contrast between the dignified *toga*-draped consul and the naked *Lupercus*, running the length of the *via sacra*, lashing the outstretched hands of women with a goatskin thong. Yet the incongruity of the contrast is a modern perception. The ancient writers appear to see nothing remarkable about it. It is never commented upon. It was natural and necessary that men adopt different social roles each marked by a different form of dress.

A man's status was established in various ways, political, social and religious, and this fact was reflected in the variety of his dress. A woman's status was established only by the nature of her sexual relationship to a man, and this also was displayed by her dress. A married woman's only acceptable dress was the *stola*, a longer, fuller version of the tunic she wore before her marriage, and the *palla*, a cloak, which covered her head and upper body and was worn over the *stola* in public. The *stola* defined the *matrona*: *Matronas appellabant eas fere, quibus stolas habendi ius erat* – 'Those who wear the *stola* are called *matronae*'.[39] In public all that was visible of a *matrona* were her face and her hands. The *palla* covered her head and arms and the *stola* reached down to her instep.[40] The bottom edge of the *stola* consisted of a wide band called the *instita*. It appears that this was an indispensable feature of the *stola*, and served to distinguish it from other variations of the tunic, and hence its wearer as a *matrona*.[41] Although by the time of Augustus, matrons could appear in public with head uncovered, in the early Republic it seems to have been regarded as a sign of great impropriety.[42] Valerius Maximus tells the story of a Sulpicius Gallus who, as late as the second century BC, divorced his wife for just such an offence, claiming that a woman's beauty was meant for her husband's eyes alone.[43] The idea that a woman's body should be covered up is also contained in a passage by Gellius, which says that it was effeminate for the sleeves of a man's tunic to reach to his wrists. Long and full-flowing garments should be worn only by women because they needed to hide their arms and legs from sight.[44] It is an interesting observation that although in the course of seven centuries the man made radical changes to the shape of tunic and *toga*, the woman's *palla* retained its original shape, and there was little change in her *stola*. Her desire for variety had to be satisfied by differences in texture, colour and decoration (Wilson 1938: 15). Differences in wealth and social status could be displayed by the ornamentation and elegance of the basic *stola* and *palla*. Cato, according to Livy, regarded such a desire in a woman to show off her wealth and standing as a dangerous form of vanity, which should be put down by law.[45]

Roman dress, therefore, was used to display status between men, as well as the ideological gulf between the male and female domains. This gulf was widened by a negative restriction: a *matrona* could not under any circumstances wear a *toga*. Conversely the *stola* was the *matrona*'s dress exclusively. Neither virgins nor prostitutes wore the *stola*. Prostitutes were explicitly forbidden it.[46] But a prostitute could wear the *toga*. In fact if the masculine form of the adjective, *togatus*, denoted a male Roman citizen, the feminine form, *togata*, denoted a prostitute.[47] By historical times, the *stola* had visually isolated the *matrona* from all other sexual categories. Of the two ritually important female categories, *matrona* and *meretrix*, it was the *matrona* that was held at a strict ritual distance. She was the 'other', the outsider that needed to be confined and contained within a domain that must never overlap the male's. The domain of the *meretrix* was not held at a ritual distance. The boundary between male and female was not quite so stark when the female belonged to the category of prostitute.

The contrasted relationship to men of *matrona* and prostitute, respectively, that the vestimentary code reveals, is a dominant theme in Rome's foundation myths as well as in some of her rituals. The *matrona* played a pivotal role in the myths concerned with the beginnings of the new state and the later political shift from monarchy to republic. The story of the abduction of the Sabine women and the story of the rape of Lucretia are of particular interest here. It is important that this whole nexus of tales about the beginnings of Rome, the birth of Romulus and Remus, the founding of the city, the aetiological tales of ancient cults, the story of the Sabine women, the exploits of Romulus, Numa and the other kings, the stories of Lucretia and Virginia and so forth, should be regarded as a body of meaningfully related discourse, rather than as separate and idiosyncratic stories. They are most usefully approached as motifs in a constantly shifting pattern of perception, as part of the raw material from which Rome created and re-created her self image.

This is my approach to the myth of the Sabine women. I treat it not as an isolated story, but as belonging to the same mythological continuum that contained the myths that I have been discussing thus far. The *matrona* that was so conspicuously absent from the story of Romulus' birth is here made the basis for the continued existence of his newly founded state. Romulus and his men might have built the city, but the Sabine women were indispensable for its prosperous continuation.[48]

Livy puts the problem succinctly:

Rome was now strong enough to hold her own in war with any of the adjacent states; but owing to the want of women a single generation was likely to see the end of her greatness, since she had neither prospect of posterity at home nor the right of intermarriage (*conubium*) with her neighbours.

(Livy, 1.9.14)

Romulus, who had tried and failed to obtain this vital right of intermarriage, finally tricked his neighbours into parting with their daughters. He invited them to a celebration of the feast of the *Consualia* and when their attention was diverted by the festivities, his men snatched the young unmarried girls away from their families.[49] The next morning, the story continues, Romulus explained to the frightened women that it was their parents' arrogant refusal to grant the Romans the right of intermarriage that had caused them

71

to resort to such tactics, and he promised them that his men intended honourable marriage. The women would, he said, 'become partners in all the possessions of the Romans, in their citizenship and, dearest privilege of all to the human race, in their children'.[50]

While the women were adapting to their roles as Roman wives and mothers, their outraged families were preparing war against Rome. Of these the biggest threat were the Sabines, the richest and most powerful of the neighbouring peoples. Neither side could gain the upper hand in the war that followed, and the casualties were mounting, when the Sabine women with great courage threw themselves between the battle lines, pleading with their husbands and fathers to desist.

> If you regret the relationship that unites you, if you regret the marriage tie, turn your anger against us; we are the cause of war, the cause of wounds and even death to both our husbands and our parents. It will be better for us to perish than to live, lacking either of you, as widows or as orphans.
>
> (Livy, 1.13.3)[51]

The men were moved by the plea. 'A stillness fell on them, and a sudden hush. Then the leaders came forward to make a truce, and not only did they agree on peace, but they made one people out of the two.'[52]

The *matrona* and the legal marriage – *iustae nuptiae* or *iustum matrimonium* – which gave her that special status were both acknowledged Roman creations. The story of the abduction of the Sabine women has as its basis this belief. It was the abduction of the Sabine women that created *iustum matrimonium*, which in turn resulted in two fundamental Roman institutions: the female category of *matrona*, and the form of legal paternity, *patria potestas*. *Iustum matrimonium* was by no means the only form of marriage in Rome. Roman marriage was a complex institution.[53] From a modern perspective it appears to have been remarkably unstructured. There was no civil marriage in Rome as we know it, nor did there exist any notion of sanctity associated with the marital bond. Legally all that was necessary for a marriage to be valid was the intention of the man and the woman – *maritalis affectio*. As John Crook puts it, 'if you lived together "as" man and wife, man and wife you were'.[54] Marriages were often entered into with great ceremony and much celebration, but none of this was legally necessary for the marriage to be valid.[55] Nevertheless the consequences of marriage varied, depending on which form of marriage the couple had entered into. And which form a man and a woman could enter into depended largely on whether or not they possessed *conubium*, the legal capacity to contract *iustum matrimonium*.[56]

Conubium was the cornerstone of Roman marriage. It was a prerequisite of *iustum matrimonium*.[57] Theoretically in *iustum matrimonium* children acquired the legal and social status of their father; in every other form of marriage they acquired the status of their mother. The father had legal authority – *patria potestas* – over his children only if they were born in *iustum matrimonium*. In other words, unless the child was born in *iustum matrimonium* he or she did not technically belong to the father's agnatic family.[58] Although all forms of marriage were valid and the notion of illegitimacy as we understand it did not exist, different forms of marriage conferred different rights and obligations on the child. From a purely religious perspective, a child not born of *iustum matrimonium*, and therefore not subject to *patria potestas*, would have no place in the family cult of his father's family and no right to intestate succession. Therefore for a man to possess offspring that legally 'belonged' to him, he had to have *conubium* with the woman he married.[59]

Conubium, *iustum matrimonium* and *patria potestas* were interrelated concepts. The wife in *iustum matrimonium* was a *matrona*. Thus only by a *matrona* could a male Roman citizen acquire a child over whom he could exercise *patria potestas*. Children born of a mother who was not a *matrona* were not subject to the *patria potestas* of their father, and were not members of his agnatic family, regardless of whether or not that father was a Roman citizen. They derived their status from their mother. Several conclusions might be drawn from this. Roman ideology recognized and legitimated the 'natural' or biological bond between mother and child. While I would hesitate to go so far as to say that it denied the biological bond between father and child, the natural maternal bond clearly superseded in importance the natural paternal bond.[60] Without *iustum matrimonium* all children would derive their status from their mother. Legally, however, they were *sui iuris* and had no agnatic kin; their relationships were all traced through their mother. This was in fact the situation which logically obtained before the abduction of the Sabine women and the invention of *iustum matrimonium*. The effect of *iustum matrimonium* was the creation of a factitious paternity, a legal bond between father and child, which not only superseded the biological bond between them but more importantly superseded the bond between mother and child. Children born in *iustum matrimonium* were not only subject to their father's *potestas*, they – the male children at any rate – became links in the chain of agnatic filiation which was held together by the transmission of *patria potestas* from generation to generation.[61] This agnatic line was the Roman *gens*.

Legal paternity was thus artificial, a fiction. 'The *paterfamilias*, or father of a family did not owe the appellation to the fact of his having fathered legitimate offspring. It was possible to have children without being a *pater familias* [i.e. if your own *paterfamilias* was alive both you and your children – by a *matrona* – would have been in his *potestas*, and you would not yourself be a *paterfamilias*]. Conversely, it was possible to be awarded the title *paterfamilias* without either engendering or adopting a child [if you were a man, the authority of *patria potestas* devolved on you when your *paterfamilias* died whether or not you had children].'[62] The mythological correlate was the suckling of the twins by the wolf, i.e. their father, Mars. Just as in the myth the feeding of the new-born babies by the wolf and the woodpecker – both symbols of Mars – undermined the mother's natural function of nourishing her baby, so *patria potestas*, the legal paternal bond between father and child undermined the natural biological bond between mother and child.

To return to the myth of the Sabine women, Livy makes it quite clear that the reason for their abduction was the denial of *conubium* by the established communities to the men of the new city. The implications of not having wives with *conubium* was not that the new Romans would not have children, but that they would not have *citizen* children. Although Roman men would have been able to reproduce themselves biologically, Rome would not have been able to reproduce herself politically. Without *conubium* and *iustum matrimonium* the children would acquire the status of their non-Roman mothers instead of their Roman fathers, and in Livy's words 'a single generation would be likely to see the end of [Rome's] greatness'. However a simple tale of abduction would not have sufficed to attest convincingly to the acquiring of *conubium* with another state. Implicit in the notion of *conubium* is the notion of equality of status. *Conubium* could not be acquired by force. If the Romans had defeated the Sabines in battle it would have put them in the rather ridiculous position of being granted *conubium* by a vanquished enemy. To allow the Sabines to defeat the Romans would not have solved the problem, and was in any case unthinkable. Instead, the Sabine women were made to intervene just when both sides seemed evenly matched and the outcome of the battle was in doubt. The result of that intervention was the combination of the two states on an equal footing. 'They [i.e. Romulus and Titus Tatius, the Sabine king] shared the sovereignty but all authority was transferred to Rome.'[63] The narrative device of the intervention of the Sabine women makes the establishment of *conubium* between themselves and the Romans plausible and the 'marriage' of the two states becomes a metonymy for *iustum matrimonium*.

The 'Sabine-ness' of the women is another feature of the myth that we tend to take for granted but which illustrates Roman ideas of *iustum matrimonium*. The Sabine women are not Roman; they are outsiders brought in to guarantee the future existence of the new city as well as their husbands' agnatic line. The central idea around which the institution of *iustum matrimonium* evolved was that the wife remained outside the agnatic family to which her husband and her children both belonged. It is widely believed that the early form of marriage, *cum manu*, had largely – but not entirely – given way by historical times to the form *sine manu*.[64] In a marriage *cum manu* a wife did become part of her husband's agnatic family. She possessed within the family the same status as her children, being in the *potestas* (technically *manus*) of her husband or his father or grandfather if they were alive. Her property, including her dowry, became the property of her husband or his *paterfamilias*, and she acquired the same rights of intestate succession within his family that her children had, while at the same time losing those rights in the family of her birth. *Cum manu* marriage was therefore an attempt to compensate for the 'alien' nature of a wife by turning her into a pseudo-daughter. Her legal relationship to her husband was analogous to that of her children to their father. Most importantly in a *cum manu* marriage, though divorce was possible, the wife could not initiate it.[65] In a *sine manu* marriage a woman remained technically aloof from her husband's agnatic family. If she had male ascendants living she remained in their *potestas* unless she had been legally emancipated. Otherwise she remained *sui iuris*, technically mistress of her own financial affairs though subject to *tutela* or legal guardianship. In a *sine manu* marriage, a woman could divorce her husband as easily as he could divorce her.[66] In a *sine manu* marriage therefore, a wife's 'alien' character was not compensated for. She remained legally a member of her own agnatic family and outside her husband's.

The tensions inherent in the position of a wife *vis à vis* her husband's family is reflected in the myth of the Sabine women. By going to war to avenge their daughters' abduction the fathers of the Sabine women reflected the power of a wife's father under whose *potestas* she remained, if she had married *sine manu*. In such a marriage the relationship of a wife to her husband's family was potentially precarious. It is generally accepted that Roman marriage was a form of political alliance at least among the elite. A father who retained *patria potestas* over his daughter after she married could in theory undermine a husband's control of his wife. Indeed the fact that a father was expected at least to participate in decisions pertaining to his daughter's affairs is illustrated in the story Plutarch tells of Hortensius' manner of allying himself by marriage with Cato. Hortensius' first suggestion was that he should marry Cato's daughter, Porcia, who was married to Bibulus. Whether Bibulus was consulted or not we do not know; it was Cato who refused Hortensius on the grounds that it was not proper to discuss the marriage of a daughter who was already married. Hortensius then suggested that he should marry Cato's own wife, Marcia, who was still young enough to bear children. This time Cato referred the decision to Marcia's father, the consul L. Marcius Philippus. When Philippus agreed, Cato divorced Marcia to enable her to marry Hortensius.[67] It is a reasonable assumption that both Porcia and Marcia were married *sine manu* and so it was their fathers rather than their husbands who ultimately decided their fate. Theoretically the law, until the time of Marcus Aurelius, allowed a father the right to force a daughter still under his *potestas* to divorce her husband, although it is doubtful if, even as early as the first century BC, this was a practical possibility if she did not want to do so.[68] In a conflict between father- and son-in-law, a woman married *sine manu*, who had a foot in both camps so to speak, would have been in a strong position to mediate. This is powerfully demonstrated in the myth of the Sabine women.[69]

Roman attitude to divorce was characterized by conflict and tension. One reason for this was the marginal position of the wife with respect to the agnatic family to which her husband as well as her children belonged. Roman marriage was, theoretically at least, a free association of a man and woman with the legal capacity to marry. Hence it was improper to enter into a contract not to divorce.[70] Nevertheless there was a clear disjunction between the ideological view of divorce and its social reality or potential reality. The traditional scholarly view of the incidence of divorce by the time of the late Republic has been that it was even by modern western standards a widespread phenomenon, at least among the elite, and in keeping with a trend towards looser moral standards and the growing emancipation of women. Recently such ideas have been challenged. It has been argued that passages taken from satirical and moralistic writing which were used to support the argument for frequent divorce were not so much accurate reflections of social events, as part of a body of misogynistic discourse.[71] Treggiari has rightly pointed out that it is impossible to compile statistics on divorce in any period in antiquity. She challenges the notion that divorce was epidemic in the late Republic and early Empire.[72] But whether or not divorce was a widespread social phenomenon by the time of the late Republic, it was certainly a socially acceptable and easily accomplished way for either husband or wife to end a marriage.

Even if divorce had not achieved the epidemic proportions suggested by most modern scholarship, the relative ease with which a marriage could, if necessary, be dissolved by either partner contributed to feelings of insecurity about marriage. This was especially the case among the elite where the financial stakes were high.[73] Since the purpose of *iustum matrimonium* was the perpetuation of the husband's agnatic line, it is quite logical that a wife was seen as fungible. Not only did the law allow her to remain technically aloof from her husband's agnatic family to which her children also belonged, but it made no great effort to ensure that she remained even nominally a part of that family. Divorce, like marriage, was a state of mind. Before the Augustan legislation all that was necessary for a formal divorce was that either husband or wife should cease to regard him or herself as married.[74] Formalities were usually observed, as they were in the case of marriage, but they were not legally necessary. The law intervened only to safeguard and distribute property as a consequence of divorce.

The ancient writers looked upon divorce with anxiety and disapproval.[75] The satirical and moralistic writers with their scathing if exaggerated diatribes against habitual and irresponsible divorce reflected a widespread and deeply rooted disapprobation. The disjunction between social practice and ideology is very clearly discernible. Despite evidence that divorce was permitted by the XII

Tables, and must have occurred at a very early date, the fact that there existed a tradition of a 'first' divorce, which some sources dated fairly late, makes that point very well. The first man to divorce his wife was, according to this tradition, Sp. Carvilius Ruga. He loved his wife, tradition insists, but she was barren. He therefore could not in all honesty swear before the censors, as he was required to do, that he had married a wife for the purpose of procreation – *liberorum quaerundorum causa*. None the less he was said to have incurred the opprobrium of his contemporaries by divorcing her. Alan Watson has argued that Ruga's was not so much the first divorce, as the first divorce of a blameless wife where the husband, himself blameless, was not required to pay a penalty.[76] According to the laws of Romulus only a husband could initiate a divorce, but only if his wife had committed the serious marital faults of adultery, poisoning of children and substitution of keys.[77] In such cases her dowry was forfeit. If however a man divorced his wife for any other reason, half his fortune was payable to his wife and the other half forfeit to Ceres. In other words the divorce of an innocent wife was blameworthy on the husband's part. Ruga's was the first case of a divorce which was 'blameless' on both sides. Ruga had to pay no penalty, but from then on it became necessary to allow the wife action for restoration of dowry. Therefore Ruga's constituted not so much the very first divorce as the boundary between the moralistic archaic form of divorce and the amoral contemporary form, which became the focus for much of the anxiety with which the *matrona* was perceived, for after Ruga divorce did not need to be justified and was not penalised.

Divorcing a wife lightly and without very good reason, was regarded with disapproval. Ruga's story is often told in conjunction with that of L. Annius who was removed from the senate by the censors of 307–6 BC for divorcing an innocent wife, who had come to him as a virgin, without seeking the advice of his friends.[78] This last omission is in contrast to Ruga who sought his friends' advice before reluctantly divorcing his wife. Divorce was necessary sometimes, but was to be undertaken only after much careful deliberation.

Religious practice did not actively penalise the divorced nor did religious ideology condemn them. But the ideal was life-long marriage.[79] The *flamen Dialis* for example was not allowed to divorce. The characteristic flame-coloured veil worn by his wife, the *flaminica Dialis*, was regarded as a symbol of permanent

marriage and formed part of the costume of a bride.[80] A potential
Vestal Virgin had to have both father and mother alive.[81] There was
no stipulation that they had still to be married to each other at the
time their daughter was chosen for the priesthood. Nevertheless
Tacitus reports that in 19 AD, when a Vestal was chosen, the daughter of Domitius Pollio was preferred to the daughter of Fonteius
Agrippa, because 'her mother had remained in the same marriage:
for Agrippa had reduced his house by divorce'.[82] A woman who
had been married only once was called *univira*, and regarded with
great approval.[83] But it must be stressed that except for the
notorious cases which formed the stuff of satire and moralistic
discourse, a woman who had married more than one husband
either on account of death or divorce did not diminish her social
stature in any way. In religious ritual *univirae* belonged to the
wider category of *matronae*, though there were rituals in which
only *univirae* participated.[84] But there is no evidence to suggest
that this signified social disapproval of women who fell outside
that category.[85]

The law of wills allowed women much greater freedom than it
did men. From an early date Roman law was concerned with property rights within families. The Furian Law on Wills, for example,
which was in existence by 169 BC, severely restricted the size of
legacies to distant relatives and non-relatives.[86] In similar vein a
child who had been disinherited without cause could try to get his
father's will invalidated. Hopkins and Burton claim that the underlying assumption allowing such suits is that fathers should treat
each child fairly (Hopkins 1983: 76 with note 58). But the law did
not regard mothers in the same light. No appeal could be made
against a mother's will until as late as the second century AD.[87] This
is consistent with the perception that the children of a marriage
'belonged' to the father. *Patria potestas* severed a child's legal relationship with its mother. Since neither she nor her property
belonged in any legal sense to the family of which her husband
and her children were a part they had no claim on it.

The Sabine women were the prototypes of the Roman *matrona*.
They were as indispensable for the perpetuation of the 'Roman'
line as the *matrona* was for that of her husband. They possessed
the virtues that a good matron was praised for. They were, in short,
the rock on which the state was built. Without them all Romulus'
diplomacy and statecraft would have been to no avail. And yet
they were never entirely a part of the state, they were always the

'Sabine women', never 'Romans'; just as a wife, regardless of the affective ties that bound her to her husband and children, stood legally aloof.

The creation of the Roman *matrona* thus ensured the continued existence of the Roman state. A *matrona* also featured prominently in the discourse surrounding the beginning of the Republic. The rape of Lucretia by Sextus Tarquinius, the son of Tarquinius Superbus, Rome's last king, was the catalyst that toppled the monarchy and created in its stead the much revered Republic. The story of the Sabine women was a relatively uncomplicated narrative, reflecting the comparatively straightforward story of the founding of Rome. The story of Lucretia reveals the complex tensions and contradictions that were inherent in the perceptions of the transition from monarchy to republic. However hated the Tarquins might have been, the earliest kings, Romulus, Numa, Servius Tullius, were revered every bit as much as the Republic itself. Their perceived contributions to religion, statecraft, and law were acknowledged and cherished as part of the Roman heritage. In the later Republic these early kings were held up as models of the Roman ideal; their simple and chaste lifestyles in particular provided a satisfying foil to the perceived corruption and extravagance of contemporary times. So there was considerable tension underlying perceptions of the establishment of the Republic. For creating the Republic was a process simultaneously of affirming and denying, undermining and re-establishing the values inherent in the Monarchy. The story of Lucretia reflects that tension. It is most usefully approached not so much as straightforward narrative – which of course on one level is what it is – but as a discourse on the kind of dangers a man could be harbouring within his house in the person of his wife, his *matrona*, however virtuous a wife she might be. The political correlate was the kind of danger the Republic could harbour in the form of ambitious men. I shall show how these two ideas were played out in the narrative. Central to the story, from this perspective, is not Lucretia herself, but male anxiety about the kind of subtle havoc a wife could create within a Roman's *domus*.

Livy's version of the story is that while the young princes were drinking in the tent of Sextus Tarquinius one day during the siege of Ardea, they fell to bragging about the relative merits of their wives.[88] Tarquinius Collatinus, not a son of the hated king but a cousin, proposed that they should ride to each of their homes unannounced, and see for themselves how their wives whiled away their husbands' absence. His own Lucretia, he swore, would win the prize in wifely virtue. And so it turned out, for while the wives of the princes were found to be carousing, Lucretia was discovered hard at work with her maids spinning wool late into the night.

Her beauty and her virtue, says Livy, created in Sextus – and this is important – the desire to debauch her by force: *Sex. Tarquinium mala libido Lucretiae* per vim *stuprandae capit.*[89] So a few days later he rode to Collatinus' house by himself and was graciously welcomed and provided with accommodation, for Lucretia suspected nothing. In the night he made his way to Lucretia's room and with sword in hand, threatening to kill her if she made a sound, he first tried to win her over with blandishments. When that failed he threatened to kill her and his slave, lay the man's body beside her and give it out that he had caught them together. At which, says Livy, 'her modesty was overcome *as with force*, by his victorious lust' – *Quo terrore cum vicisset obstinatam pudicitiam* velut vi *victrix libido.*[90] The next day Lucretia summoned her father and her husband with witnesses. She told them what had happened and her intention of killing herself, although she herself had had no adulterous intentions.

> They seek to comfort her, . . . by diverting the blame from her who was forced to the doer of the wrong. They tell her that it is the mind that sins not the body; and that where purpose has been wanting there is no guilt.
>
> (Livy, 1.58.9)

But having made them swear that they would avenge her dishonour, she stabbed herself and died.

Why does Lucretia kill herself? A husband was by law allowed to kill with impunity an adulterous wife.[91] But the victim of rape was not guilty of a criminal offence and was totally exonerated from blame in the eyes of the law.[92] The Christian apologists and their followers saw Lucretia as a sinner. Her sin was the involuntary sexual pleasure – as they saw it – of the woman even as she is being violated.[93] Bryson contrasts St Augustine's interpretation of the story of Lucretia with that of Livy: the Christian interpretation (Lucretia secretly seduces) opposed to the pagan (she was raped). The Christian interpretation easily accounts for Lucretia's suicide.

Bryson suggests that the pagan writers and especially Livy saw the rape of Lucretia as a public crime. Lucretia commits suicide in order to exact vengeance not of a personal but a political nature. 'It is not . . . a private matter, but an affair of state and its outcome will be the overthrow of the state' (Bryson 1986: 164). This interpretation however does not account for the complexity of meaning inherent in the story of Lucretia and the subtle interplay of the notions of home and state.

The key to Lucretia's suicide in Livy's narrative is the notion of *vis*, force. I argued in the last chapter that for lawful sexual intercourse, such as intercourse within marriage, the notion of *vis*, if not its physical reality, was a necessary mediating factor. The myth of the seduction of Bona Dea by her father showed the failure of force and its replacement with guile in the case of manifestly unlawful intercourse such as incest. Inherent in Lucretia's story is the notion that intercourse mediated by *vis*, even if not strictly lawful, rendered the woman blameless. If Sextus Tarquinius had subdued her by simple force her suicide would have been meaningless. But he does not subdue her, she submits to the fear of disgrace. There are no undertones of involuntary sexual pleasure, no notion of sin in the Christian sense. Yet in the last resort Lucretia, however honourable, was seduced rather than raped. Sextus' intention was to conquer her through force – *per vim* – but in fact he does so as though by force – *velut vi*. So Lucretia is and is not guilty of adultery. An adulteress would have been killed by her husband or her father. Lucretia killed herself. Her last words are poignant: 'though I acquit myself of the sin, I do not absolve myself from punishment; not in time to come shall ever unchaste woman live through the example of Lucretia'.[94]

The oath that Brutus compelled the Romans to swear reconciles Lucretia's story with the founding of the Republic.

> To begin with, when the people were still jealous of their new freedom, he obliged them to swear an oath that they would suffer no man to be king in Rome, lest they might later be turned from their purpose by the entreaties or the gifts of princes.
>
> (Livy, 2.1.9)

Brutus' fear was that the Republic could be destroyed not through force – for a state that prided itself on its military prowess violence presented few terrors – but by seduction. This could happen only in a monarchy. While an individual king could be all that was desirable in a ruler, monarchy as an institution could fall prey to corruption. Correspondingly, as revealed by Lucretia's story, while a virtuous wife such as she had been brought honour and prosperity to a man and his family, marriage as an institution could lead to misery and destruction. Lucretia conjured up simultaneously the picture of the chaste, industrious wife and the woman whose sexuality could, however involuntarily, threaten her husband and his house.

Women continued to play a prominent part, both individually and collectively, in the stories that helped define 'Romanness'. Many of these tales constituted the aetiology of the foundations of temples or rituals, thus ensuring that they remain part of popular self-perception. They portrayed women both as contributing positively to the welfare of the state and as serving to undermine its institutions, thus reflecting the same sort of tensions that existed in the rhetoric of misogyny. The festival of the Carmentalia, for example, was instituted because the Roman matrons, angered at being deprived of the privilege of riding in carriages, performed abortions on themselves in order to punish their husbands by denying them children. The senate restored to them the right to ride in carriages and instituted the rites to Carmenta on the ides of February to ensure the birth of healthy babies.[95] But while tales such as this confirmed a man's worst fears about women, there were others that featured women as saviours of the state. An example is the aetiological story of the founding of the temple of Fortuna Muliebris. The temple commemorated the action of the women who persuaded Coriolanus to desist from an attack on Rome. But Livy's account of the incident gives an interesting insight into male attitudes towards collective action by women, even when it was for the good of the state.

> Non inviderunt laude sua mulieribus viri Romani – adeo sine obtrectatione gloriae alienae vivebatur – momnomentoque quod esset templum Fortunae muliebri aedificatum dedicatumque est.

> Men did not envy the fame the women had earned, – so free was life in those days from disparagement of another's glory – and to preserve its memory the temple of Fortuna Muliebris was built and dedicated.[96]

Women were always the 'other' – *alienae* – and even when their actions saved and preserved the state, men regarded them with a sense of unease.

WIFE AND PROSTITUTE IN RITUAL

Two temples standing side by side; two festivals, one marking the beginning, the other the end of a related series; two goddesses: Ceres and Flora. Their relationship to agricultural enterprise has been demonstrated and widely discussed.[97] In this section I shall discuss a different aspect of the cults: the ways in which they were used to define and categorize the sexuality of women. I shall show that their respective rituals reflected attitudes towards the categories of 'wife' and 'prostitute' similar to the ones that were discernible in myth. The cults of Ceres and Flora, concerned with the wife and the prostitute respectively formed the ritual counterpart to the ideals encapsulated in the myths concerned with female sexual status. But ritual in this case is not simply a reflection of myth. It adds an important new dimension to the perception of the female in Roman antiquity. 'Wife' and 'prostitute' were two separate ritual categories, but they were also facets of a common female sexuality. The cults of Ceres and Flora were separate cults, but to the extent that they were concerned with the sexuality of women, they were mutually interdependent for the creation of meaning. The ideal of the wife that found expression in the cult of Ceres was limited by the ideal of the prostitute that found expression in the cult of Flora and vice versa. The ritual features of the two cults provided a foil for each other.

To begin with it will be helpful to analyse the function of Ceres in marriage. She was intimately connected with the marriage ceremony. In poetic expression the symbol of the torch was used to evoke the wedding. Virgil describes Amata's frenzied efforts to prevent Lavinia's marriage to Aeneas thus:

> . . . et natam frondosis montibus abdit
> quo thalamum eripiat Teucris taedasque moretur.

[She] hides her daughter in the leafy mountains, thereby to rob the Teucrians of their marriage and to delay the torches [i.e. the wedding].[98]

84

Ovid also uses the metaphor of the torch to express the belief that weddings that were celebrated while cult was being offered to the dead – i.e. during the festivals of the Feralia and the Caristia – were unlucky,

> dum tamen haec fiunt, viduae cessate puellae:
>   expectet puros pinea taeda dies,
> nec tibi, quae cupidae matura videbere matri
>   comat virgineas hasta recurva comas.

But while these rites are being performed, ye ladies change not your widowed state. Let the torch of pine wait till the days are pure. And O thou damsel who to thy eager mother shalt appear all ripe for marriage, let not the bent back spear comb down thy maiden hair.[99]

Propertius has Cornelia speak of her transition from maiden to wife in this way:

> mox, ubi iam facibus cessit praetexta maritis . . .

And soon when the maiden's garment yielded to the torches of marriage . . .[100]

The torch was evidently a commonly accepted metonymy for marriage. The torch of marriage was connected explicitly with Ceres:

> Facem in nuptiis in honorem Cereris praeferebant.

At weddings the torch was carried in honour of Ceres.[101]

The central element in the ceremony of a Roman wedding was the nocturnal procession in which the new bride was conducted to her husband's home – the *deductio ad domum*. This part of the ceremony was important for two reasons. I have already observed that no ceremony, religious or legal was necessary for a marriage to be valid. All that was necessary – provided the parties had legal capacity to marry – was intent – *affectio maritalis*.[102] Strictly speaking a marriage need not even be consummated to be legal. However it was essential that the wife take up residence in her husband's home; this was a *sine qua non* of a valid Roman marriage.[103] The *deductio ad domum* constituted public notice of the marriage and the new status of the bride. It signified that the subsequent co-habitation of the couple was a valid marriage, that legal capacity to marry had been established, and that *affectio maritalis*, something impossible to demonstrate, must be assumed. It left no room for doubt that the woman was henceforth a *matrona* and that her children would be subject to the *patria potestas* of her husband or his *paterfamilias*. Although ceremonies accompanying a first marriage often differed from those accompanying remarriages, the *deductio* was a common feature in both.[104]

The most striking feature of the *deductio* was the torches.[105] The number of torches probably depended on the size and splendour of the procession. Their purpose was of course functional, but at least one had a symbolic value.[106]

> Patrimi et matrimi pueri praetextati tres nubentem deducunt; unus qui facem praefert ex spina alba, quia noctu nubebant; duo qui tenent nubentem.

> Three young boys whose parents were still alive, led the bride; one headed the procession with a torch of white pine – for the Romans celebrated marriages by night – and two held the bride's hands.[107]

According to Pliny the *spina alba*, white pine, was 'the most auspicious tree for supplying wedding torches, because according to the account of Masurius, it was used for that purpose by the shepherds who carried off the Sabine women'.[108] I suggest that it was the torch made of *spina alba*, carried at the head of the procession and evocative of the story of the Sabine women – the original *matronae* – that also constituted a sacred symbol of Ceres. It was to this torch that Festus was referring when he said that a torch was carried in honour of Ceres at weddings. It would appear that Ceres was perceived to be particularly concerned with the status of the bride, the new *matrona*. In this section I shall show that Ceres' connection with the wedding was directly related to her concern for lawful sexual intercourse as defined by marriage. The *matrona* was the embodiment of such a definition. A man's sexuality was not at all constrained by marriage. Marital fidelity was never a requirement for a husband. It was imperative for his wife.

There was only one temple of Ceres in Rome.[109] But it was dedicated not just to Ceres alone, but to the triad, Ceres, Liber and Libera.[110] Each deity occupied a separate *cella* within the building. The most important festival of Ceres, the Cerialia, was likewise held in honour not just of Ceres, but of the triad.[111] The three deities were closely associated. It is helpful to analyse that association in terms of the concepts of gender and sexuality.

Liber's connection with viticulture and wine has been widely studied.[112] He was credited with the discovery of wine and its introduction into society. We saw in connection with the use of wine at the festival of the Bona Dea, that wine was a symbolic expression of masculinity; it represented the male principle. The cult of Liber supports that hypothesis. Augustine, for example, described the cult of Liber thus: 'I come now to the rites of Liber, a god whom they have put in charge of moist seeds; this includes not only the juice of fruits, among which wine somehow holds first place, but also the semen of animals.'[113] In charge of wine and semen Liber represented maleness. Libera, the third member of the triad is presented as the perfect female counterpart of Liber. As Liber was to the male, Libera was to the female: 'Under the name of Liber let him preside over the seeds of men, and as Libera over the seeds of women.'[114]

But Liber and Libera represent not simply the principles of masculinity and femininity, but sexual intercourse itself.

> They say that the god Liber gets his name from Liberating, because it is through his favour that males in intercourse are liberated from or relieved of, the semen which they emit. For women they say that the same service is performed by Libera, whom they also identify with Venus; for they think that the woman also emits seed. Hence in the temple of Liber they dedicate to the god the male sexual organs and in the temple of Libera, the corresponding female organs.
>
> (Aug., *de Civ. D.*, 6.9)[115]

Liber and Libera were complementary deities. But there was also a third element to the cult – Ceres. Ceres was, moreover, its most prominent figure. I suggest that her function was that of ordering and regulating the sexuality that Liber and Libera represented. To put it another way, the concept of sexual intercourse as represented by the couple Liber–Libera was mediated by Ceres. In terms of gender and sexuality the cult of the triad represented not simply sexual intercourse, but intercourse regulated by marriage.

Ovid recorded a belief that Liber was the discoverer not only of wine but also of honey.[116] I argued, following Detienne, in connection with the representation of honey at the festival of the Bona Dea, that honey was used as a symbolic expression of the ideal of chastity within marriage. I wish to suggest here that this myth of Liber might most usefully be read in those terms. That is, that the male sexuality of Liber was contained within the concept of marriage. Even though men were free to have relations with women other than their wives, a man's relationship with his wife, as we shall see, was ritually mediated.

The story that Liber discovered honey was very likely an aetiological myth that was meant to explain the practice of sacrificing cakes infused with honey at the Liberalia.[117] The Liberalia, celebrated on 17 March was, as far as we can tell, in honour of Liber only.[118] Neither Ceres nor Libera are mentioned in connection with this festival. The Liberalia marked a Roman male's rite of passage from boyhood to manhood; it was the day on which boys, with much ceremony and celebration, formally adopted the *toga virilis*.[119] Historians describing this transition tend to stress – and rightly so – the political, military, legal and financial responsibilities that the new adult male would henceforth assume.[120] It is noted only in passing that for men the ceremony of formally donning the *toga virilis* was equivalent to marriage for women. The suggestion is that marriage, while of crucial importance to women, was less important to men. Empirically this is true. The consequences of the formal transition from childhood to adulthood were very different for men and for women. But from an ideological perspective it was marriage that marked the transition from childhood to adulthood for both men and women. *Conubium*, as we have seen, was a *sine qua non* of a valid Roman marriage. Another necessary factor was puberty.

> There could be no legal marriage in Rome between persons under the age of puberty. The male must be *pubes*, the female *viripotens*. In the earliest law, however, it is impossible to speak of 'an age of puberty,' since puberty was determined by actual inspection of the body. Out of respect for their modesty, this practice was at a remote period discontinued in the case of girls and the fixed age of twelve settled upon; but boys continued to be examined, probably in connection with the *tirocinium fori* when they assumed the dress and political privileges of men.
>
> (Corbett 1930: 51)[121]

Technically a boy was not considered a man until he was considered capable of sexual intercourse. And in connection with the formal transition into adulthood, capacity for intercourse was equivalent to the legal capacity for marriage. Before a boy was regarded as a man, ready to take on the multifarious privileges and responsibilities of legal adulthood, his fitness for marriage had either to be demonstrated or assumed.

The ceremonies that accompanied a boy's coming of age and a bride's wedding day had at least one significant symmetrical feature. On the day that a Roman boy put aside his *toga praetexta* for the *toga virilis* he also wore a specially woven tunic, the *tunica recta*, so called because it was woven on an old-fashioned loom, from top to bottom, with the weaver standing rather than seated.[122] A bride on her wedding day also wore the *tunica recta*. She also symbolically discarded the *toga praetexta* of her childhood.[123]

We do not know how rigidly social practice adhered to these traditions. Although the day of the Liberalia was by tradition the day on which boys adopted the *toga virilis* it was possible to hold the ceremony on some other day.[124] Similarly the tradition of wearing the *tunica recta* may or may not have been regularly observed. But the important thing is that the traditions existed. The *tunica recta*, the garment ideally worn by both boys and girls while they were undergoing the rite of passage into two very different sorts of adult world, marks the symmetry of perception with which the transitions were regarded. Just as the bride's *tunica recta* evoked the circumstances of a boy's rite of passage, the boy's evoked a bride's. Marriage was as much part of a boy's future as of a girl's. The difference was that it was the only future for a girl. To return to the Liberalia, I suggest that the tradition that a boy assume the *toga virilis* on that day, was meant as a ritual statement that he was now physically capable of marriage. In keeping with his varied duties as a citizen he was expected on that day, accompanied by his friends, to visit the major temples in Rome, of which the temple of Ceres, Liber and Libera was just one.[125] But the day on which the ceremony took place was meant specifically to evoke Liber and sexuality limited and regulated by marriage; this idea was inherent also in the garment that was worn on the occasion, the *tunica recta*.

In the rest of this section I shall explore a fundamental difference in the way that Roman religion categorized men and women in terms of their sexuality. Put succinctly, women were polarized into two starkly contrasted groups according to how their sexuality was expressed: wives, whose sexuality was constrained and regulated; and prostitutes who were promiscuous. Men were not categorized in this way. As far as rituals of gender and sexuality were concerned, men constituted a single group. Nevertheless, religious ideology constructed an asymmetry in the way that men related to the two female groups. Lawful sexual intercourse was invariably presented in terms of a mediating factor. We have already seen that violence was one such factor. In the cult of the triad, Ceres, the figure connected with the marriage ceremony, mediated between the sexuality of Liber and Libera. By contrast a man's relations with a prostitute needed no mediation. This I shall show by comparing the cults of Ceres and Flora. I shall also show that the female categories of 'wife' and 'prostitute' were defined in terms of each other. They were seen as opposed but complementary aspects of a common female sexuality.

The cult of Liber–Libera formally acknowledged a man's sexual role within marriage. But in terms of the marriage ceremony, Ceres, as symbolically represented by the torch of *spina alba*, appears to have been concerned with the woman only. The three examples I gave of the metaphorical representation of the wedding in terms of a torch all refer to marriage from a woman's point of view.[126] Nor, to the best of my knowledge, is there an example of a man referring to his marriage in these terms. Also Romulean law appears to have connected Ceres specifically with the wife; a man who divorced his wife without just cause forfeited half his property to his wronged wife and the other half to Ceres.[127] Within the cult of Ceres, Liber and Libera, although Liber received cult as the discoverer of wine, no wine was allowed in the rites of Ceres.[128] This served to create a negative association of Ceres with the male element in marriage, thereby emphasizing her association with the female.

Ceres' connection with *matronae* is most clearly demonstrated in the rite of the *sacrum anniversarium Cereris*. In 216 BC following the Roman defeat at Cannae, the senate limited the period of mourning to thirty days so that the *matronae* might observe the *sacrum anniversarium Cereris*.[129] We have very little information about this rite,[130] but enough to be able to place it very plausibly within the pattern that has emerged of the role of Ceres within marriage. It too was concerned with the sexuality of the *matronae* as a ritual category. Its rites were performed exclusively by *matronae*. Although the cult of Ceres, Liber and Libera presented the concept of sexuality within marriage from the perspective of both male and female, the *sacrum anniversarium Cereris* distanced the sexes from each other. Not only were men not present at the rite, but the women had to abstain from sexual intercourse with their husbands for nine days prior to and during the rite itself.[131] The distance between husband and wife was emphasized by the fact that the husband was not required to be celibate during his wife's absence at the rites. His sexuality was not ritually confined in any way.[132] There was thus no parallelism between the sexuality of husband and wife, such as was expressed by the cult of Ceres, Liber and Libera. The *sacrum anniversarium Cereris* might also usefully be contrasted with the festival of Bona Dea. Bona Dea's festival categorized women only according to their gender: women as opposed to men. The rites were not limited to any one particular female sexual category. Although men were ostentatiously removed from the scene of the festival, their presence was symbolically acknowledged. At the *sacrum anniversarium Cereris*, by contrast, men were excluded at every level, actual and symbolic. The exclusion is particularly pointed because the men so excluded were the husbands from whom the participants derived their status as *matronae*.

From a ritual perspective, the most striking consequence that marriage as an institution had for women was that it divided them. The married woman was selected out from the category of the female that the festival of Bona Dea presented. Marriage redefined her. She was henceforth defined not by her gender alone, but by the curbing of her sexuality. Her sexuality and its potential, her ability to bear children, were at the disposal of a single man, her husband. His sexuality, however, was not similarly constrained. Marital chastity was not a requirement for the married man. Marriage did not divide men into two sexually distinct groups.

At the opposite pole to the ritual category of the *matrona* was the category of the prostitute. The cults of Ceres and Flora together provided the ritual representation of this opposition. To begin with, the temple of Ceres, Liber and Libera and the temple of Flora stood side by side, constituting a visual expression of the relationship of the two cults. *Libero Liberaeque et Cereri iuxta Circum Maximum* . . . eodemque in loco *aedem Florae* – 'The temple of Ceres, Liber and Libera stood next to the Circus Maximus . . . *in the very same place* stood the temple of Flora.'[133] Chronologically the cults were related to each other by a symmetry of opposition. The Cerialia constituted the beginning, the Floralia the end of a consecutive series of festivals all avowedly dedicated to the success of agricultural enterprise.[134] They were both the responsibility of the plebeian aediles. Thus Cicero as aedile elect:

> I am now an aedile elect; and I understand the position in which the nation's will has placed me. With the utmost diligence and solemnity I am to celebrate the holy festival of Ceres, Liber and Libera. By holding the solemn festival of our Lady Flora I am to secure her favour for the people and commons of Rome.
>
> (Cic., 2 *Verr.*, 5.14.36)

The parallel features of the cults of Ceres and Flora serve to emphasize the sharp contrast in the nature of their respective rites. The *ludi scaenici*, one of the ritual features of the Floralia,[135] was marked by excessive drunkenness, ribaldry and licentiousness.[136] Although the actors on stage were prostitutes, the Floralia was not a festival of prostitutes as much as a celebration of the idea of prostitution itself. The ritual actors were not simply the prostitutes whose lewdness on stage provoked the moral outrage of writers such as the younger Seneca, St Augustine and Tertullian, they were the prostitutes and their audience together. The salacious jokes, the drunkenness, the general ribaldry that emanated from the audience were as much a part of the rite, as the suggestive miming of the prostitutes.[137] That it was not just general obscenity, but prostitution that was the issue here is suggested by Tertullian:

> The very prostitutes, the victims of public lust are produced on the stage, . . . they are paraded before the faces of every rank and age; proclamation is made of their abode, their price, their record, even before those who do not need the detail.
>
> (Tert., *De Spect.*, 17)

The distinction here between prostitutes and prostitution is subtle but significant. Prostitutes presented as a female sexual category undoubtedly played an important role. But the focus of the rite was the ritual presentation of the idea of prostitution, which necessarily included the way in which men related to prostitutes.

The categories of *matrona* and prostitute formed dual but opposed aspects of a common female sexuality. Both derived their status from a single male category: men were both husbands to *matronae* and clients to prostitutes. However, the *sacrum anniver-*

sarium Cereris and the Floralia reveal the difference in the way that the two relationships operated. The ritual distance between husband and wife, in a relationship ritually mediated, was exaggerated by the absence of men at the rite of Ceres. Similarly the exaggerated obscenity at the Floralia at which men and women participated together on equal terms, showed by contrast the expression of a relationship unfettered by notions of ritual distance and mediation.

The Floralia also provided a vivid visual contrast to the festival of the Cerialia which took place a few days earlier. Ovid remarks on the different appearance of the women at each festival. 'Why is it that whereas white robes are worn at the festival of Ceres, Flora is neatly clad in attire of many colours?'[138] Ovid is referring here to the Cerialia, but white appeared to have been worn at the *sacrum anniversarium Cereris* too.[139] The lighting at each festival provided added visual contrast. The Floralia was extravagantly lit. Cassius Dio mentions an occasion where at least five thousand torches were used to provide light at the Floralia.[140] Torches were a necessary component of any nocturnal activity, including the Cerialia. But ordinary torchlight, enough to see by but not deliberately excessive, has the effect of deepening the surrounding darkness, giving an overall impression of lightlessness rather than light. The brilliant lighting at the Floralia was not only an expression of the exuberant nature of the rites, it formed a further point of contrast with the recently celebrated festival of the Cerialia. Finally, the drunkenness at the Floralia also provided a contrast to the rites of Ceres, at which wine was not even offered as a libation.

Thus the cults of Ceres and Flora were related by a symmetry of opposition. They ritually articulated the explicit polarization of the categories of *matrona* and prostitute in religious ideology. The attitude to wives that found expression in the literary, legal and mythological traditions was acted out in ritual. In the rites of Ceres and Flora, both men and women acted out and experienced the ideological division of women into sexual categories.

Part III

VENUS' ROLE IN
ROMAN RELIGION

INTRODUCTION TO
CHAPTER 3

The ritual participants in the cults of Ceres, Flora and Bona Dea were segregated according to categories defined by gender and sexuality. Categorization of ritual participants was a fundamental feature of Roman religion. The categories were multifarious and varied from cult to cult and from ritual to ritual. Female participants were always defined in terms of their sexuality. Female ritual categories were not limited to those I examine in this book, however. For example, one category that is beyond the scope of this book but is none the less extremely important is the category of mothers. Where women were concerned, religion was exclusively preoccupied with their sexuality and its implications. By contrast the religious representation of men reflected their varied social and political roles. They were hardly ever defined exclusively by gender or sexuality. For example, at the festival of Bona Dea men constituted a symbolic sexual and political presence. Both roles were acknowledged and woven into the fabric of the rite. Military power and military domination were also themes in Roman cult and were represented in ritual by men. We will see this phenomenon in the cults of Venus that I examine in this chapter.

The rituals connected with the cults of Ceres and Flora and of Bona Dea were similar in that they all treated ritual categories as separate, self-contained and ritually distanced from one another. The defining feature of these category-specific rituals was their exclusiveness. Prostitutes were not allowed to participate in the *sacrum anniversarium Cereris*, for example, and matrons *qua* matrons had no ritual role at the Floralia. The festival of Bona Dea was celebrated as a festival for women only. But exclusiveness was not the only way in which categorization was made ritually manifest. In contrast to the deliberate exclusiveness of cults such as

Bona Dea's we also see cults which easily accommodated different ritual groups in a single festival, and sometimes even in a single rite. This tendency is most apparent in the cults of Venus where we see the integration of disparate categories under the aegis of a single ritual. In the cult of Venus Verticordia, for example, wives and prostitutes *qua* wives and prostitutes appear to have participated together in a single ritual designed to celebrate a common sexuality. The separate categories were recognized, but no ritual barrier was erected between them. Venus represented an ideology best described as one of inclusiveness or of integration. This ideology extended beyond the female categories represented in the cult of Verticordia. In other cults of Venus – the two examined here are the cults of Venus Obsequens and Venus Erycina – sexually defined categories operated together with male centred representations of military power and dominance. There is no apparent difficulty in the assimilation, no attempt that we know of to explain or justify the phenomenon. The cults of Venus appear to have been merely a competing model for the treatment of ritual categories.

3

VENUS

Why is it that the women, when they adorn in their houses a
shrine to the women's goddess, whom they call Bona Dea,
bring in no myrtle, although they are very eager to make use
of all manner of growing and blooming plants?

(Plut., *Quaest. Rom.*, 20)

Plutarch's question was a hoary old chestnut in the ancient world.
Many writers attempted to account for what they saw as a great
puzzle.[1] Roman religion is full of ritual features that seem bizarre to
us today, but that never aroused curiosity or comment among
contemporary writers beyond a simple documentation of them.
Therefore so much attention devoted to an apparently trivial
feature in a single cult is striking. But at second glance the association – even a negative one – between myrtle and Bona Dea turns
out to be not so trivial after all. Myrtle was Venus' plant. The
intimate association between Venus and myrtle is widely attested in
literature.[2] Myrtle also took on, by association with Venus, all the
connotations of sexual love that she evoked.[3] But it never had
independent symbolic value. Its presence in myth and ritual always
evoked Venus.

The most popular aetiology for the exclusion of myrtle from
Bona Dea's festival was the story that Bona Dea was beaten by
Faunus with rods of myrtle. In the accounts of Plutarch, Arnobius
and Lactantius, Bona Dea was Faunus' wife who was beaten by her
husband with myrtle because she drank a large quantity of wine.[4]
In Macrobius' version she was Faunus' daughter. She refused his
incestuous advances and he plied her with wine and beat her with
rods of myrtle in a vain attempt to force her to submit. Despite the
slight variations in narrative detail, the relationship between Bona

Dea and Faunus is the reason offered by all four writers as to why wine was disguised as milk at her festival, and myrtle excluded. Implicit in these accounts is the belief that myrtle, like wine, represented the male principle which was overtly rejected at Bona Dea's festival. Myrtle and wine are thus given a symmetric symbolic value in these accounts. The pervasive force of the belief that myrtle was connected with Venus makes this interpretation superficially plausible. Indeed Plutarch explicitly makes the connection between myrtle and Venus in the context of the cult of the Bona Dea.

> Is it because they remain pure from many things, particularly from venery, when they perform this holy service? For they not only exclude their husbands, but they also drive every-thing male out of the house whenever they conduct the customary ceremonies in honour of the goddess. So, because the myrtle is sacred to Venus, they rigorously exclude it.
>
> (*ibid.*)

But though the literary accounts give symmetrical symbolic value to wine and myrtle, their ritual relationship is asymmetrical. Wine, though disguised, was an essential element of the rite of Bona Dea. It represented the male principle, which though overtly excluded from the rite, was covertly included.[5] But myrtle was entirely excluded. Its absence was underscored by the presence of all sorts of different plants. The house where the festival took place was decorated with 'all manner of growing and blooming plants' except for myrtle. If myrtle, like wine, was meant to represent the male principle, its absence would have been symbolic of a total rejection of the male, overt and covert. To read both wine and myrtle as symbolically representative of men results in the appear-ance of a fundamental inconsistency within the cult.

But the pervasiveness of the belief that myrtle was associated with Venus makes it improbable that it had a different evocation in the cult of the Bona Dea. The association with Venus, however, does not always necessarily evoke ideas of sexual love, and in a cult of women, ideas of men. The contention of this chapter is that Venus' significance in Roman religion was not confined to the role she played as custodian of the domain of sexual relationships. The representation of Venus as patron deity of sexual relationships was merely the most widely acknowledged manifestation of a much more complex role. It was not only the categories of male

100

and female that Venus united. Her broader function was to draw together into a single system the various categories – whether defined sexually, politically or socially – that other cults and rituals separated. The cults of Venus provided an alternative model for the ritual treatment of categories: a model based on inclusiveness rather than exclusiveness.

Myrtle was also associated with Venus in contexts other than sexual love. For example, generals celebrating an *ovatio* wore a chaplet of myrtle rather than the laurel of the triumphator. Why? Gellius says that one of the reasons why a general was awarded an *ovatio* rather than a triumph was if he had won an easy victory owing to a quick surrender. 'For such an easy victory they believed that the leaves sacred to Venus were appropriate on the ground that it was a triumph not of Mars but of Venus.'[6] But he also gives other reasons why an *ovatio* might be granted rather than a triumph: if war had not been declared in due form and therefore not waged with a legitimate enemy, or waged with adversaries of low status such as slaves or pirates. Such victories were not necessarily easy. Nevertheless they too could result in an *ovatio*.[7]

Pliny also associates Venus and myrtle in a context that has nothing to do with sex. He tells a story of two myrtle trees called the patrician myrtle and the plebeian myrtle that once grew in the precinct of the shrine of Quirinus. As long as the patricians were the more powerful faction in the state the patrician myrtle flourished while the other withered, but when the plebeians grew strong their myrtle tree grew green while the patricians' turned yellow. Although the connection with Venus is not made explicit here, it is clear from the structure of the passage as a whole that in this instance too, an intuitive appeal was being made to the acknowledged association between myrtle and Venus, whom Pliny calls the 'guardian spirit of the tree who presid[ed] over unions'.

fuit ubi nunc Roma est iam cum conderetur, quippe ita traditur, myrtea verbena Romanos Sabinosque, cum propter raptas virgines dimicare voluissent, depositis armis purgatos in eo loco qui nunc signa Veneris Cluacinae habet: cluere enim antiqui purgare dicebant. et in ea quoque arbore suffimenti genus habetur, ideo tum electa quoniam coniunctioni et huic arbori Venus praeest, haud scio an prima etiam omnium in locis publicis Romae sata, fatidico quidem et memorabili augurio. inter antiquissima namque delubra habetur Quirini, hoc est ipsius Romuli. in eo sacrae fuere myrti duae ante aedem ipsam per longum tempus, altera patricia appellata, altera plebeia. patricia multis annis prae-valuit exuberans ac laeta; quamdiu senatus quoque floruit, illa ingens, plebeia retorrida ac squalida. quae postquam evaluit flavescente patricia, a Marsico bello languida auctori-tas patrum facta est, ac paulatim in sterilitatem emarcuit maiestas. quin et ara vetus fuit Veneri Myrteae, quam nunc Murciam vocant.

At the time of the foundation of Rome myrtles grew on the present site of the city, as tradition says that the Romans and Sabines, after having wanted to fight a battle because of the carrying off of the maidens, laid down their arms and purified themselves with sprigs of myrtle, at the place now occupied by the statues of Venus Cluacina, *cluere* being the old word meaning 'to cleanse'. And a kind of incense for fumigation is also contained in this tree, which was selected for the purpose on the occasion referred to because Venus the guardian spirit of the tree also presides over unions, and I rather think that it was actually the first of all trees to be planted in public places at Rome, fraught indeed with a prophetic and remarkable augury. For the shrine of Quirinus, that is of Romulus himself, is held to be one of the most ancient temples. In it there were two sacred myrtles, which for a long time grew in front of the actual temple, and one of them was called the patrician's myrtle and the other the plebeian's. For many years the patrician's tree was the more flourishing of the two, and was full of vigour and vitality; as long as the senate flourished this was a great tree, while the plebeians' myrtle was shrivelled and withered. But afterwards the plebeians' myrtle grew strong while the patricians' began to turn yellow, for from the Marsian war onward the authority of the fathers became weak, and by slow degrees its grandeur withered away into barrenness. Moreover there was also an old altar belonging to Venus Myrtea, who is now called Murcia.[8]

I shall start out with an a priori assumption that the exclusion of myrtle from the cult of Bona Dea was meant to evoke Venus. The thesis of this chapter will be that the cult of Bona Dea appealed not to Venus' widely attested connection with sexual love, but to her more fundamental religious function of which the connection with sexual love was only one expression, that is the function of bringing together disparate ritual categories.

The cult of Venus Verticordia, which I shall look at first, is structured according to sexually defined categories. Female sexuality was central both to the foundation legends and to the rites. The cult operated in terms of sexually defined categories. It categorized gender into male and female, and further categorized the female according to sexual status. But the ritual treatment of these categories in the cult of Venus was quite different from their treatment in the cults of Bona Dea, Ceres or Flora. Rather than excluding one category or another, the cult, while acknowledging the existence of the categories, included them as equal participants in its rites. Venus Verticordia represented the ritual union not simply of male and female, but of ritually exclusive categories. It thus provided a competing model to cults such as Bona Dea's which operated on a principle of ritual exclusion.

The cults of Venus Obsequens and Venus Erycina were also concerned with ritual categories, but not only with those that were sexually defined. What little we know about the cult of Venus Obsequens shows an easy assimilation of the quite unrelated ideas of military success and adulterous matrons. The cult of Venus Erycina encapsulated the essence of militaristic ideology, and at the same time was made to be a cult favoured by prostitutes. Venus Erycina contained both categories without apparent conflict or tension, and they both contributed in equal measure to the way in which the cult was perceived.

To conclude I shall address the question of how the cults of Venus and Bona Dea, as components of the same ritual system, were related meaningfully by their antithetical approach to a common ritual element.

VENUS VERTICORDIA

Two foundation legends provided a frame of reference for the perception of the cult of Venus Verticordia in ancient times. Sometime in the late third or early second century BC – the exact date is uncertain – a statue was dedicated to Venus Verticordia by the chastest matron in Rome, in this case Sulpicia, daughter of Servius Sulpicius and wife of Fulvius Flaccus. The Sibylline books had prescribed the dedication as a cure for the prevailing licentiousness of women. The hope was that matrons and unmarried girls would more readily turn from licentiousness to chastity.[9] The second legend was connected with the dedication of a temple to Venus Verticordia in 114 BC. A Roman knight and his virgin daughter were returning to Apulia from the Roman games when the girl was struck by lightning and killed. Her tunic was pulled up to her waist, her tongue protruded and the trappings of her horse were scattered around her. The meaning of this dreadful prodigy turned out to be that three Vestal Virgins had been guilty of unchaste conduct in which many members of the equestrian class were implicated. All the offenders, male and female, were duly punished and a temple was built to Venus Verticordia.[10] According to both Ovid and Valerius Maximus, the temple and statue that respectively figured in each story were offered to the goddess in the hope that she would correct the wanton ways of women and make them chaste. This, said Ovid, was the explanation of the cult title itself: Verticordia, Changer of Hearts.[11]

Each legend dealt with a separate aspect of the cult – the dedication of the statue and the dedication of the temple; each also dealt with areas of female sexual morality which had different implications for the collective welfare of the Roman state. There was much more at stake in the virginity of a Vestal Virgin than in the *pudicitia* of a *matrona*.[12] But the two stories are, none the less, complementary rather than competing perceptions of the cult. They are both characterized by an extraordinary level of exaggeration: hyperbole is a common feature of both stories. Consider for example the concept of the chastest matron. How are the degrees of chastity to be identified? One is either chaste or unchaste. Indeed we are never told what Sulpicia did to deserve the honour of being deemed the chastest matron. Elsewhere in stories about women's sexuality, chastity is defined in absolute terms. An example is the story of Claudia Quinta, who single-handedly drew to Rome along the Tiber the ship containing the statue of the Magna Mater.[13] Her dress and manner had given rise to rumours of unchastity but the goddess, by the miracle, proved her chaste. In other words, her behaviour, though it did not conform to prevailing norms of matronly conduct, did not make her less chaste than her fellows. The same dichotomy between chastity and unchastity operates in the story of Lucretia, as we saw. The question at issue was not to what degree her chastity had been compromised, but whether after she had submitted to Tarquinius' threats she could regard herself as chaste at all.[14]

The second story is superficially very different from the first, but in fact it is thematically consistent. The temple, it was believed, was built to expiate the *crimen incesti*, the transgression of Vestal Virgins who had broken their vow of chastity. This story is extraordinary for a number of reasons. The virginity of the Vestals had very special implications for Rome. A Vestal did not merely have to be chaste, she had to be a virgin. A simple loss of virginity by a single Vestal would cause the collapse of the state if not properly expiated. A Vestal's lapse from this strict ideal of virginity could never be concealed for any length of time, because the gods themselves by means of prodigies would reveal it. In the foundation legend of the temple of Venus Verticordia, not just one but three of the six Vestals were found to have been guilty of having had sexual relations with men. More startling in the context of the culture of the Vestals was that whereas one of the three was found to have had a single lover, the other two had had relations with large numbers of Roman knights. This is Dio Cassius' account:

> Three had known men at the same time. Of these Marcia had acted by herself, granting her favours to one single knight. . . . Aemilia and Licinia, on the other hand, had a multitude of lovers and carried on their wanton behaviour with each other's help. At first they surrendered themselves to some few privately and secretly, telling each man that he was the only one favoured. Later they themselves bound every one who could suspect and inform against them to certain silence in advance by the price of intercourse with them, . . . So besides holding commerce with various others, now singly now in groups, sometimes privately, sometimes all together, Licinia enjoyed the society of the brother of Aemilia and Aemilia that of Licinia's brother.
>
> (Dio Cass., 26.87)

In the context of the Vestals this account of sexual excess of orgiastic proportions is bizarre. Dio's account suggests that the transgressions took place over a period of time, increasing in promiscuity as they went along. But according to the common belief about the Vestals, one lapse by one woman was enough for the state to begin to lose its stability. And just in case the signs of impending political disaster were missed, the fire in Vesta's temple, which it was the Vestals' duty to tend unceasingly, would spontaneously extinguish itself – a certain sign that one of its priestesses was no longer a virgin. Seen against the prevailing ideology of the Vestals the most striking characteristic of the story is the extraordinary degree of exaggeration. It is presented as a historical account, and it is possible that the temple of Verticordia was built in expiation of Vestal transgression. But I suggest that the details have been exaggerated and that the exaggeration had some functional purpose in connection with the cult of Venus Verticordia.

That functional purpose has to do, I suggest, with ritual categories. The two narratives feature matrons and Vestals. But there is a third implicit category involved – prostitutes. In Dio's description the Vestals act like prostitutes. Dio could have described a brothel in the same terms. An unchaste matron, i.e. a matron who has sexual relations with men other than her husband, is also prostitute-like. Both stories thus present a blurring of the boundaries of the distinct sexual categories. The stories also imply that such blurring of ritual boundaries is dangerous and needs to be ritually expiated. Hence the dedication of the statue and the temple. What is important is that the expiation was accomplished through Venus – Venus who could integrate disparate categories without compromising the ritual boundaries that defined them. Venus provided the mechanism that other cults lacked for restoring the ritual *status quo* when the categories were compromised. Consider for a moment the cults that operated on a principle of ritual exclusiveness. The cult of Ceres had no mechanism with which to deal with prostitutes, nor the cult of Flora with matrons. As for Vesta, her cult was indistinguishable from virginity itself. Vesta, as we shall see, was represented by the sacred fire in the *aedes Vestae* which spontaneously extinguished itself at the first whiff of Vestal unchastity.

Venus' significance in Roman religion thus lay in her perceived ability to integrate disparate categories. Pliny, in the passage quoted above (see pp. 101–2) on the plebeian myrtle and the patrician myrtle, says that Venus presided over unions, *coniunctioni . . . Venus praeest*. Although the reference here is to the marriage of the Sabine women, *coniunctio* does not necessarily denote marriage or indeed any other type of sexual union. In Pliny's passage *coniunctio* provides the point of transposition of ideas from the way myrtle and therefore Venus was made to operate in the myth of the Sabine women, to the way it was used in the story of the patrician and plebeian myrtles. The patricians and plebeians formed two competing factions of the state. The myrtle, in this case, functioned as a common symbol, which simultaneously affirmed the separate status of each faction yet united them as members of a single polity.

The cult of Venus Verticordia, however, was not concerned with political factions but with sexual categories. But like the patrician myrtle and plebeian myrtle the cult also had integration as its theme. It is important to note that in integrating disparate categories the cult of Venus does not deny the existence of the categories. Ritual categorization was a defining feature of Roman cult. Venus simply provided an alternative way of treating those categories. But the integrity of the separate categories was never compromised; their boundaries never blurred. It is worth reiterating that the cult of Venus Verticordia was not even overtly a generic cult of women, as was Bona Dea's cult, but of women separated into the same ritual groups that functioned separately in other cults within the Roman system. The hyperbole which characterized the two foundation legends drew attention to this feature of the cult. The exaggeration of the differences between the groups served to reiterate their independent existence within the cult.[15]

We now turn to the ritual connected with the cult of Venus Verticordia. Her festival took place on 1 April each year. Ovid provides the most detailed account:

> Rite deam colitis Latiae matresque nurusque
> et vos, quis vittae longaque vestis abest.
> aurea marmoreo redimicula demite collo,
> demite divitias: tota lavanda dea est.
> aurea siccato redimicula reddite collo:
> nunc alii flores, nunc nova danda rosa est.
> vos quoque sub viridi myrto iubet ipsa lavari:
> causaque, cur iubeat – discite! – , certa subest
> litore siccabat rorantes nuda capillos:
> viderunt satyrii, turba proterva, deam.
> sensit et opposita texit sua corpora myrto:
> tuta fuit facto vosque referre iubet.
> discite nunc, quare Fortunae tura Virili
> detis eo, calida qui locus umet aqua.
> accipit ille locus posito velamine cunctas
> vitium nudi corpori omne videt;
> ut tegat hoc celetque viros, Fortuna Virilis
> praestat et hoc parvo ture rogata facit.

nec pigeat tritum niveo cum lacte papaver
    sumere et expressis mella liquata favis;
cum primum cupido Venus est deducta marito,
    hoc bibit: ex illo tempore nupta fuit.
supplicibus verbis illam placate: sub illa
    et forma et mores et bona fama manet.
Roma pudicitia proavorum tempore lapsa est:
    Cymaeam, veteres, consuluistis anum.
templa iubet fieri Veneri, quibus ordine factis
    inde Venus verso nomina corde tenet.

Duly do ye worship the goddess, ye Latin mothers and brides, and ye, too, who wear not the fillets and long robe [i.e. the *stola*]. Take off the golden necklaces from the marble neck of the goddess; take off her gauds; the goddess must be washed from top to toe. Then dry her neck and restore to it her golden necklaces; now give her other flowers, now give her the fresh-blown rose. Ye, too, she herself bids bathe under the green myrtle, and there is a certain reason for her command; learn what it is. Naked, she was drying on the shore her oozy locks, when the satyrs, a wanton crew, espied the goddess. She perceived it and screened her body by myrtle interposed: that done, she was safe, and she bids you do the same. Learn now why ye give incense to Fortuna Virilis in the place steamy with warm water. All women strip when they enter that place, and every blemish on the naked body is plain to see; Fortuna Virilis undertakes to conceal the blemish and hide it from men, and this she does for a little incense. Be not reluctant to take poppy pounded with snowy milk and liquid honey squeezed from the comb; when Venus was first escorted to her ardent spouse, she drank that draught: from that moment she was a bride. Propitiate her with supplications; beauty and virtue and good reputation are in her keeping. In the time of our forefathers Rome had fallen from a state of chastity, and the ancients consulted the old woman of Cumae. She ordered a temple to be built to Venus, and when that was duly done, Venus took the name of *Verticordia*, Changer of the Heart, from the event.[16]

The festival was clearly an all-female affair, although there is no record of an overt exclusion of men, no explicit ritual prohibition of males such as we find in the rites of Bona Dea, and no prescriptions for secrecy.[17] Nor can an argument be made for the symbolic presence of males at the rites, such as I made in the case of Bona Dea. Nevertheless, the whole point and purpose of the rites of Venus Verticordia presupposes the existence of men, not as politically dominant, but in the role of sexual partners of the female participants. The whole ritual was centred around the importance of the physical relationship between male and female. Although males did not participate in the rite as a ritual category, they played a fundamental role in the construction of the ideology of the cult.

Vestal Virgins featured in the foundation legend of the temple, but they did not participate directly in the rites as far as we know. The ritual categories of women that did participate were matrons and prostitutes. The joint participation in a rite of matrons and prostitutes, especially given the nature of the ceremonies, has led to much controversy in modern scholarship. There is general agreement, however, as to the existence of a schism in the cult; it is widely believed that there were two separate cults, one to Venus and one to a goddess called Fortuna Virilis.[18] The debate takes off from this point, and is about the nature of the division, and of each cult. The reason for this interpretation is not only the mention of two categories of worshippers, but also, seemingly, of two different deities, Venus and Fortuna Virilis. We have only two instances of the mention of Fortuna Virilis: by Ovid and by Verrius Flaccus in the *Fasti Praenestini*. According to the note on the *Fasti Praenestini* the festival on 1 April was in honour of Fortuna Virilis. There is no mention of Venus – if we ignore Mommsen's interpolation,[19] and I shall show in a moment why I think we should. On the other hand Macrobius,[20] Plutarch[21] and Lydus[22] all say that the festival was dedicated to Venus. Ovid is the only ancient writer to mention both Venus and Fortuna Virilis in the same context. In my opinion the modern debate on the cult is gratuitous because the foundation on which it is constructed, namely the existence of a schism in the cult, is flawed. The festival on 1 April was a single festival in honour of a single goddess.

Ovid is clearly describing a single ceremony. The opening lines are perfectly clear and unambiguous: *Rite deam colitis Latiae Matresque nurusque/et vos, quis vittae longaque vestis abest*. There are two categories of participants in the cult: matrons and prostitutes. They both offer cult to a single goddess, *deam* colitis (my emphasis). There is no reason to doubt that the various stages of the ritual were performed by all participants together: the washing and drying of the cult statue, the ritual bath under the myrtle, the offering of incense to Fortuna Virilis in the baths. Schilling sees the passage about Fortuna Virilis as an interpolation of a description of a second cult into a general description of the rites of Venus.[23] But there is no reason for such an interpretation. It is merely a continuation, after a brief aetiological digression, of the injunction for the ritual bath. The bathing under myrtle was to take place in the baths. There is no suggestion whatsoever that this was limited to the prostitutes. On the contrary Ovid makes it perfectly clear that all the women participated in this part of the ceremony – *accipit ille locus posito velamine* cunctas (my emphasis). In fact *cunctas* is the clearest possible marker that this is not an interpolation but a continuation of the description. For the passage as a whole is couched in the form of ritual injunctions to two categories of worshippers functioning together, and *cunctas* invokes both categories simultaneously. The passage then continues smoothly with the third ritual injunction, the drinking of the sacred potion with an aetiological explanation invoking Venus.

Fortuna Virilis, I suggest, is nothing more than a cult title of Venus. It is not a name meant to denote a separate entity. Fortuna Virilis has the same force as Verticordia. Ovid uses the name to refer to Venus. His account also suggests that Verticordia might have been the later title for an older cult of Venus Fortuna Virilis. He links the cult title Verticordia very specifically with the events set forth in the foundation legends. But it is not clear which story he has in mind. The general falling off of standards of sexual conduct seems more in keeping with the story of the dedication of the statue. But he specifically refers to the dedication of the temple, which took place about a hundred years after the statue was dedicated. By Ovid's time at any rate, it was a single cult. The entry in the Praenestine calendar marks out the ritual as devoted to Fortuna Virilis rather than to Venus Verticordia. But why this particular epithet? The Praenestine calendar, as it was inscribed – i.e. ignoring Mommsen's interpolation – offers a clue: 'Women in crowds supplicate Fortuna Virilis, and women of humbler rank – *humiliores* – do this even in the baths, because in them men exposed that part of the body by which the favour of women is sought.' Lydus also says explicitly that women at this festival bathed in the men's baths.[24] Although this was an all-female festival the rites were meaningless without the tacit acknowledgement of the existence of men. Men played no part in the rites, but they necessarily formed a sexual category in terms of the cult. We have already seen something akin to this take place at the rites of the Parilia, where although there was no evidence for the participation of women, the rituals that the men performed depended for their meaning on the capacity of women to bear children.[25]

The female categories in the cult were defined according to sexuality and their relationship to each other was symmetrical. Unlike in the cults of Ceres and Flora, the rites were not designed to underscore the differences in function and behaviour of the two categories. On the contrary they performed the same ritual and they performed it together. The male category was one of gender rather than sexuality and it occupied a different position *vis à vis* each of the female categories. The cult of Venus Verticordia presided over the way each of these female categories related to the single male category. For example, a *matrona*'s relationship to a single man, her husband, would differ from the relationship of a prostitute to men. As for virgins and especially the Vestals, their relationship to males, marked by strict prohibition, would again differ markedly from the other two categories. I suggest, therefore, that the cult title Fortuna Virilis was meant to invoke and include within the cult the male principle that was fundamental to its meaning. Moreover, Fortuna Virilis was invoked, according to Ovid, in the baths themselves, so that the blemishes on the naked female body might be made invisible to men. Verrius Flaccus, as we have already seen, in a complementary exegesis, invokes male sexuality as the reason why Fortuna Virilis was worshipped by women in the men's baths.

It must by now be clear why Mommsen's interpolation is misleading and why it is unnecessary to construct a model of two competing cults in order to explain our evidence on the cult of Venus Verticordia. The evidence all points in the direction of a single cult to a single goddess. Verrius Flaccus' statement that the *humiliores* bathed in the men's baths does not necessarily make an argument for a schism of the cult. *Humiliores* does not necessarily refer to prostitutes but simply to a class which was economically, socially and legally underprivileged.[26] A possible explanation, offered tentatively here, that would reconcile the evidence of Verrius Flaccus and Ovid is that the festival, though open to women of all ranks, was in practice celebrated only by women of the lower classes: the *humiliores*.

111

To turn briefly to the rites themselves, Ovid mentions three ritual prescriptions: first, the statue of the goddess was to be stripped, washed and re-adorned; second, the women themselves were to bathe under boughs of myrtle; and third, they were to drink a ritual potion. What is immediately striking about Ovid's description is the perception of the close affinity between goddess and worshipper. The distance usually maintained between the two is here transcended. The cult statue, signifier of the deity, was undressed, washed and adorned just as the women undressed, bathed and adorned themselves.[27] The tantalizing question, for which we unfortunately do not have an answer, is whether the ritual bath of the worshippers and the washing of the statue took place simultaneously. The stated purpose of the ritual bath is also significant. Blemishes on the naked female body would thereby be hidden by Fortuna Virilis from the eyes of men. On one level the implication of this is that it would enhance the women's desirability. But it also implies that the women would be endowed with the quintessential quality of the goddess – physical perfection. Apparently the power of Venus Verticordia to unite disparate categories operated even with regard to this fundamental division of deity and mortal. Within the confines of the ritual, goddess and worshipper were united in a common sexuality.

The symmetry between the goddess and her followers was maintained in the remaining prescriptions of the cult. Ovid provided an aetiological myth to explain the necessity for bathing under myrtle. Once, after a bath, Venus used a myrtle bough to screen herself from the lewd gaze of satyrs. The women recreated this incident in the mythology of the goddess by bathing under myrtle. Similarly they drank the ritual potion of poppy pounded with milk and honey in imitation of the potion drunk by Venus as a mark of her sexuality: 'when Venus was first escorted to her ardent spouse she drank that draught: from that moment she was a bride'.

In the cult of Venus Verticordia it is possible to discern all the categories defined by gender and sexuality that we have encountered in the rites of Bona Dea, Ceres and Flora. Even the exceptional status with which the virginity of the Vestals was endowed in Roman ideology has been assimilated into the cult. Most interestingly, we have here a recognition of the male as a sexually defined rather than a politically defined category. In recognizing these various categories and operating in terms of them, the cult of

Venus Verticordia – and, as I shall shortly argue, other cults of Venus as well – remained within the ideological framework that linked the cults of the Bona Dea, Ceres and Flora. But what set the cult of Venus Verticordia apart within that framework, was the manner in which it treated the ritual categories. It operated, as I have already observed, on a principle of inclusion rather than of exclusion, thereby offering an alternative model albeit within the same system.

VENUS OBSEQUENS AND VENUS ERYCINA

We have very little evidence about the cult of Venus Obsequens. Her temple near the Circus Maximus was believed to have been the oldest temple of Venus in Rome.[28] It was built by Q. Fabius Maximus Gurges, who, when he dedicated the temple in 295 BC, gave the goddess the cult title 'Obsequens' because she had proved propitious towards him during his campaign against the Samnites.[29] Livy said that the temple was built on the advice of the Sibylline books, which had been consulted because of alarming prodigies that took place after the Samnite war had been successfully completed.[30] Fabius Gurges built the temple with money collected in fines from women convicted of adultery. It is not clear whether the prodigies were believed to have been caused by the adultery and whether the temple was a means of appeasing the goddess.

The only other piece of information that we have about this cult is that the anniversary of the temple fell on 19 August, which was also the day of the Vinalia Rustica. We know nothing about the ceremonies that marked the observance of the anniversary. All we have is the foundation legend. It suggests that Venus Obsequens was concerned with at least two areas of human activity: war and its successful outcome, and the sexual morality of *matronae*. The concern for matronal chastity was something Obsequens shared with the cult of Venus Verticordia. But the cult of Verticordia was exclusively devoted to sexual categories. In the cult of Obsequens good matronly conduct and successful military activity were given equal value. The connection, if any, between these two spheres of conduct is hard to discern, at least to the modern eye. None the less these were the two perceptions – bearing in mind that there could well have been others connected with the rites that we know nothing about – that were evoked by the cult of Venus Obsequens. The absence of any evidence about the nature of the rites precludes any insight as to how these seemingly unrelated themes were played out. At the very least the cult of Verticordia suggests a high probability that both categories – women as matrons, men as soldiers – would have participated in them.

The cult of Venus Erycina is more widely attested. It reveals concerns similar to those of the cult of Obsequens. The power of the Roman state, defined politically and militarily, and the concerns of prostitutes both came under the aegis of Erycina. Venus Erycina was imported into Rome from Sicily. The cult of Venus of Eryx in Sicily was regarded as being of very great antiquity and of great and enduring power. Diodorus Siculus describes it as follows:

> A man may well be filled with wonder when he stops to sum up the fame which has gathered about this shrine; all other sanctuaries have indeed enjoyed a flush of fame, but frequently sundry happenings have brought them low, whereas this is the only temple which, founded as it was at the beginning of time, not only has never failed to be the object of veneration but, on the contrary, has as time went on ever continued to enjoy great growth.
>
> (Diod. Sic., 4.83)[31]

The cult was rich and powerful but, more importantly, it was seen to have been adopted by a succession of significant individuals and powerful groups to their advantage: first Eryx, then Aeneas, both sons of Venus, the Sicanians, the Carthaginians and finally the Romans.

The Romans were not content with merely adopting the cult. Although after the capture of Sicily in the first Punic war they were able to lay claim to the sanctuary, they re-created the cult of Eryx in Rome itself. The circumstances under which they did so, make it easy to overlook the significance of the move from a ritual perspective. The devastating defeat at Lake Trasimene in 217 BC was believed to have been at least partly the consequence of religious neglect. Q. Fabius Maximus, the recently appointed dictator, recommended consultation of the Sibylline books, which in turn prescribed a host of religious measures to be taken, including the dedication of a temple to Venus Erycina.[32] It is easy to lose Venus Erycina in the crowd of other deities that were to be supplicated in one way or another on this occasion. But in fact, this particular measure was in many ways the most remarkable. Venus, for one

114

thing, was honoured twice. She was to share in the *lectisternium*, the ritual banquet offered to a dozen deities, which was another of the measures prescribed at the time, and where traditionally she was paired with Mars. But this was, for want of a better way of putting it, a generic Venus, rather than a representative of a special cult. The implications of the temple to the special cult figure, Venus Erycina, were different. This cult was established and indeed derived its name from a geographical location far away from Rome. It might have constituted Roman territory by this date, but that did not make it part of Rome.[33] In this respect it was not different from the Mater Magna of Pessinus, Cybele, who was transferred to Rome in 204 BC, in circumstances very similar to those which had led to the adoption of the cult of Erycina a few years earlier.[34] Nor was it different from the cult of Juno of Veii, which had been transferred to Rome at the beginning of the fourth century BC. But the manner in which the cult of Venus Erycina was transferred to Rome was strikingly different in that there was an absence of the ritual circumstance and symbolic action that marked the transition of both Juno and Cybele.[35]

Juno of Veii was moved to Rome in 396 BC after Veii had been captured by Camillus. Her adoption was an example of the custom of *evocatio* whereby a non-Roman deity was formally invited to transfer his or her allegiance to Rome. In this instance Camillus had 'evoked' both Juno and Apollo.[36] Livy thus describes the way in which Juno was moved to Rome:

When the wealth that belonged to men had now been carried away out of Veii, they began to remove the possessions of the gods and the gods themselves, but more in the manner of worshippers than of pillagers. For out of all the army youths were chosen and made to cleanse their bodies and to put on white garments, and to them the duty was assigned of conveying Juno Regina to Rome. Reverently entering her temple they scrupled at first to approach her with their hands, because this image was one which according to Etruscan practice none but a priest of certain family was wont to touch; when one of them, whether divinely inspired or out of youthful jocularity asked, 'wilt thou go, Juno, to Rome?' – whereat the others all cried out that the goddess had nodded assent. It was afterwards added to the story that she had also been heard to say that she was willing. At all events we are told that she was moved from her place with contrivances of little power, as though she accompanied them voluntarily, and was lightly and easily transferred and carried safe and sound to the Aventine, the eternal home to which the prayers of the Roman dictator had called her; and there Camillus afterwards dedicated to her the temple which he himself had vowed.

(Livy, 5.22.3–7)[37]

There is a considerable degree of symbolic action involved here. For example, the men chosen to transport the goddess were carefully selected; Livy is careful to distinguish this event from pillage. Then there is the ritual purification, the donning of special garments, the initial reluctance to touch the statue, even the initial *evocatio* – all this must be read as a way of marking out a boundary that a deity moving from one religious system to another would have to cross. The climax of the ritual and its most important feature was the consent of the goddess herself to the move. Merely to have carried the statue away to Rome would not have made Juno Regina Roman. The gods could not be acquired by plunder. The crossing of a ritual boundary of any kind, whether internally within a single religious system, or from one system to another, needed to be ritually marked out.

This point is made even more emphatically in the case of Cybele, the Magna Mater. In the transmission of her story we see similar sorts of ritual elements as in the story of Juno, but presented with a greater degree of elaboration. There was a lot more at stake in the adoption of this ritual which contained a much greater degree of non-Romanness than did the cult from Veii. The extraordinary nature of the symbolic action surrounding the arrival of the cult of the Magna Mater reveals an underlying anxiety about the introduction of a cult which in the form of its sexually anomalous priests, the castrated *Galli*, contained at least one element that no ritual manipulation could assimilate into the Roman religious system.

There are many literary versions of the story of how the black stone, the image of the Magna Mater, was brought to Rome from Pergamum. The stories vary with respect to the peripheral details.[38] But the core of ritual circumstance that marked the extraordinary nature of the transition is consistent across the different versions. First, there was an actual physical object that had to be transferred

– the black stone, the symbol of the goddess. Next, although the move had been prescribed by the Sibylline books, the goddess herself had to signify formally her willingness to make the change. And so we find Attalus, King of Pergamum, at first unwilling to accede to the Romans' request until the goddess herself conveys to him her desire to move to Rome.[39] So far the story is not very different from that of Juno. But from this point on it becomes much more elaborate. I shall use Ovid's version for the discussion here not only because it is the most vivid description we have but also because it appears to have been the version that was enacted on the stage. It is a reasonable supposition that the version seen constantly on stage would have been the most familiar.[40]

The ship bearing the black stone from Pergamum was greeted at Ostia by a vast throng of people, which Ovid describes in terms of ritual and political categories: the men are categorized into *equites*, senators and plebeians; the women into matrons (*matres . . . nurusque*), virgins (*natae*), and finally the special category of Vestal Virgins. But at Ostia the ship stuck fast in the mud and could not be moved to Rome. The collective efforts of the male population failed to budge it. Then Claudia Quinta, a nobly born matron with an undeserved reputation for being unchaste, stepped forward and prayed to the goddess to vindicate her: 'They say I am not chaste . . . if I am free of crime give by thine act a proof of my innocence, and chaste as thou art do thou yield to my chaste hands.'[41] The goddess heard her and with barely an effort, Claudia Quinta drew the ship to Rome.

Bremmer has suggested that this incident was an example of a rite of passage marking the transition of the goddess from one location to another. By putting this story in a general context of rites of passage, he suggests that the ship sticking in the mud, for example, should be seen as an instance of the ritual reluctance that marks the passage of an individual from one domain to another; Claudia Quinta he sees as the marginal figure that commonly, in these cases, is made to overcome the ritual difficulty.[42] Bremmer is surely correct in interpreting the incident as a rite of passage, a ritual acknowledgement of the danger inherent in passing from one domain to another, and the mechanisms by which the danger may be neutralized. But the introduction of this cult to Rome does not fit easily into Bremmer's general cross-cultural theoretical framework. It is more helpful to analyse the incident in terms of the particular empirical framework of Roman ritual and ideology.

The non-Roman nature of the rites of the Magna Mater have long been recognized. However, the stress has most commonly been placed on the noisy, freakish nature of the rites: the clashing of cymbals, the beating of drums, the howls of the *Galli*, her eunuch priests. All this is seen as being out of step with the *gravitas* of the Roman, and this is the standard explanation offered for the rule that no Roman citizen was allowed to join the priesthood of the *Galli*.[43] I suggest that the notion that these rites were intrinsically offensive to the Roman ideal of *gravitas* has been exaggerated by modern scholarship.[44] Noisy, clamorous processions formed the stuff of the state's ritual apparatus. We only have to imagine the atmosphere at a triumph, for example, the procession headed by a garishly dressed general, his face daubed with rouge, followed by extravagantly displayed spoils of war and his raucous, ribald army.[45] Not much *gravitas* there, or at any rate not the sort that would make squeamishness about the Magna Mater's rites a plausible proposition. Or consider the *Salii*, a college of priests consisting of well-born men, who processed through the streets at various times during the year, leaping, singing and clashing their sacred shields; or the *Luperci*, again men of the elite, who ran naked in the street lashing onlookers with strips of hide, their foreheads smeared with blood and milk. Lurid rituals were clearly not foreign to Romans and we must look elsewhere for an explanation of the obvious Roman perception of the 'otherness' of the Magna Mater.[46]

I suggest that the explanation is the castration of the *Galli* – not so much the act itself, but the fact of it. The reason that no Roman was permitted to join the priesthood was that a castrated male was an aberration in terms of the system of ritual categories. A *Gallus* was considered to be neither man nor woman. *Semimares* is the word Ovid used.[47] This perception was encouraged by the customary appearance of these priests:

> [H]e wore a long garment, mostly yellow or many-coloured with long sleeves and a belt. On their heads these priests wore a mitra, a sort of turban, or a tiara, the cap with long ear flaps that could be tied under the chin. The chest was adorned with ornaments and sometimes they wore ornamented reliefs, pendants, ear-rings and finger rings. They also wore their hair long which earned them the epithet of 'long haired'; . . . on the day of mourning for Attis they ran around wildly with dishevelled hair, but otherwise they had their hair

dressed and waved like women. Sometimes they were heavily made up, their faces resembling white-washed walls.

(Vermaseren 1977: 97)

From a ritual perspective it was not the fact that they looked strange, but that they looked pseudo-feminine that set the *Galli* apart. As we have seen, dress was used on many different occasions to mark a man out both politically and ritually.[48] This demarcation of roles occurred in so extreme a fashion that a consul could in the appropriate context even appear naked – as a *Lupercus*. But for a man to dress in feminine garb was in the most profound sense un-Roman. Castration and the feminisation that went with it would have made a *Gallus* a ritual anomaly. There was no place for him in the ritual scheme. He could not be both a *Gallus* and a *Roman*.

This fact is made strikingly clear by an anecdote related by Valerius Maximus (7.7.6). A priest of Cybele, a *Gallus* named Genucius, was instituted heir under a will. The praetor granted him *bonorum possessio*, thus allowing him to take his inheritance. The testator was the freedman of one Surdinus, who appealed to the consul to set aside the praetor's decision. The consul did so on the grounds that since Genucius was castrated he could be regarded as neither man nor woman (*Genucium amputatis sui ipsius sponte genitalibus corporis partibus neque virorum neque mulierum numero haberi debere*). A non-Roman citizen could not inherit under the will of a Roman. If Genucius had not been a citizen, the praetor would not have granted him *bonorum possessio* in the first place. Therefore Genucius was a citizen who had disobeyed the senatorial decree forbidding Roman citizens to become *Galli*. But castration had deprived him of the status of citizen, not in a legal sense, but in a ritual sense. This explains both the decision of the praetor to grant *bonorum possessio* and the decision of the consul to abrogate the grant.

I suggest that it was this that made the entry of the Magna Mater to Rome, desirable as it was, ritually dangerous. The device of the ship sticking in the mud of the Tiber was not meant to suggest the goddess' reluctance to cross Rome's ritual boundary. Rather it signified the reluctance of the Roman religious system to accept a cult with elements so fundamentally at variance with its own ritual scheme.

The mechanism by which the danger posed by Cybele's arrival was neutralized was the vindicated chastity of Claudia Quinta. An unchaste *matrona*, like a castrated man, was a ritual anomaly: there was no place for her in the religious scheme of things. She was neither *matrona* nor prostitute. Claudia Quinta's vindication was a signifier of the health or the wholesomeness of the Roman system of ritual categories and declared it robust enough to receive the foreign element without being contaminated by it. It established the ritual integrity of the collectivity that Magna Mater was entering. The chaste matron, embodied by Claudia Quinta, was not the marginal figure of Bremmer's theory but indeed represented a central and vital element of the religious system.[49]

The cult of Venus Erycina, by contrast with both the cult of Magna Mater and Juno of Veii, is striking because of the dearth of ritual circumstance attending its introduction into Rome. We have the barest minimum of detail: a temple was vowed to Venus Erycina by Q. Fabius Maximus, as prescribed by the Sibylline books; two years later, he dedicated it, having been appointed *duumvir* for the purpose of so doing. The only other prescription of the Sibylline books was that the dictator himself, as the most important individual in the state, should dedicate the temple.[50] That was all that was apparently necessary for Venus Erycina to be brought to Rome. No statue or other physical object made to symbolize the goddess was deemed necessary to root the cult in Rome. Even after the establishment of Venus Erycina in Rome, her cult in Sicily continued to flourish, with the Roman state itself contributing to its great renown. Diodorus Siculus writes,

> The consuls and praetors, for instance, who visit the island, and all Romans who sojourn there clothed with any authority, whenever they come to Eryx, embellish the sanctuary with magnificent sacrifices and honour, and laying aside the austerity of their authority, they enter into sports and have conversation with women in a spirit of great gaiety, believing that only in this way will they make their presence there pleasing to the goddess. Indeed the Roman senate has so zealously concerned itself with the honour of the goddess that it has decreed that seventeen cities of Sicily which are most faithful to Rome shall pay a tax in gold to Aphrodite and that two hundred soldiers shall serve as a guard of her shrine.
>
> (Diod. Sic., 4.83)

Tacitus says that Tiberius undertook to restore the ancient temple at Eryx though the actual work seems to have been carried out under Claudius.[51]

The ancient writers saw the adoption of the cult by Rome as unproblematic since Aeneas was believed to have been connected with it, or as Diodorus Siculus puts it, since the Romans traced back their ancestry to Venus. But despite the special relationship that was believed to exist between Rome and Venus, Erycina was a foreign cult in much the same way as Juno of Veii was. I suggest that it was the general ritual function of Venus that obviated the necessity for any rite of introduction. We have already seen that internally, within the Roman ritual framework, Venus was seen to unite ritually disparate categories. But it was not merely the boundaries that demarcated ritual categories within the Roman system that Venus could straddle. The cult of Venus Erycina demonstrates that she could just as easily straddle the boundary that marked a Roman from a non-Roman cult.

We do not know what sorts of rites were carried out in the temple of Venus Erycina in Sicily. Nor do we have a clear account of the rites of Venus Erycina in Rome. There were two temples of Erycina in Rome: the temple vowed by Q. Fabius Maximus was built on the Capitoline.[52] We know very little about it and nothing at all about the sort of rites that were deemed appropriate to it. The temple of Venus Erycina which is better known to us is the one dedicated thirty-four years later by L. Porcius Licinius, who had vowed to construct it during the Ligurian war.[53] This temple, situated near the *porta Collina*, is the only one mentioned by Strabo when he says that the cult of Eryx was re-created in Rome.[54] Despite the separate temples the fact that the anniversary of the dedication of both temples fell on the same date – 23 April – suggests that the cult of Venus Erycina was seen as a single ritual entity. Nevertheless, it appears that nobody was quite clear as to the ritual nature of the day because it was also the day of the festival of the Vinalia Priora. The name Vinalia, says Varro, had nothing to do with Venus: 'The Vinalia from wine – *Vinalia a vino* – ; this day is sacred to Jupiter, not to Venus.'[55] But the very emphasis on the fact that Venus had no role in the festival is in itself suggestive. Varro could only have been trying to refute a perception of his time that the Vinalia was a festival of Venus. Support for this interpretation comes from Ovid. He writes about 23 April,

I will now tell of the festival of the Vinalia; . . . Ye common girls, (*vulgares puellae*) celebrate the divinity of Venus: Venus favours the earnings of ladies of a liberal profession. Offer incense and pray for beauty and popular favour; pray to be charming and witty; give to the Queen her own myrtle and the mint she loves, and bands of rushes hid in clustered roses. Now is the time to throng her temple next the Colline gate; the temple takes its name from the Sicilian hill.

(Ov., *Fast.*, 4.863–872)

The Vinalia, which Varro said was dedicated to Jupiter, now turns out to be a festival celebrated by prostitutes and dedicated to Venus. But five lines later Ovid asks, 'Why then, do they call the Vinalia a festival of Venus? And why does that day belong to Jupiter?' Twenty-one lines later, following an aetiological explanation, which I shall return to in a moment, he exasperatingly concludes: 'Hence [i.e. because of the wine that Aeneas paid out to Jupiter] the day is called the Vinalia: Jupiter claims it for his own, and loves to be present at his own feast.'

Was the day sacred to Jupiter or to Venus? This was the problem as the ancient writers saw it. Was there a symbolic link between these deities and if so, how was it defined? This is the problem we need to address. The traditional approach has been to accept the ancient problem on its own terms and attempt to reconcile the evidence.[56] I suggest that we would do better to take the confusion itself as evidence for the nature of the cult of Venus Erycina. That is to say the confusion was not a manifestation of ignorance as to the significance of the day, but was itself a ritual feature of the cult. The uncertainty and confusion about the nature of the festival of Erycina must be seen in terms of the way that cults of Venus operated within the system of ritual boundaries.

The undisputed features of the festival are that 23 April was the anniversary of both temples of Erycina at Rome; there was a festival of prostitutes dedicated to Venus; and the day was known as the festival of the Vinalia. The dispute is about the patron deity of the Vinalia, which name was derived from wine. Ovid offers an explanation as to why the Vinalia was sacred to Jupiter. Mezentius, the Etruscan king, had agreed to help Turnus in his war against Aeneas on condition that he receive the year's vintage. Aeneas learning of this bargain offered the year's vintage to Jupiter himself if he, Aeneas, was favoured in battle. He was favoured, Turnus was defeated, and the Vinalia commemorates the event. The story is repeated by Plutarch, but with significant variations in detail. In the *Roman Questions* he asks, 'Why on the festival of the Veneralia [*sic*] do they pour out a great quantity of wine from the temple of Venus?'[57] In reply he relates approximately the same story as Ovid about Aeneas and Mezentius. But in this case the vintage was promised by Aeneas not to Jupiter but to 'the gods'. Not only does Plutarch make no mention at all of Jupiter, but he also says that the sacrifice of wine took place at the temple of Venus. The epigraphical material is no less confusing. While the *Fasti Antiatini Veteres* and the *Fasti Caeretani* mention Venus Erycina and Venus respectively, the *Fasti Praenestini* mentions Jupiter.[58]

There is never any suggestion that the day might be dedicated to both Jupiter and Venus, each receiving separate cult sacrifice. Instead it appears that a choice had to be made between the two deities. None of the accounts of the festival suggest a natural association between Venus and Jupiter. Varro and Plutarch both demand that a choice be made. Varro explicitly rejects Venus' significance on this day, claiming that the day was sacred to Jupiter. Plutarch, by putting the problem in terms of the same myth which Ovid used to legitimate the importance of Jupiter at the Vinalia, and yet not mentioning Jupiter at all, implicitly rejects his significance and claims the day for Venus. Moreover, by calling the festival Veneralia instead of Vinalia he clearly invokes Venus. Ovid contradicts himself in the course of twenty-four lines, leaving the question as to whether the Vinalia belonged to Jupiter or to Venus in effect an open one. Finally, none of the epigraphical material suggests that the day was sacred to both deities – it too demands that a choice be made. But nobody quite knew which deity to choose or why, and the overall impression is one of dual perception. Although never overtly acknowledged, Jupiter and Venus were both significant on this day. The controversy in itself, the very demand that a choice be made, presupposes this. The controversy also demonstrates the lack of formality in the association. There are many instances of deities being associated in cult or ritual in various ways. In this book alone we have seen Hercules and Bona Dea, Ceres and Flora, Ceres and Liber, Liber and Libera – yet in each case, there was some attempt made to legitimate the association, to provide a justification in myth or rite. Aetiological myth linked Hercules and Bona Dea, various cultic ritual devices linked the other pairs and the triad of Ceres, Liber and Libera. In the case

of Venus and Jupiter we see no such attempt. There are two possible explanations for this. Either it was an association that was so
natural that it did not need formal legitimation; or there was no
formalized cultic association of the sort apparent in the cases
where we saw an attempt at legitimation being made. Given that
the result was confusion and controversy I suggest that the latter is
the more likely explanation.

The two deities were clearly associated, but that association was
not legitimated or formalized either by a myth or by a particular
ritual practice or injunction. The uncertainty arose in the exegetical
writing precisely because of the absence of a legitimating device.
The way in which Plutarch frames the question is particularly
instructive. One almost feels, when reading it in the context of the
other evidence and looking specifically for a legitimating device,
that an opportunity has been missed. The sacrifice of the wine at
the Vinalia – Plutarch calls it the Veneralia, but it is clearly the same
festival – took place outside the temple of Venus. This would have
ritually connected Venus and Jupiter, except that Jupiter is not
mentioned at all. Plutarch says the vow was made 'to the gods' –
tois theois. The structure of Ovid's account compounds the ambiguity. Was the presiding deity Venus? Jupiter? Both? Thus although
the evidence appears to demand that a choice be made, the nature
of the evidence is such that a choice is impossible. If we try to
reconstruct the ritual of 23 April from the evidence we have, we
are left with the following scenario: at the temple near the Colline
gate prostitutes offered cult to Venus; outside one of the temples,
either the one by the Colline Gate or the one on the Capitoline, a
large quantity of wine was sacrificed. The problem is that the wine
was not sacrificed to Venus. That is about the only fact on which
there is general agreement. To slip for a moment into a somewhat
crude analysis of *mentalité*, the participants at the rite had in one
way or another to confront the ambiguity inherent therein. They
might have made a deliberate choice between the deities, accepted
the involvement of both or made no attempt to reconcile the
dilemma. But it is indisputable that both Jupiter and Venus were, in
one way or another, invoked – perhaps evoked would be a better
word – at the rite. The confusion and uncertainty were a part of the
ritual structure of the festival.

The absence of clearly delineated parameters for the ritual significance of the Vinalia is consistent with the model of Venus that
I have presented in this chapter. It is an extreme expression of the

124

logic of the model. When categories are not kept separate but are drawn together, confusion must sometimes result. But it is important to understand that this was a ritualized confusion, an inherent component not merely of the rite at the temple, but of the day in general. The festival of prostitutes at the temple of Venus Erycina took place on a day that was perceived as commemorating an event that was in terms of Roman self-identity primordial: the divine legitimation of Aeneas' establishment on what might best be described – in ritual terms – as proto-Roman soil. In Ovid's terms, a festival of Venus was celebrated on a day sacred to Jupiter. As far as ritual categories were concerned, the motifs of military and political power implicit in the aetiological myth of the Vinalia as well as the foundation legends of Erycina's temples would have operated in the general perception of the significance of the day, side by side with the motif of a festival of prostitutes. It might appear to us, as it did to the ancient exegetists, to have been a muddle. But it was a ritual muddle, as much part of the nature of the day as licentiousness was part of the Floralia. The cult of Venus Erycina appears to have taken the ideology of inclusion to its logical limits.

VENUS AND BONA DEA

We come full circle back to Plutarch's question: why was myrtle excluded from the rites of Bona Dea? Or to put it another way, why were Venus and Bona Dea so incompatible that the incompatibility had to be ritually demonstrated?

Venus and Bona Dea represented different ways in which ritual categories were treated in cult. The cults of Venus integrated disparate and apparently unrelated categories within a single ritual entity. Venus' most enduring characterization as the goddess of sexual love was, I have suggested, just one facet of a broader function of integration. The hallmark of the festival of Bona Dea, by contrast, was its elaborately flaunted exclusiveness. I suggest that the rejection of myrtle from the cult was an affirmation of this distinction. It represented a deliberate distancing of the cult from the ideology of integration represented by Venus.

Plutarch's was not the only attempt, as we saw, to explain the exclusion of myrtle from the festival of the Bona Dea: the two stories of Faunus and Bona Dea were also used for this purpose. Macrobius describes Bona Dea as the daughter of Faunus, who refused her father's incestuous advances and was beaten by him with twigs of myrtle. Hence myrtle was excluded from her rites. We can give an account of this in terms of the integrative function of Venus. The beating with myrtle symbolized the attempt to draw together the opposite ritual categories of male and female. But we are dealing here with incest. Incest, particularly between father and daughter, could never be mediated by any ritual device.[59] Even Venus could not bring those two categories together. This seemingly trivial story was in fact a powerful rejection of the integrative function of Venus and a legitimation of the function of exclusion for which Bona Dea stood. It provided an account of one aspect of human behaviour that never could be reconciled.

The second myth which has been transmitted by Plutarch, Arnobius and Lactantius provided a somewhat weaker exegesis for the rejection of the integrative principle. Bona Dea is here the wife of Faunus, who was beaten by him with myrtle twigs for drinking wine. I have argued that wine was to be understood as a symbol of the male principle, which was overtly at least excluded from Bona Dea's rites. By drinking wine Bona Dea undermined the principle of separation of gender categories on which her rites were based. Here myrtle was used to punish a ritual offence rather than as an instrument to force the commission of one. It was an apt punishment, for myrtle was the symbol of an ideological position that the cult of the Bona Dea eschewed. As an instrument of chastisement its effect was to identify the nature of the offence: that is the failure to respect the boundary between male and female. Its function in this myth as in the other one was to distance the two competing ideologies of Venus and Bona Dea.

The cults of Venus viewed in these terms play a very important role in the dynamics of the Roman religious system. In their variant treatment of ritual categories the cults of Venus provided a foil to those defined by exclusivity. The dynamic interplay of function between these various cults constituted a system of meaningful interrelations which formed the very basis of Roman religion.

Part IV

THE VESTALS AND ROME

INTRODUCTION TO CHAPTER 4

The Vestal Virgins were Rome's most extraordinary religious phenomenon. At any given time there were six Vestals who might range in age from early childhood to extreme old age. A newly selected Vestal had to be between six and ten years old and was committed to serve for a period of thirty years. After that she was free to leave the priesthood but could choose to serve until her death. Many chose to remain. The Vestals were virgins *extraordinaire*. Virginity was not merely a necessary attribute of the Vestals, it was reified. Individually and collectively the Vestals were an embodiment of virginity. This chapter explores the reasons for this phenomenon and its implications for the Roman collectivity.

The most conspicuous aspect of the priesthood was the live interment of a Vestal who was suspected of having lost her virginity. This fact more than any other underscores sharply the extraordinary character of the Vestals. Suspicions of unchastity and its almost inevitable aftermath – burial alive – arose typically during periods of political instability. The loss of a Vestal's virginity was a sign that all was not well with the state's relationship with its gods. The only way that that relationship could be repaired was by the ritual of live interment. A Vestal's perceived physiological virginity had a tremendous power. It was a signifier of the political stability of the state as well as the instrument which restored stability when crisis threatened. Two questions inform the analysis of this chapter: First, how was the physiological fact of virginity transformed into this extraordinary power? Second, what was the essential character of this transformed virginity? Did it have some ritual purpose besides its function of maintaining political stability?

Ritual and legal rules combined to create an artificial entity called a Vestal Virgin – *virgo vestalis* – from a little girl who was ten years old at most. The most important and most conspicuous of the ritual rules was the injunction to observe uncompromising chastity. In a society where procreation was of fundamental importance, this injunction alone served to set these women apart from their fellows. But it was complemented by legal rules which were unique to the Vestals and had the effect of setting them apart not only from female citizens, as the injunction to virginity did, but from male Roman citizens too. In this chapter I examine the way in which ritual and law operated in tandem to set the Vestals apart from every other ritual category and to render them unique.

Finally an analysis of the most important of the Vestals' ritual duties suggests a reason for this complex construction of the Vestal and shows why she was supremely qualified to be a signifier of political stability. My thesis is that because the Vestals were set apart from the collectivity and could not represent any single ritual category, they were able to represent the whole. In a ritual sense the Vestals *were* Rome.

4

THE USES OF VIRGINITY
The Vestals and Rome

She that hath broken her vow of chastity is buried alive near the Colline gate. Here a little ridge of earth extends for some distance along the inside of the city wall; . . . Under it a small chamber is constructed, with steps leading down from above. In this are placed a couch with its coverings, a lighted lamp, and very small portions of the necessities of life, such as bread, a bowl of water, milk, and oil, as though they would thereby absolve themselves of the charge of destroying by hunger a life which had been consecrated to the highest services of religion. Then the culprit herself is placed on a litter, over which coverings are thrown and fastened down with cords so that not even a cry can be heard from within, and carried through the forum. All the people there silently make way for the litter, and follow it without uttering a sound in a terrible depression of soul. No other spectacle is more appalling nor does any other day bring more gloom to the city than this. When the litter reaches its destination, the attendants unfasten the cords of the coverings. Then the high priest, after stretching his arms towards heaven and uttering certain mysterious prayers, brings forth the culprit, who is closely veiled, and places her on the steps leading down into the chamber. After this he turns away his face as do the rest of the priests, and when she has gone down, the steps are taken up, and great quantities of earth are thrown into the entrance of the chamber, hiding it away, and making the place level with the rest of the mound.

(Plut., *Num.*, 10)

Public, often gory, often lingering death, in battles, executions, or in the arena was by no means an unfamiliar spectacle in ancient

Rome. Therefore Plutarch's description of the execution of a Vestal Virgin convicted of losing her virginity is, to say the least, unexpected. What surprises is the evocation of an atmosphere of sombreness surrounding the meticulous ritual of execution. Particularly poignant is the description of the heavy silence, born of overwhelming emotion, which must have been in such marked contrast to the everyday bustle and din of the city.

The Vestals were different; different from any other phenomenon of Roman life or ritual. They were six women ranging in age from early childhood – a new Vestal had to be between six and ten years old – to middle age and beyond. They were defined by their virginity. Indeed they could be described as virginity personified. There was no such thing as a non-virgin Vestal. Such a phenomenon was a dangerous anomaly and was made to disappear from the Roman state in the fashion Plutarch so vividly describes. The most striking aspect of the implications of a Vestal's virginity, however, is that it was largely taken for granted. Ancient writers scratched their heads over why myrtle was excluded from the cult of Bona Dea, but nobody asked why it was just these six women and no others who were so cruelly put to death if they were suspected of losing their virginity. Nobody asked, because everybody knew the answer: the Vestals were different.

But how were they different and why were they different? The Vestal Virgins have been the object of a great deal of careful scholarly scrutiny in modern times. But modern scholars, like their ancient counterparts, also largely take for granted the injunction that the unchaste Vestal must be buried alive, as well as the circumstances of the burial. But this is not only the most striking aspect of the priesthood, it is extraordinary even in the context of the Roman religious system itself. In no other instance that we know of was the transgression of a ritual injunction ever punishable by death. The lack of collective emotion on ritual occasions was until fairly recently considered good enough reason to deny Roman ritual the status of religion. The burial of the unchaste Vestal, as Plutarch represents it at any rate, appears to violate both norms. What was the special significance of the virginity of the Vestals and why did the loss of it provoke so extraordinary a reaction?

The starting point of such an inquiry must be the ritual of interment. This is the most salient feature of the Vestal phenomenon, and the one most frequently alluded to in the ancient literature. Historical accounts are peppered with references to Vestals put to death on suspicion of unchastity. Moreover the ritual never changed. For a Vestal Virgin the consequences of a determination that she was no longer a virgin were always the same: live interment.

The first thing to note is the complexity of the ritual. The ritualistic nature of the punishment of the Vestal is all the more striking when compared with the way her alleged lover was punished. He was publicly flogged to death, without ceremony as far as we can tell.[1] The manner of the Vestal's punishment was in fact used to construct an elaborate fiction – the fiction that the unchaste Vestal, who was killed for her loss of virginity, was not really killed at all. The underground chamber into which she descended was provided with 'very small portions' – i.e. symbolic quantities – of what is necessary to sustain life. There was clearly no realistic assumption that these would keep the woman alive for any length of time, yet by a ritual fiction she was not actually put to death. She went down the steps ostensibly of her own accord, into a – symbolically – habitable room. The pontiffs averted their gaze and did not see her descend. Finally, all traces of the chamber were erased.[2]

What was the ritual nature of an unchaste Vestal? Wissowa's suggestion, which has gained wide acceptance, was that she was regarded as a *prodigium*, 'like a two-headed child or any of the other indications given to the Roman people of unhealthy relations with heaven'.[3] But others have pointed out that there are fundamental differences between the nature of *prodigia* and unchaste Vestals.[4] Most significant from the perspective of the present discussion are the differences in procedure that were used to respond to the problem of *prodigia* and the problem of the unchaste Vestal. First, *prodigia* were usually dealt with by the *decemvii* and the *haruspices*.[5] There are instances where some of the expiatory rites were recommended by the pontiffs, but these were rare. However, it was the pontifical college alone that tried and condemned a suspected Vestal. This is of fundamental importance. Of the *haruspices'* involvement in expiation of prodigies, MacBain writes, 'In no other society, ancient or modern, has a priesthood of foreign nationality been permitted to enjoy such an intimate relationship to the religious – and sometimes political – life of the people.'[6] We shall see shortly why it would have been inappropriate to have 'foreign' religious functionaries involved with the regulation of the Vestals. The second point is the manner in which an unchaste Vestal was disposed of. Unfortunates born with marked physical deformities such as so-called two-headed

133

children, or children without eyes or noses, or androgynes, were from time to time labelled *prodigia* and destroyed. However, the manner of their disposal contrasted markedly with the manner of the disposal of an unchaste Vestal. Androgynes, for example, whose status as *prodigia* was based on their ambivalent sexual status, were cast out of the city. Most of the cases recorded by Obsequens were sewn up in sacks and thrown into the sea.[7] The unchaste Vestal, however, was buried within the city. This is all the more remarkable because there was a rule going back to the XII Tables that nobody's remains must lie within the boundaries of the city.[8] The Vestals were the only category in whose case the exception to the rule was the norm. Apparently, the Vestal who had transgressed and thereby put the state in the gravest jeopardy nevertheless retained the privileges granted to her colleagues, who by guarding their virginity guaranteed the state's peace and prosperity. Finally, according to Plutarch, priests – *hiereis* – made offerings to the dead Vestals – the ones who had been buried alive, that is – at the spot where they were buried.[9] The interpretation of an unchaste Vestal as a *prodigium* raises more problems than it solves.

Significantly – and this is perhaps the most important factor relating to the punishment of a Vestal – the burials typically took place during times of severe political crisis. Tim Cornell observes that we have only two recorded instances of Vestals being punished for unchastity during the period between the first Punic war and the end of the Republic.[10] The two instances occurred in 216 and 114 BC. Both took place against the background of intense emotional upheaval following news, on each occasion, of the annihilation of the Roman army. It is striking that not only are these the only two known examples of execution of Vestals for this period, but that they also coincide with two of the three known instances of human sacrifice ever recorded in Rome.[11] On each occasion two Greeks and two Gauls were buried alive in the Forum Boarium. This was a source of embarrassment to Livy at least, who described it as something uncharacteristic of Roman ritual.[12] From a modern perspective there might appear to be an analogy between the burial of the unchaste Vestal and the burial of the victim of human sacrifice. All were victims of the current crisis and ensuing panic. But it is important that Livy appears to see no such analogy. The burial of unchaste Vestals was a necessary, even vital part of Roman ritual, but the burial of the Greeks and the Gauls was an embarrassing lapse from the Roman ideal.

The virginity of a Vestal was a powerful force. It was qualitatively different from the chastity of a matron or from general injunctions for sexual continence. A Vestal's virginity represented life and death, stability and chaos for the Roman state. This cannot be overstated.[13] It is important to remind ourselves that virginity *per se* was not of great importance in Roman society.[14] Not all erring virgins were punished in this way. This is critically important. The virginity of a Vestal was more than mere physical virginity. Physical virginity was of course a necessary part of the ritual persona of the priestess. But it was only a signifier of a much more complex, abstract, and politically charged ideal of virginity that was peculiar to the Vestals.[15] By losing her physical virginity, the Vestal more importantly betrayed the ideology of her unique status. To put it another way, not only did she cease to be a virgin, but more importantly, much more importantly, she ceased to be a Vestal. That was what the ritual of her punishment acknowledged. This ideological virginity, as I shall call it, is the crux of the problem of the Vestal Virgins. On the foundations of physical virginity was constructed an ideology of a unique religious function. To understand it we have to understand the nature of that construction. We need to recover the complex of meanings with which the physical virginity of the Vestals was invested.

THE TRANSVALUATION OF VIRGINITY

A Vestal's virginity was indispensable for the political well-being of Rome. But – and herein lies a paradox – the loss of her virginity was equally indispensable for the political well-being of Rome. A single lapse by a single priestess threatened the very existence of the state. In such an event the only way to restore the *status quo* was to rid the state of the offending Vestal in the manner described by Plutarch. The flip-side of this was that when the political stability of the state was under threat the possibility that a Vestal might have been unchaste provided a convenient mechanism for averting the threat. Virginity was an indispensable requirement for a Vestal because the potential loss of that virginity was every bit as vital for the welfare of the polity as virginity itself.

If the loss of a Vestal's virginity portended such dire consequences for the state, why were no measures ever taken to protect the women from the temptation and the opportunity of transgressing? A Vestal was not in any sense secluded. On the contrary, not only did her ritual duties regularly take her away from the *Atrium Vestae*, where she lived with her five colleagues, but her social life does not appear to have differed materially from that of the average upper-class Roman woman. For example, we know that Vestals could attend dinner parties. Dio Cassius records an instance of a Vestal being insulted while returning from a dinner party because she had not been recognized as a Vestal.[16] Superficially there appears to have been a sharp disjunction between the extreme form of the punishment of an unchaste Vestal and the lack of measures taken to protect her chastity.

The manner in which a Vestal's transgression was revealed effectively side-stepped the thorny problem of determining whether or not the woman really had lost her virginity. The gods themselves revealed her crime by means of *prodigia*.[17] We do not know the exact procedure of the pontifical court that thereafter tried the suspect whose unchastity was thus revealed. It is a reasonable assumption that the evidence considered was purely circumstantial. The woman appears to have been present at the trial and allowed to defend herself. One of the criticisms that the younger Pliny makes about the trial of the Vestal Cornelia by Domitian is that it was held in her absence.[18] It is important to note that the *prodigia* which signalled a Vestal's transgression were usually reported in times of serious political instability. As I have already noted, there are only two recorded instances of a Vestal being punished for unchastity between the first Punic war and the end of the Republic.[19] On both occasions the accusations were made in the aftermath of disastrous defeats of the Roman army. The trial of the two Vestals Opimia and Floronia in 216 BC followed the near annihilation of the Roman army by Hannibal at Cannae.[20] The trials of Aemilia, Licinia and Marcia in 114 BC came in the wake of the destruction of the army of C. Porcius Cato by the Scordisci in Thrace.[21] These defeats gave rise to intense and widespread emotional upheaval in Rome itself.[22] The religious measures taken to quell the panic were not merely extensive, they were extreme, even to the point of human sacrifice, as we saw. It is against this background of religious frenzy that we must view the accusations of unchastity against the Vestals. In both cases more than one Vestal was involved. This is in itself significant because just one lapse by one Vestal was sufficient to put the security of the state in jeopardy. In 114 especially, the women were represented as indulging in veritable orgies of sexual licence.[23]

136

In 216 both women were found guilty by the pontifical college that traditionally tried such cases. One committed suicide and the other was buried alive in the prescribed fashion. One of the alleged seducers was flogged to death and we know nothing of the other. The official proceedings in 114 are even more suggestive of scapegoating. After the traditional pontifical court had acquitted one of the women, the tribune Sex. Peducaeus set up, by popular decision, a court to re-try the Vestals claiming that the decision of the pontiffs had been too lenient.[24] This was an extraordinary measure. The exclusive authority of the pontifical college and especially of the Pontifex Maximus over the Vestal Virgins was an ancient tradition, believed to have been established as far back as the time of Tarquinius Priscus.[25] The significance of the proceedings in 114 rests in the clear determination to find the Vestal guilty.[26] Seen in the context of the political turbulence of the time, and the frantic religious activity that accompanied it, it is not difficult to suggest an explanation. The ritual burial of the guilty Vestal, as described by Plutarch – repeated three times in 114, or more accurately in the period between 115 and 113 – would have been a powerful antidote to feelings of impending catastrophe. This could also explain why such occurrences were so rare. The execution of a Vestal was a desperate measure, taken in times of extreme crisis, as a last resort. It would have been difficult to sustain the kind of emotion described by Plutarch if the spectacle had been a familiar one.

The Vestal Virgin and the Vestal who had lost her virginity were both, and in equal measure, vital for the welfare of the polity. The sexuality of the Vestal was inseparable from the welfare of the state. If the state was in trouble the spectacle of the burial of an unchaste Vestal would restore hope for its recovery. If the state was peaceful and prosperous the Vestals were clearly chaste. The younger Pliny illustrates this well in his description of the trial and execution of the Vestal, Cornelia, by Domitian. It was a charge trumped up by Domitian, said Pliny, 'from an extravagant notion that exemplary severities of that kind did honour to his reign'. What is significant about this account is the manner in which Cornelia protested her innocence: 'How could Caesar think I am polluted when as long as I carried out my sacred duties he has conquered and triumphed?' – *Me Caesar incestam putat, qua sacra faciente vicit, triumphavit?*[27] To make a modern analogy, the virginity of the Vestals was the insurance for the welfare of the state.

But it would be belying the complexity of the structure of the priesthood to see in it merely a cynical device to counter political and social upheaval. It was not only in times of crisis that a Vestal's virginity was called into question. A Vestal had not only to be chaste in fact, she had to appear to be so if she was not to incur the dangerous suspicion of unchastity. For example, Plutarch says that Crassus caused the prosecution of the Vestal Licinia by associating with her too closely.[28] Both Crassus and Licinia were tried and acquitted, for it turned out that all he wanted to do was buy at a bargain price some property that she owned. Livy records that the Vestal Postumia was put on trial because her attractive appearance and free and easy manner had aroused suspicions of unchastity.[29] She also was acquitted with the warning to dress and behave in a manner 'more suitable to sanctity than coquetry'. However, the evidence of 216 and 114 BC shows plainly that the Vestals were used as scapegoats in extreme situations.[30]

The functional aspect of the Vestals' virginity gives rise to a more fundamental problem however. It is not enough to say that their virginity was intimately related to the welfare of the polity. It is necessary to examine the dynamics of that relationship. I shall approach the question through the notion of ideological virginity that I have delineated. For the moment and purely for analytical purposes we must regard this, an artificial construct, as separate from physical virginity. In reality the two were intertwined; the virginity of the Vestals was a single, not a dual phenomenon. Ideological virginity was founded on the fact of physical virginity and was constructed by means of the complex set of rules that governed and bound the priesthood.

One caveat: virginity here must not be understood in terms of chastity or purity or any other concept merely denoting approved sexual behaviour. It must be regarded in the strict physiological meaning of the term.

A complicated and detailed set of rules governed the lives of the Vestal Virgins. To begin with not everybody was qualified to be a Vestal. The qualifications for a prospective Vestal were quite rigorous. She had to be aged between six and ten; be free of any kind of physical blemish or impediment; to have father and mother both living – *patrima et matrima*; and to be in *patria potestas*. This last injunction was further qualified. Her father should not have been emancipated in any way from the *potestas* of his father, which

THE USES OF VIRGINITY

meant that if the girl's grandfather was alive she would have to be, like her father, in his *potestas*.[31]

The rule that required her to be in *patria potestas* and *patrima et matrima* had the effect of placing the potential Vestal within the context of a Roman family ideally conceived. This requires clarification. *Patria potestas* was a legal artifact, as we have seen.[32] It was designed not merely to transmit property and absolute legal authority over one's descendants through the male line, but was also a means of providing a male Roman citizen with legitimate children. From a legal perspective the paternal and maternal ties were asymmetrically defined. The maternal bond was natural: a woman's children were hers by virtue of the fact that she had given birth to them. The paternal bond was legal: a man's children were his only if they were born of a wife with whom he had *conubium*, i.e. his *matrona*, within the form of marriage known as *iustum matrimonium*. Such children, and they alone, derived their status from their father. Over them, and over their descendants acquired in the same fashion, a man wielded absolute authority – *patria potestas*. They became his heirs at law – *sui heredes* – the males inheriting upon his death not only a share of his property, but also *patria potestas* which they in turn would exercise over their direct descendants. It is important to recall that *patria potestas* was potential as well as actual. A male Roman citizen acquired the right to exercise *patria potestas* the moment that his *pater* died – or the moment he was legally emancipated from his *pater's potestas* – regardless of his age, and regardless of whether or not he himself was a father. But that power could not be exercised except over children born in *iustum matrimonium*. Thus *patria potestas* signified legally recognized Roman paternity. This is important. The law appears to have ignored the biological bond between father and child. Children born to a man outside *iustum matrimonium* – for example, the children of his concubine – were not automatically subject to his *potestas*. He had to adopt them legally in order to make them his own. Even more striking is the fact that children born to a man's *matrona* automatically came under his *potestas* even if he demonstrably could not have fathered them. A eunuch had the right to marry, and children born to his wife were legally his.

Patria potestas was also a continuous chain of power, passed down from father to son, linking through the generations the agnatic line. This continuous line of filiation could be deliberately severed

139

but ideally would continue indefinitely in an unbroken chain. The prospective Vestal had not merely to be in *patria potestas*, but in *patria potestas* thus ideally conceived. Strictly speaking even if her father had been emancipated from the *potestas* of his father, she would remain in the *potestas* of her grandfather unless she herself had been formally emancipated. But that evidently was inadequate. It was the ideal that the rule invoked, even if, spanning as it did only three generations, the ideal was expressed symbolically.

It is also important to note that the maternal and paternal relationships were mutually exclusive. Depending on the circumstances, one took precedence over the other. The maternal bond, the natural or biological relationship between mother and child, was, to use a concept familiar to contract lawyers, the default rule.[33] A child at birth derived its status – including citizenship – from its mother, unless it had been born in *iustum matrimonium*. The effect of *iustum matrimonium* and its legal corollary, *patria potestas*, was to override the maternal bond or at least the legal implications of it. A *matrona*, especially if married *sine manu*, had no legal claim on her children nor they on her. Yet despite the legal implications, it would be silly to deny the importance of the maternal bond. The biological tie of mother and child was certainly recognized even if considered subordinate in this single instance. The necessity for the potential Vestal to be *matrima* must be interpreted, I suggest, as a recognition of that relationship. The girl needed to fit correctly into the framework of paternal and maternal relationship as it was defined socially and legally in Rome. The context of the ideal Roman family from which she had to be removed had to be perfect. She had to be unblemished not merely physically but socially too.

But from the precise moment that she was admitted to the priesthood all ties with her family were broken. By removing her from a 'perfect' family the rule underscored the complete severance of her familial ties. On a purely physical level, she moved from her family home to the *Atrium Vestae*, the official residence of the Vestals, where she would henceforth live. This physical distancing from her own family, however, was symbolic of a much more fundamental removal from the social matrix in which the individual family was embedded. This was effected chiefly by the manner in which she was removed from the *potestas* of her *paterfamilias*, whether father or grandfather.

Virgo autem Vestalis *simul* est capta atque in atrium Vestae

deducta et pontificibus tradita est, *eo statim tempore* sine
emancipatione et sine capitis minutione e patris potestate exit
et ius testamenti faciundi adipiscitur.

As soon as the Vestal is chosen, escorted to the atrium *Vestae*
and delivered to the pontiffs, she *immediately* passes from the
control of her father without the ceremony of emancipation
or loss of civil status, and acquires the right to make a will.[34]

The change in the new Vestal's status was dramatic. Gellius focuses
on two aspects of it: the instantaneous nature of the conversion,
and the fact that the change took place without the normal
procedures of *emancipatio* or *capitis deminutio*.[35] This apparently
simple legal exception had enormous consequences for the Vestal.
It made her in legal terms unique. The legal status of the Vestal was
designed to set her apart from the common experience of every
other Roman citizen, male and female.

The Vestal was freed from *patria potestas* without undergoing
capitis deminutio. There were several ways in which the ordinary
Roman citizen could be freed from *patria potestas*. When one's *pater*
died or if he – the *pater* – underwent *capitis deminutio* in any of the
three degrees, the tie of *potestas* was severed. In the Vestal's case
neither of these situations applied. She became free immediately –
eo statim tempore – and not on the death of her father; nor, obviously, had her father undergone *capitis deminutio* as that would
automatically have disqualified his daughter. The tie of *patria potestas* could also be artificially severed while the *pater* was still alive
and had not himself undergone *capitis deminutio*. This necessitated
the ceremony of *emancipatio*.[36] For a woman, marriage *cum manu*
also had the same effect. However, both *emancipatio* and marriage
cum manu meant that the child underwent *capitis deminutio*. In the
Vestal's case the tie was broken without either *emancipatio* or
capitis deminutio. Anybody inclined to think that the legal status of
a Vestal was in any way analogous to male status[37] need only
compare the little girl with her father, who, if his own father were
still alive, was still in *patria potestas*, and subject to all its legal
incapacities, to see how untenable such a notion really is. The
contrast between a Vestal and the average Roman citizen, male or
female, could not have been more sharply contrived.[38]

The consequences of a Vestal's freedom from *patria potestas* set
her apart from all other Roman citizens. There was no fundamental
difference between the legal capacities of men and women as long

as they were *in potestate*. The *pater's* power over both sons and daughters was, in theory, absolute. However, once they became free from *potestas* the relative legal capacities of men and women changed radically. As far as intestate succession to property was concerned, sons and daughters *in potestate* had identical claims on their *pater*. But it was more than property that a son acquired on his *pater's* death. It was only on the death of his father, as I have already observed, not when he himself became a father, that *patria potestas* gave a son both legal autonomy and legal authority over children born in *iustum matrimonium*. It is worth repeating that regardless of age and regardless of whether or not he himself had children, a man acquired this legal capacity on the death of his *pater*. Until he reached puberty he was *in tutela*, subject to a guardian. But thereafter his legal autonomy was unrestricted. His children, over whom he had *potestas*, were *sui heredes*, his heirs at law, and they had first claim in intestate succession. A woman's situation was radically different. As one of her father's *sui* her claims on his property were no different from that of her brothers', but she did not inherit as they did the power which would have given her personal autonomy and authority over her descendants. A woman could never possess such power. Her children were never in her *potestas* and hence were not her heirs at law. If she had married *sine manu* her property went to her agnates, that is those who had been in her father's *potestas*. If she had married *cum manu* her children might inherit her property not because they were her children, but because she and they were in the *potestas* of the same man. When viewed in this schematic way it becomes clear that *patria potestas* operated on every level of family structure. The implication of the rule as set forth by Gellius is that the Vestal was removed not merely from the sphere of authority of her individual *pater*, but from the whole structure of *patria potestas* to which everybody else was subject in one way or another. That, I suggest, is the explanation of the fact that the institutions of *emancipatio* and *capitis deminutio* were bypassed in the case of the Vestals. They were required only if a person was leaving the authority of his *pater*, and – in the case of a man – acquiring that same authority in his own right; they were also required if a person was moving from the authority of one individual to that of another, for example in cases of adoption or – for a woman – marriage *cum manu*. In the case of the Vestal they became meaningless.[39]

From the moment that a little girl was chosen by the *pontifex maximus* to be a Vestal Virgin she stood aloof from the rest of Roman citizenry. The legal rules operated to create in her a unique legal entity. Ideological virginity endowed this entity with the corresponding ritual uniqueness. The six Vestals could not identify either legally or ritually with any other category in Rome. I shall show that by being excluded from every other category of the collectivity, whether the group was defined legally, ritually or in some other way, a Vestal became a symbol of the whole. Her identity lay only in Romanness. She was and could be nothing else.[40]

The rules by which property was transmitted at death were different for a Vestal and reflected her extraordinary status. It was the Roman state that was a Vestal's sole heir at law; her agnatic family had no legal interest in her property.[41] The collectivity as represented by the state became for a Vestal the surrogate of the agnatic kin, who, had she not been a Vestal, would have been her heirs. For, from the moment that she became a Vestal, she had no kin. The testamentary powers of a Vestal were also consistent with her unique status. A woman who was free from *patria potestas* had no power, theoretically, to conduct affairs of business, including making a will, without the supervision and consent of a *tutor*. A man's autonomy was similarly restricted only until he reached puberty. Thereafter he could write his will without the need for it to be endorsed by a *tutor*. So could a Vestal from the day that she entered the priesthood at six to ten years of age. Although the testamentary powers of a Vestal and a man *sui iuris* were superficially similar they were products of very different legal contexts. A man's testamentary privileges were a product of his status within the kinship system based on the institution of *patria potestas*. The Vestal's privileges were a product of her status outside the system. To put it another way, a man's testamentary privileges were positively defined, a Vestal's negatively. To take an analogy from medicine, it is as though two very different diseases were to present with the same symptoms. A physician who failed to make a differential diagnosis could not hope to cure them both.

The legal rules effected a Vestal's separation from the family both individually and institutionally. This 'separateness' manifested itself in various ways. For example when a Vestal became ill she was sent for nursing not to one of her female relatives but to the home of a selected matron.[42] Similarly at the *Parentalia*, a festival devoted especially to the worship of dead ancestors, it has been plausibly conjectured that the Vestals collectively offered cult at the tomb of a legendary Vestal, Tarpeia.[43] A Vestal could have no ancestors of her own. Just as the collectivity stood to her in the position of agnates, only former Vestals could be regarded as her ancestors.

None the less a Vestal's natural relationships were sometimes invoked, even exploited. In 143 BC, the Vestal Claudia used her sacred status to protect her triumphing father from the tribune, who would have dragged him down from his chariot and prevented his triumph.[44] Even more significant is the way in which Cicero in defence of Fonteius exploits the fact that Fonteius' sister was a Vestal.

> A Vestal Virgin casts her arms about the brother of her blood
> – *germanum fratrem* – imploring your protection,
> gentlemen, and that of the Roman people. She has devoted
> so many years to propitiating the immortal gods on behalf of
> you and your children that she may well today propitiate
> your hearts when she appeals on behalf of herself and her
> brother. What protection, what comfort is left to the poor
> lady if he is taken from her? Other women can bear protec-
> tors for themselves, they can have in their own homes a
> companion and a participant in all life's chances; but to this
> maiden what can be dear or delightful save her brother?
>
> (Cic., *Font.*, 21)

This might have been tear-jerking rhetoric but it could only have worked if a Vestal's natural relationships were generally acknowl-edged. But this does not necessarily undermine the legal effect of a Vestal's status. What it does do is reveal the disjunction between social practice and cultural ideology. Social practice might on occa-sion mask the ideal, but it does not invalidate it. A Vestal was no longer her father's heir, but he could if he chose leave her intestate portion to her in the form of a bequest. That this implied the acknowledgement of kinship did not in any way undermine the rule that artificially denied that kinship. A Vestal's position *vis à vis* her family was legally contrived. But as in the case of the maternal bond within *iustum matrimonium*, a legal rule did not necessarily undermine affective ties nor the acknowledgement of those ties. This tension inherent in a Vestal's situation is illustrated for example by a set of dedicatory inscriptions to a Vestal named Flavia Publicia. Some of the inscriptions record filiation, some do not.[45]

As the legal landscape changed over time and relative legal capacities were adjusted, the rules governing the Vestals were adjusted too, in order that their special status be maintained in the face of change. For example, as a result of the restrictions placed by Augustus on the unmarried and childless, the Vestals would have lost some of the legal rights, specifically rights of inheritance, that they had previously enjoyed.[46] Augustus countered this effect by granting the Vestals the *ius liberorum*.[47] A contemporary legal artifice was thus used to maintain the Vestals' time honoured status.

The ritual position of the Vestals reflected their legal status. The Vestals as we know were not in any way secluded. They had public religious functions to perform and their social activities did not appear to have been restricted at all, except of course by the injunction to be and appear to be chaste. In appearance however the Vestals were again different, marked out from the rest of society by distinctive dress and appurtenances.[48] The most conspicuous visual attribute of a Vestal as she appeared on the public streets was that she was accompanied by a *lictor*.[49] A *lictor* was a symbol of office. Certain magistrates were accompanied in public by lictors, but not all. The tribunes, for example, were not accompanied by lictors.[50] Priests were generally not accompanied by lictors although we know from Festus that the *flamen Dialis* was.[51] But Festus implies that this was not a traditional privilege of priests. The *flamen* had a *lictor*, he says, on account of his sacred duties, or perhaps, more generally, on account of his sacredness – *sacrorum causa*. A *lictor* was a symbol of power, secular in the case of magistrates, sacred in the case of the *flamen Dialis* and the Vestal Virgins. From the perspective of common perception a Vestal on the streets, accompanied by a *lictor*, would have been a unique figure, instantly recognizable as a Vestal. Positions of power in Rome were occupied exclusively by men. The Vestals were the only women who were accompanied by a symbol of power.[52] The visual impact of the Vestal in the public streets was similar to the impact of the legal rules on her status. It kept her aloof from the common experience of any and every other category in Rome.

A Vestal's personal appearance was also distinctive. Her hair was always worn in a style unique to the Vestals: the so-called *sex crines*. The only surviving passage on the *sex crines* is partially corrupt.[53] But it suggests that the hairstyle was a very old one, that it was worn by Vestal Virgins and brides and that it had to do in some way with chastity. This is all we know about the *sex crines*. But we do have a fair amount of evidence for the dress of a Roman bride. A bride's dress predictably symbolized in all sorts of ways the fact that she was undergoing, in Van Gennep's terms, a rite of passage from virgin to wife. A bride's traditional tunic, the *tunica recta*, was, for example, identical to that worn by a boy on the day he attained manhood.[54] A bride's girdle was tied with a special knot, the *nodus Herculaneus*, which could only be untied by her new husband.[55] She also wore the *flammeum*, a veil the 'colour of Jupiter's lightning' which was otherwise only worn by the *flaminica Dialis*.[56] Her hair was dressed in the style known as the *sex crines*, which we know was also the hairstyle of the Vestals. There is an obvious symmetry between the *flammeum* and the *flaminica* and the *sex crines* and the Vestals. Festus says of the *flammeum*, 'The bride is wrapped in it on account of the good omen because it is always worn by the wife of a *flamen* who is not allowed to divorce' – i.e. the *flaminica Dialis*.[57] The bride's dress marked her transitional status by invoking aspects of other rituals which were appropriate to her position. Her tunic was evocative of the male ritual of transition from childhood to adulthood; the *flammeum* of the ideal *matrona*, the *flaminica Dialis*. And the *sex crines* as worn by the bride was meant to evoke the virginity of the Vestals. The *flammeum* and the *sex crines*, symbols *par excellence* of virginal and matronal status, announced the ambivalent status of the virgin about to become a *matrona*. But as worn by the Vestals the *sex crines* had a deeper symbolic value. The *sex crines* was the peculiar badge of the Vestals just as the *flammeum* was the badge of the *flaminica*. It was a permanent attribute of the Vestals and as worn by them it was a marker of both their physical and ideological virginity. Visually it marked out a Vestal as a Vestal and not simply as a virgin, in much the same way as the *flammeum* worn by the *flaminica* served to identify her as the *flaminica* and not simply a *matrona*.

It is not easy to determine the nature of a Vestal's garment. There is no surviving literary reference to it. Beard, relying on sculptural evidence, identified their dress as the *stola*.[58] But this is by no means certain. The literary evidence for the *stola* strongly suggests that the extra length was achieved by sewing on a wide band, often of a contrasting colour, called the *instita*, to the bottom of the tunic.[59] But the *instita* rarely appears on sculpture, leading some scholars to surmise that it might originally have been painted on.[60] There can be no certainty about a Vestal's dress. It is impossible to

tell whether it was recognized as a *stola*, or whether it was merely
an extra-long tunic which was worn only by the Vestals. However,
even if we were to assume for argument's sake that the Vestal did
in fact wear the *stola*, it would not have diminished in any way the
uniqueness of her appearance: the *sex crines* and the *lictor* were a
unique and distinctive combination which served to distinguish the
Vestals and set them apart visually.

VIRGINITY AND THE RITUAL REPRESENTATION OF ROMAN INTEGRITY

Against a background of Roman legal and cultural codes, the Vestal
stands aloof uncompromisingly virginal. Her physical virginity, the
sine qua non of her religious office, was exaggerated into an ideology of virginity that put her outside each individual social domain.
I have suggested that this enabled her the better to represent the
collectivity as a whole, to be a symbol of Roman integrity. In this
section we shall see how her ritual duties and obligations effectively accomplished this function.

Livy calls the Vestals *venerabiles et sanctae*.[61] The reason, he
says, was their virginity. The effect of this sacred virginity on the
woman herself was that her individual potential for sexuality and
procreation was suppressed. Ideological virginity was designed to
suppress that potential. For example, a Vestal's tenure of office
was not necessarily lifelong. The priesthood demanded only thirty
years of service. After that time she was free to marry, i.e. resume
the 'normal' life that the priesthood had interrupted.[62] The thirty
years of her service was, however, a critical thirty years as far as
her sexuality and procreative potential were concerned. As Beard
has pointed out it corresponded roughly to the period of a
woman's fertility.[63] Few priestesses did in fact avail themselves of
the opportunity to relinquish an arduous and potentially deadly
office, but the rule remained. The requirement that a Vestal serve a
minimum of thirty years effectively circumscribed that period in
the woman's life when she was at her most sexually active and
fertile, precisely in order to suppress her sexual potential. The
difference between a Vestal and an unmarried girl was that the
latter's virginity would, in the normal course of events, evolve
naturally into active sexuality. A Vestal's virginity, by contrast, was
inactivated precisely during that period when such an evolution
would normally have taken place. She was allowed to give up her

sacred office only when her sexual potential was waning. One of the ways that ideological virginity isolated the Vestal was by de-sexualizing her. The tension between a Vestal's sexual potential and its implacable suppression invested the woman with a peculiar religious power. It now becomes easier to understand the extraordinary response to the suspicion that a Vestal had lost her virginity. A Vestal's unchastity was a sign of the dangerous resurgence of her sexual potential. It was also a sign that the constraints imposed on that potential – i.e. ideological virginity – had failed. The loss of her physical virginity removed the foundation upon which the ideal of a Vestal Virgin was constructed. It bears repeating – again – that the peculiar gravity of a Vestal's crime was not merely that she had ceased to be a virgin, but that she had thereby ceased to be a Vestal.

The power inherent in a Vestal could on occasion achieve miraculous proportions. A Vestal's prayer, for example, was believed to have the power to root to the spot a runaway slave, provided that he had not left the city.[64] There are also legendary tales of Vestals who cleared themselves of suspicions of unchastity by performing miracles. Aemilia, who had incurred the suspicion when the sacred fire was extinguished, caused the fire to blaze up again by laying her sash on the cold hearth. Tuccia carried water in a sieve from the Tiber to the forum without spilling a drop.[65] The miracles were regarded as Vesta's own vindication of her priestesses. In the rest of this chapter I shall show how the Vestals' power was harnessed as a guarantor of stability and integrity for Rome.

The Vestals' most conspicuous duty was tending the hearth fire in the temple, the *aedes Vestae*. Indeed the literary accounts describing the founding of the priesthood by Numa say that this was the very reason for the priesthood.[66] Virgins were seen as peculiarly suitable for such a task because like the fire, they were pure and undefiled.[67] The fire was also a potent symbol for the chastity of the Vestals and its consequence, the stability of the Roman state. They had to tend it ceaselessly for its extinguishing might be a sign of their unchastity and presage disaster for the city.[68] If it was determined that it was indeed such a sign a Vestal would be tried and punished in the customary fashion. If the fire had been extinguished merely through a Vestal's negligence, she was whipped by the *pontifex maximus*.[69]

The motif of fire dominated the cult of Vesta. Indeed the *aedes*

Vestae contained no cult statue; the fire itself was regarded as the representation of the goddess.[70] But there was more to the relationship between the virgin priestesses and the hearth fire of Rome itself than the devotion of priestess to deity and the homologous relationship marked by purity. Fire, as we have already seen, was sometimes considered a symbol of male procreative power.[71] Varro calls it the symbolic equivalent of semen.

> The conditions for procreation are two: fire and water. Thus these are used in the threshold in weddings, because there is union here. And fire is male, which the semen is in the other case, and water is the female because the embryo develops from her moisture, and the force that brings their binding is Venus.
>
> (Varro, *Ling.*, 5.61)

That this symbolism extended to Vesta's fire is suggested by the stories of the birth of Romulus (in some versions) or Servius Tullius (in others), who was believed to have been fathered by a phallus which appeared in the hearth fire.[72] The king in whose hearth the phallus appears orders his daughter, on the advice of a soothsayer, to have intercourse with the phantom. When she persuades a slave girl to take her place her angry father would have both girls put to death but is prevented by Vesta herself. The slave girl subsequently gives birth to Romulus or Servius depending on the version of the story. Thus Vesta's fire had dual symbolic value: on the one hand it evoked the idea of sexual purity in the female, on the other it represented the procreative power of the male. This tension between sexual avoidance and sexual power that was inherent in the sacred fire was also inherent in the ideology of a Vestal's virginity.

While fire by itself symbolized male procreative power, fire and water together as I have already observed were symbols for life itself. In the passage quoted above Varro saw in water an equivalent of the procreative power of the female. Festus expressed the same idea but in broader terms:

> Water and fire are both denied to condemned men and accepted by brides. The reason is probably because these two substances contain the very stuff of human life. Therefore, those returning from a funeral sprinkle themselves with water and step over fire.
>
> (Festus, p. 3 L)

This symbolism occurs in legal rules as well. The *Digest* states that there were two modes of capital punishment: death and exile. The exile was stripped of his Roman citizenship and banished from the city. The loss of citizenship, which was symbolically equivalent to death, was indicated by the exile being denied fire and water. Any other form of banishment was not *exilium* but *relegatio* and did not entail loss of citizenship.[73] It was therefore not a form of capital punishment. The symmetry between death and exile was effected by the symbol of fire and water.

A Vestal's primary task was tending the fire of Vesta. The fire had to be tended constantly for if it went out the consequences were terrible for both Vestals and City. But a Vestal's daily chores also involved the ritual use of water. Each day a Vestal had to perform the laborious task of fetching water from a spring to purify the *aedes Vestae*. This was no ordinary spring, but the one which watered the field where the *ancile* had fallen from heaven.[74] The *ancile* was a shield, a pledge of Roman power – *pignus imperii* – from Jupiter to Numa. There were several *ancilia* for Numa had copies made in order to foil a potential thief. These were all ceremoniously paraded by the *Salii* at various times each year, including 1 March, the old Roman New Year,[75] the day when Vesta's fire was also formally rekindled.[76] Both the hearth fire of Vesta and the *ancile* were central to the very existence of Rome, and were symbolic of Roman identity and stability. The Vestals' daily duties of tending the fire and of purifying the temple with water from the spring connected with the *ancile* had equivalent value. The prominent place given to fire in the cult and the dramatic consequences of the Vestals' failure to tend it made it the more significant feature, and by far the better known. But the two elements of fire and water in the cult must be seen as parallel. They were both part of the daily ritual. Also, the symmetry between fire and water is evident in the mythical tales of Vestals. The stories of Aemilia and Tuccia reveal the same parallelism, one making proof of her virgin status with fire, the other with water.[77]

In the very repetitiveness of their daily rituals connected with fire and water the Vestals symbolically affirmed the continuation not just of Roman power but of Roman life itself. No wonder then, that an interruption of the ritual, the most conspicuous sign of which was the extinction of the fire, caused such dismay. The intimate relationship between a Vestal's virginity and the sacred fire is underscored by the fact that the loss of virginity was signified by the loss of the fire – the spontaneous extinction of the fire. We must recall that if it was determined that the fire had gone out simply because of a Vestal's negligence, her chastity was not impugned. But the spontaneous extinguishing of the fire and a Vestal's unchastity were equivalent occurrences, both omens of disaster. The offending Vestal, like the sacred fire, had to be 'extinguished' before the state could repair its fractured relationship with the gods. The culprit disposed of, a new fire formally rekindled and a new and unblemished priestess chosen, represented anew a state of harmony.[78]

This interpretation of the relationship between Vestal and fire helps explain some puzzling features of the cult. For example, it makes sense of the fiction that the unchaste Vestal was not really put to death but was placed in a 'habitable' room. She was not 'killed' in the same way that the fire did not 'die'. And like the fire which was kindled anew, pure and unpolluted, the Vestal was restored in the person of a new little recruit likewise pure and unpolluted. The relationship between Vestal and fire also suggests a reason as to why the unchaste Vestal was buried within the city and not cast out. The fiction that she was not actually killed, as well as the fiction that her tomb was not really a tomb, meant that the rule against burial in the city was not violated. Also, although the emergence of a Vestal's carefully suppressed sexuality made her unfit for her duties, it did not make her completely devoid of sacredness. Sexuality was, after all, a quality inherent in fire itself. This also explains why priests continued to offer sacrifice over the place where she had been buried alive.

The relationship between the Vestals and the sacred fire also suggests an explanation of the old puzzle that the process of trial and execution of a Vestal did not fit into the normal framework of criminal law.[79] Despite the fact that *crimen* was the word used to refer to a Vestal's sexual lapse, it was not, I suggest, regarded as a crime in the ordinary sense. I propose the somewhat radical idea that the reason the Vestals did not have recourse to the usual mode of capital trial, was because they were thought of as transcending even the category of citizen. The most striking disparity between the rights of a Vestal and the rights of a citizen was that ever since the passage of the *lex Valeria* in 509 BC, a citizen, when faced with a capital charge, had recourse to the *ius provocationis ad populum*.[80] A Vestal did not. It must be said immediately that it is nowhere stated that the Vestal was not a *civis*. In fact, as we saw, she did not undergo *capitis deminutio* in any degree when she became a Vestal, while loss of citizenship usually involved *capitis deminutio* either *maxima* or *media*. The idea of loss of citizenship also sits uneasily on a figure meant to be a symbol of the state. Instead, I suggest that she *transcended* the status of *civis* as long as she was a Vestal. This made it possible to circumvent the procedure that was always necessary before an execution could be carried out. The Vestal's burial was not an execution in the ordinary sense. She was not put to death. The underground chamber in which she was interred contained, in Plutarch's words, 'very small portions of the necessities of life'.[81] Her death occurred spontaneously, just as the fire went out spontaneously.

The sentence of death was imposed on a Vestal not by a judicial but by a religious body, the pontifical college.[82] The right of the *pontifex maximus* and the pontifical college to pronounce judgement on a Vestal was one of the main reasons that scholars have argued that the *pontifex* was her pseudo-*paterfamilias*. The role of the pontifical college was seen as analogous to the role of the family council and the fact that the *pontifex* participated in the ceremony of live burial as analogous to a *pater*'s *ius vitae necisque*. However, I have shown in my discussion of a Vestal's privileges with regard to property that the notion of pseudo-*paterfamilias* is untenable.[83] The suggestion that the Vestal transcended even the category of *civis*, has much greater explanatory power for the fact that the normal criminal procedure was circumvented in her case. In the following discussion of the palladium we shall see how such isolation and its concomitant extraordinary status enabled her to perform a unique function.

The Vestals' isolation from the incidents of categorization, which included the category of *civis*, gave them unique ritual status. The palladium, like the *ancile*, was regarded as a surety of the power of Rome – *pignus imperii Romani*.[84] It was kept in the *aedes Vestae*, but unlike the *ancile* was never displayed in public. In fact only the Vestal Virgins were allowed to see it or to touch it.[85] In this regard it was different from the sacred fire which was on open view in the temple. The secrecy that shrouded the palladium led to the speculation that in fact it did not exist and that the temple contained nothing more than the fire.[86] But the belief that there was indeed something secret, sacred and powerful that the Vestals guarded in their temple was more pervasive. It was also believed to have been originally a pledge of Trojan power, which was brought to Italy by Aeneas after the sack of Troy.[87] It was a symbol of the continuation of power, reaching backward as well as forward in time.

The question is what *imperium Romanum* meant in the context of the palladium and the *ancile*. Did it refer to Roman power over her empire, her dominance over other nations and continuous aggrandizement, or only to her continuing existence? To make a political analogy, was the power of the palladium related to the *imperium domi* or the *imperium militiae*? A passage in Livy suggests an answer.[88] In it Camillus argues against moving Rome to the site of Veii after the sack of the city by the Gauls in 390 BC. The argument is based almost entirely on religion, on the impropriety of carrying out Roman rites away from Rome. But it also suggests that the palladium and the *ancile* could not be moved from Rome at all. Their religious potency operated only on the site of Rome itself. A permanent move to Veii would have necessitated abandoning them. They were guardians of Rome, pledges of Roman *imperium*. Moving them to the site of Veii would make them Veientine and therefore powerless. Rome could not be Rome on the site of Veii. To leave them behind on a site that was no longer Rome, would also deprive them of power. The notion of *imperium* that these cult objects represented was more akin to the notion of the *imperium domi*. It did not extend beyond the limits of the city. The palladium and the *ancile* were assurances of the continuing existence of the collectivity and the integrity of Roman sovereignty.

These two pledges of Roman sovereignty, the *ancile* and the palladium, had in common an aura of mystery. Both were concealed, albeit in different ways, from the population at large. The palladium was kept altogether out of sight, while the 'real' *ancile* was hidden among the fakes. Nobody at all was able to identify the genuine *ancile*. This made the Vestals unique in their function of guarding the palladium, in their ability to see it and touch it with full knowledge of its import. Again I suggest that it was their isolation from all factional interests that qualified them to perform this extraordinary function. It made them, like the palladium, symbols of Roman integrity. They also were pledges for the continuing existence of Rome. Their powers also extended only to the bounds of the city. We saw that their prayers could stop a runaway slave, but only if he had not left the city. This was perhaps another reason why they were buried within the city, even when they were buried alive for unchastity. Outside the city, in the space that was not Rome, as it were, a Vestal was as meaningless as the palladium.

A third ritual obligation of a Vestal was the preparation of *mola salsa*, ground, salted spelt which was an essential part of every Roman sacrifice. The meal was sprinkled on the head of the sacrificial victim before it was killed. Indeed *mola* by itself could constitute a sacrifice.[89] The word *immolare*, 'to sacrifice', derives, says Festus from *mola*.[90] And Pliny writes, 'no sacrifice is carried out without *mola salsa*'.[91] The custom was an ancient one attributed, as many religious traditions were, to Numa.[92]

The preparation of *mola salsa* was the task of the Vestals exclusively. No other individual at all was allowed to participate. Ironically, the fact that no other women were allowed to participate in the preparation of *mola salsa* has been used to bolster the argument that women typically occupied a marginal position in Roman religion.[93] The fact is that making *mola salsa* was neither a male task nor a female task. It was a Vestal's task. And it was a Vestal's task by virtue of her singular ritual status.

The reason that it was exclusively the task of the Vestals was that *mola salsa* was an essential component of all Roman sacrifice. But all sacrifice did not involve the participation of the collectivity as a whole. More often than not one or other of a ritually defined group was excluded from a specific sacrifice. The sacrifice to Hercules at the *Ara Maxima*, for example, excluded women, that to the Bona Dea excluded men. Festus mentions a ritual formula where at certain sacrifices the *lictor* would formally exclude strangers, prisoners, women and virgins.[94] And although in all cases there is no specific evidence for sacrifice, we have seen that in ritual the categories would sometimes remain separate, sometimes mingle. Roman ritual taken as a whole was an ever-shifting pattern of different permutations and combinations of categories. But *mola salsa*, made ceremoniously by the Vestal Virgins, was an indispensable component of every sacrifice, regardless of who participated and who was excluded. Its function was to make every sacrifice, however exclusive in other respects, nevertheless representative of the collectivity. To put it another way, *mola salsa* symbolically included the ritually excluded.

The Vestals were supremely qualified to prepare *mola salsa*. They, being unable to represent any individual ritual category, could without ambiguity or equivocation represent the state as a collectivity. Their ritual relationship to *mola salsa* was similar to their relationship to the sacred fire and the palladium. *Mola salsa*, the sacred fire, the palladium, were all endowed with the same

154

ritual significance – they represented Rome, as did the Vestals.⁹⁵

By means of the *mola salsa* the Vestals symbolically participated in every sacrifice in Rome. Analogous to the use of *mola salsa* is their symbolic participation in the rite of the Parilia.⁹⁶ The Parilia, which celebrated among other things the founding of Rome, consisted not of a single central rite, but a series of celebratory rituals held throughout the city. What unified these individual rituals was the *suffimen* which was provided by the Vestals and which was central to the sacrifice. *Suffimen* were the ashes of unborn calves which had been ceremoniously burnt by the *Virgo Vestalis Maxima* at the Fordicidia. A little of this ash, possibly sprinkled on the fires, was an important element of the individual rituals.⁹⁷

There were other rituals where the Vestals participated actively rather than symbolically. Here too the Vestals' presence served to legitimate the rite, to make it essentially Roman. An example is their participation in the rite of Bona Dea. The Vestals' presence at the festival was further legitimation of a rite that did contain potentially subversive elements.⁹⁸ The paradox of a rite that was secret and nocturnal and held in a private house rather than in a temple also being *pro populo* was manifestly weakened by the participation therein of the Vestals. Although space is insufficient here to examine all such examples of the Vestals' duties, I suggest that the model constructed in this chapter would be a fruitful approach to the problem of their ritual functions within apparently disparate cults.

The temple, the *aedes Vestae*, also conformed to the symbolic pattern that I have been tracing throughout this chapter. It was perceived to be of extreme antiquity, but it was not a consecrated *templum*. The chief significance of this fact was that decrees of the senate could not be made there. According to Varro decrees of the senate might lawfully be made only in a place which had been specifically marked out as a *templum* by an augur. Areas of the *curiae* Hostilia, Julia and Pompeia had to be so marked because they were not consecrated places. On the other hand all sacred places were not necessarily *templa*. Varro's specific example for such a place is the temple of Vesta.⁹⁹ It is not possible to recover all the implications of the *aedes Vestae* not being consecrated as a temple, but I would like to suggest a reason, in terms of my model of the Vestals, as to why a decree of the senate might not be made there. On the face of it the *aedes Vestae* might well appear to have been a pre-eminently suitable place for the issuing of senatorial decrees. For I have argued that the Vestals were the perfect embodiment of Rome. However, the Vestals derived that status from their freedom from the potentially divisive categories of which Rome consisted. Evidently this included the senate. It is an interesting commentary on the senate that even on the level of ritual ideology they were not perceived as unequivocally representative of the collectivity. That was the unique function of the Vestals.

Finally this analysis provides a plausible explanation for the presence of a Vestal Virgin within the complex structure of the myth of the birth of Romulus. It made him simultaneously Roman and non-Roman: non-Roman for all the reasons I suggested in chapter 2; Roman because although Rhea Silvia was a Vestal of Alba Longa, yet the fact that she was a Vestal would necessarily evoke everything a Roman Vestal connoted. Conversely, the fact that a Vestal was the mother of Rome's founder played its part in the structuring of a figure that was the embodiment of Rome.

CONCLUSION

It is helpful to approach Roman religion as a system, as an inter-dependent network of meaningfully related cults. The richness and complexity of meaning with which each individual cult is endowed can best be appreciated when it is seen in the context of the religion as a whole. Meaning is generated not only from within each cult but also from the way in which it is related to other cults in the system. The cults of Ceres, Liber and Flora are particularly good examples of this process. Le Bonniec (1958) and Bruhl (1953) in particular have demonstrated the significance of the cults of Ceres and Liber respectively, as independent entities. But seen in relationship to each other and to the cult of Flora the meanings thus independently generated acquire a new dimension, a greater depth and complexity. Ceres, Liber and Flora are of course easy cases. The way in which they were structured invites comparison. Ceres, Liber and Libera for example, occupied the same temple. Flora's temple stood next door, in Tacitus' words in the very same place, *eodem in loco*. The other easy case for us, because the ancient commentators themselves pointed the way, was Bona Dea and Venus. Why was myrtle, Venus' plant, not used at the festival of Bona Dea? It was Plutarch's question before it became ours. But most of the time the interconnections need to be teased out in a process fraught with difficulty. For one thing we are in danger of missing relationships within cults that might have been intuitively acknowledged in antiquity. But more damaging perhaps is the risk of over-zealously creating relationships which perhaps never existed. There are no easy answers. Gaps, inadequacies and over-simplifications are inevitably a part of writing ancient history. But I have tried to suggest two ways in which to steer clear of possibly anachronistic explanations or rationalizations.

157

The first is the concept of categorization. Roman religion was organized around categories. Rituals were defined by their participants. In this book I have focused on categories that were defined by gender and sexuality. It is a fair assertion that the way in which women were ritually defined always encompassed in some way their gender and sexuality. Men were rarely thus defined. In the rites of Venus there were glimpses of the ways in which men participated: the story of the patrician myrtle and the plebeian myrtle hinted at a political distinction, while the cults of Venus Obsequens and Venus Erycina both ritualized the notion of military prowess. Implicit in the lictor's cry as reported by Festus, *hostis, vinctus, mulier, virgo exesto*, we have the suggestion of male citizens as a ritual category, in some instances. So one way of trying to identify related cults within the system is to compare the categories of participants whenever possible.

It is important to note that different cults used categorization in different ways. The cults of Bona Dea, Hercules Invictus at the *Ara Maxima*, Ceres and Flora all operated on a principle of ritual exclusivity. Sometimes the exclusion of other categories was rigid and strictly enforced; witness Bona Dea and the Clodius affair. The *sacrum anniversarium Cereris* was another rite that was strictly exclusive, confined as it was to *matronae*. In these cults exclusion operated in terms of the physical absence of the excluded category. At the Floralia, which was undoubtedly a festival of prostitutes, the exclusivity was less rigid. The Floralia was a stage performance with actors – prostitutes – and audience. I showed that the men in the audience had a ritual role to play. But given the nature of the festival – a public stage performance – it is more than likely that the audience contained women who were not prostitutes. In fact this is an area where ritual categorization was not a perfect mirror of social categories. For there were surely individual women who were both *matronae* and prostitutes. It is possible that some women participated in different cults that were marked by exclusivity by virtue of their multiple status. But that does not change the nature of the cult itself. The Floralia was a ritual manifestation of prostitution regardless of whether some of the women who participated in the cult were also technically *matronae* as well. It was an exclusive cult in that it did not recognize any other category of women. The distinction becomes clear when we compare the Floralia to the cult of Venus Verticordia. The cults of Venus, I argued, operated in a way antithetical to the model of exclusivity.

CONCLUSION

Venus served an integrative function in Roman religion, by
acknowledging yet bringing together disparate categories within
the same ritual. In the cult of Venus Verticordia prostitutes and
matronae qua prostitutes and *matronae* performed the rites
together. The Vestals, I argued, were unique. By transcending all
other ritual categories they became representatives of the unity, the
integrity of the state. They were simultaneously symbols of its
soundness and instruments for healing its rifts.

A second way to avoid the trap of anachronistic explanations is
to see Roman religion itself as part of a system. I suggested that
cultural institutions in general are also usefully perceived as a
system. In particular I used legal rules, vestimentary codes, myth,
poetry in its various genres, and historiography to demonstrate
consistency with the patterns that emerged from the analysis
of ritual. I do not suggest that this is a foolproof method for avoid-
ing anachronism or falsity. But to invoke again the metaphor of
Monet's cathedral, if it is possible to demonstrate that the different
perspectives reveal the same cathedral, that at least lends plausibility to the analysis.

It is clear that women's role in Roman religion was not a marginal
one. I have shown that they participated in important public rituals
and festivals of the civic calendar. This takes us back to the question I began with: why did Roman women never acquire a legitimate constitutional role? It is important to realize that this is a
modern question. There is no evidence that it was ever an issue in
antiquity. When men feared political action by women they were
not afraid that they would have to cede a degree of power to
women. Rather they feared that women would destroy the structure
of society itself. That for example is the fear that Cato expresses, as
we saw, in the debate over the repeal of the Oppian law. The
political domain was exclusively male. Women could never share it;
they could remain outside (which is what did happen) or they
could destroy it (which is what men feared could happen).

Though modern, the question is a valid one. For there is a
remarkable affinity between women like Hortensia, Cornelia,
Servilia or Sempronia just to name a few, and modern western
women. These were all women who were eminently capable of
playing a constitutional role, and indeed who did affect the course
of events through either the politics of protest or the politics of individual influence. But they appear to have accepted unquestioningly

159

their position outside the domain of legitimate authority. Thus, for example, Hortensia protesting before the triumvirs a tax imposed on the personal wealth of some of the richest women in Rome: 'Why should we pay taxes when we have no part in the honours, the commands, the state-craft for which you contend against each other' (App., *B. Civ.*, 4.5.34). Her words are echoed by Livy through the tribune Valerius. Valerius was arguing that the Oppian law should be repealed and the women allowed their baubles: 'No offices, no priesthoods, no triumphs, no decorations, no gifts, no spoils of war can come to them. Elegance, adornment, finery – these are a woman's insignia' (Livy, 34.7.8–9). In other aspects of their lives women did over the years achieve a very great degree of equality with men. A most important factor in this process was the effective freedom from the constraints of tutelage, for the *tutor* early on became little more than a legal formality. When Augustus released the mother of three children – four for a freedwoman – from the requirements of a *tutor*'s supervision of certain legal trans-actions, his innovation was little more than the discarding of a formality. In effect there were already mechanisms in place to allow women to circumvent the will of their *tutores*. If a *tutor* refused assent to a particular transaction a woman could apply to the authorities to force him to assent. If he was absent she could not only get one temporarily appointed, but could choose him herself. Indeed it has been noted that though we know a good deal about the business transactions of Cicero's wife Terentia, we do not know who her *tutor* was (Crook 1967a: 115). These women were wealthy, independent, sophisticated in matters of politics and finance, yet they never sought political legitimation, which with the hindsight conferred by two thousand years of intervening history, seems today like a logical progression.

The lesson from Roman religion was, as I showed, that women never had a ritual identity independent of their relationship to men. In one sense this is not peculiar to Rome. Women have always been classified according to their sexuality. Even today women are classified according to the stages of their sexual development into roughly pre-menarche, post-menarche and post-menopausal stages. Ostensibly this serves a medical function, but it would be naïve to suggest that there were no social and cultural undertones to classifications of this nature. In Roman ritual, however, sexual classification was endowed with extraordinary symbolic significance. Nowhere is this more apparent than in the case of the Vestals. Apart from their daily ritual duties a Vestal's everyday existence was not very different from the ordinary upper-class Roman matron. They attended dinner parties and the public games, and they did have friendships and social and business relations with men despite the danger that these might lead to allegations of unchastity. They were not secluded, nor was their social behaviour formally inhibited except for the necessity to preserve both the appearance and reality of chastity. Yet their identity was encompassed entirely by the fact of their virginity. Whatever individual personality they possessed was effaced by their sexuality. Occasionally we get a quick glimpse of the individual woman behind the Vestal façade, accompanied by a reminder of the high price she might well have to pay for individuality. For example, Livy's account of the trial of the Vestal Postumia suggests a woman with a vivacious manner and a fondness for self-adornment. In themselves these traits were not offensive. However, they could and in this case did give rise to suspicions of unchastity. Postumia was tried and acquitted but admonished to dress and behave with greater circumspection. For Vestals virginity was all-encompassing.

The Vestals were, of course, an extreme case. But women never fully escaped the implications of ritual categorization. We know very little indeed of individual Roman women, of their lives, their interests, their achievements. In Moses Finley's memorable phrase they were indeed the 'silent women of Rome' (Finley 1968). But those few individuals who did survive in historical accounts, always and without exception regardless of their personal achievements, derived their identity from their relationship to one or more prominent men. These women were first and foremost wives, mothers, daughters, sisters or even mistresses of some noteworthy man. Whatever their achievements, they were subordinate to that defining relationship. Roman women lacked an independent identity. This was particularly true of *matronae*, the group otherwise most qualified for a constitutional role. Although in a *sine manu* marriage a woman was not legally or financially subordinate to her husband, her identity in large measure depended on his. A woman is rarely introduced in historical writing without an accompanying litany of her male relationships: her father, her husband or husbands if she had been married more than once, her sons or her brothers, depending on the relative political prominence of each.

I suggest that this lack of an independent identity was a major factor in the failure of women to achieve a constitutional role in the Republic. Their facelessness prevented them from becoming a political force in their own right, regardless of their qualifications for the part. Women were politically powerful, as Bauman so cogently demonstrates, but they were content to act through their menfolk (Bauman 1992). It would be simplistic to regard women's exclusion from a constitutionally defined political role as male imposed. We have no evidence that women ever fought for an independent, legitimate political role. Rather women's position was the result of a shared ideology. In the religious domain in particular, women, divided into sexual categories, acted out time after time, year after year, the ritual implications of male defined identity. Ritual repeatedly reinforced the status quo and legitimated the male defined status of women.

NOTES

INTRODUCTION

1 See e.g., Hawley and Levick 1995; Bauman 1992; Dixon 1992 and 1988; Kertzer and Saller 1991; Rawson 1991; Treggiari 1991b; Gardner 1986a, to list but a tiny sampling of what's on offer.
2 I refer only to women of the privileged classes.
3 See Hallett 1984: 91–96.
4 An excellent example for the political influence wielded by women comes from Cicero (*Att.*, 15.11). Following the assassination of Caesar, Brutus and Cassius were given the derisory administrative posts of overseeing the corn supply in Asia and Sicily respectively. Cicero describes a meeting attended by the two men, their wives, Servilia, who was Brutus' mother and Cassius' mother-in-law, and Cicero himself among others, to decide what should be done about it. Although the men appear powerless to act, Servilia takes it upon herself to ensure that the appointment to the corn supply be withdrawn from the senatorial decree (*Servilia pollicebatur se curaturam, ut illa frumenti curatio de senatus consulto tolleretur*). For the rest see e.g., Cic., *Brut.*, 58.211; Plut., *C. Gracch.*, 19; App., *B. Civ.*, 4.5.32–33; Sall., *Cat.*, 25.
5 See for example, Cato's speech against the repeal of the Oppian Law in Livy, 34.2–4; see also Appian's description of the reaction to Hortensia's speech before the triumvirs, App., *B. Civ.*, 4.5.34. I discuss this issue in some detail in chapter 2.
6 *Contra* Crook, 'In Roman public life, . . . even in public religion – except for the Vestal Virgins – women played virtually no part.' Crook 1986b: 83 *et seq.*
7 This metaphor was inspired by the title of an article by Guido Calabresi and Douglas Melamed. See G. Calabresi and A. D. Melamed, 'Property rules, liability rules and inalienability: one view of the cathedral', *Harvard Law Review*, 1972, vol. 85, pp. 1089–1128.
8 See e.g., Scheid 1992a; Cazanove 1987.
9 Scheid gives a vivid account of the extraordinary position of the *Flamen Dialis*. Scheid 1986.
10 Livy, 1.7.3; Dion. Hal., *Ant. Rom.*, 1.40.3.

11 Livy, 1.7.3.
12 Plut., *Quaest. Rom.*, 18; *ibid.*, *Sull.*, 35.1; *ibid.*, *Crass.*, 12.2.
13 Ov., *Fast.*, 3.167 *et seq.*
14 Livy, 1.20.4; Dion. Hal., *Ant. Rom.*, 2.70–71; see also Ov., *Fast.*, 3.259 *et seq.* For an account of the rituals performed in Rome on this day, see Scullard 1981: 85–87.
15 See e.g., Livy, 27.37; *ibid.*, 31.12.9.
16 Most of the translations have been taken from the Loeb Classical Library where available, with occasional minor alterations. Works not available in the Loeb Classical Library are my own translations unless specifically attributed.
17 The fate of the Bacchanalian conspirators in 186 BC is an example, if an extreme one, of the ruthlessness with which undesirable religious activity could be suppressed by the authorities.

1 THE CULT OF BONA DEA

1 Cic., *Att.*, 1.12; Plut., *Caes.*, 9–10.
2 The source material on the Bona Dea has been conveniently assembled. See Brouwer 1989.
3 Cic., *Att.*, 1.13.
4 See for example, CIL 6.(1).60; *ibid.*, 64. For a comprehensive survey of the epigraphic sources see Brouwer 1989: 15 *et seq.*
5 Plut., *Quaest. Rom.*, 60; Gell., *N.A.*, 11.6.1.
6 It was customary for devotees of Hercules to sacrifice a tithe of their fortune at the *Ara Maxima* (Plut., *Quaest. Rom.*, 18). The sacrifice took the form of a public feast. Plutarch says that Crassus, when consul in 70 BC, feasted the people at 10,000 tables at a sacrifice in honour of Hercules. *Ibid.*, *Crass.*, 12. See also *ibid.*, *Sull.*, 35.1.
7 Gell., *N.A.*, 11.6.1.
8 I discuss these mechanisms below. See pp. 40 *et seq.*
9 According to this story Carmenta, the prophetic goddess and mother of Evander, came late to the celebration of the new rite, to the annoyance of Hercules who therefore excluded all women from his altar forever. Plut., *Quaest. Rom.*, 60.
10 Festus, p. 3 L. See also Quint., *Inst.*, 2.16.6.
11 Festus, p. 3 L.
12 Plut. *Quaest. Rom.*, 1; marriage with fire and water appears to have represented the quintessentially Roman form of marriage, *iustum matrimonium*, where the man and woman possessed *conubium*, the legal capacity to marry. (See p. 72 *et seq.* for a discussion of *conubium*.) In order to reassure the abducted Sabine women that their marriages would be 'lawful' Romulus promised them marriage 'with fire and water' (Dion. Hal., *Ant. Rom.*, 2.30.6). The concept of *iustum matrimonium* is difficult to translate into modern institutions of marriage. Marriages where *conubium* did not exist were not in any sense unlawful. They merely entailed different legal consequences as we shall see below. The ceremony involving fire and water was almost certainly a part of marriage by *confarreatio*. It is highly likely

that it was a part of the ceremonies of other forms of marriage as well. See Corbett: 1930: 73 *et seq.*

13 See for example, Ov., *Fast.*, 4.786–792; Pliny, *H.N.* 2.103.222; Festus, p. 77 L. The symbolism of fire and water seems to have operated in much the same way in Greek ideology as well. In Aristotle's *Problemata*, 4.28.880a, 12 *et seq.*, for example, he asks,

> why is it that in summer men are less capable of sexual intercourse and women more so? The answer is, that the heat of summer balances the wet and cold nature of females, and strengthens their sexual drive, while men who are naturally hot and dry are weakened by excess of heat in the summer.

For a study which argues that the hot and dry, in Greek religion, is perceived in terms of enhanced male sexual potency, while the cold and the wet is seen in terms of impotence, see Detienne 1977.

14 Macr., *Sat.*, 7.6.15–18.
15 Verg., *Aen.*, 8.184 *et seq.*; Ov., *Fast.*, 1.543 *et seq.*
16 The order of the labours of Hercules never varies in the sources. They are: 1. the Nemean Lion; 2. the Lernean Hydra; 3. the Cerynitian Hind; 4. the Erymanthian Boar; 5. the Augean stables; 6. the Stymphalean birds; 7. the Cretan Bull; 8. the Mares of Diomedes; 9. the girdle of Hippolyte; 10. the cattle of Geryon; 11. the apples of the Hesperides; and 12. Cerberus. See e.g., Apollod., *Bibl.*, 2.5.
17 This was not the universal view of Cacus. Dionysius of Halicarnassus describes him as a robber, *Ant. Rom.*, 1.39; Livy simply calls him a shepherd, Livy, 1.7.5. However, the narrative details of both these versions are consistent with the version of Ovid and Virgil. In Ovid and Virgil the poetic transformation of Cacus into a figure of fantasy has the effect of defining the character not of Cacus so much as of Hercules. When the *Ara Maxima* was founded Hercules was not yet a god. The poets' version of the tale brings the figure of Hercules closer to the divinity that was worshipped at the altar. See also Small 1982.
18 In some versions of the story the cult is founded by Evander in honour of Hercules. See Dion. Hal., *Ant. Rom.*, 1.40.6; Tac., *Ann.*, 15.41; Strab., 5.3.3. See also Platner and Ashby: 1929 (hereinafter Platner–Ashby), *s.v. Herculis Invicti Ara Maxima.*
19 *Cacus, Aventinae timor atque infamia silvae/non leve finitimis hospitibusque malum* – 'Cacus, the terror and shame of the Aventine wood, to neighbours and to strangers no small curse.' Ov., *Fast.*, 1.551–552.
20 See e.g., Prop., 4.11.15; Macrob., *Sat.*, 1.21.4.
21 Verg., *Aen.*, 8.193–195 (my emphasis).
22 Verg., *Aen.*, 8.241–246.
23 Ov., *Fast.*, 1.564.
24 *Ibid.*, 565 *et seq.*
25 Verg., *Aen.*, 8.225–227.
26 See Dion. Hal., *Ant. Rom.*, 1.39.2; Livy, 1.7.5.
27 The comparison between the dragging of the cattle backwards and the rock suspended in iron is a legitimate one. It is a comparison that

is valid both internally – within Virgil's story alone – and externally – when we compare Virgil's story with Ovid's. Note that the only two occasions in Virgil's account when Hercules is baffled is when there is no evidence of the theft of the cattle and when he is confronted by the barrier to the cave. As for the comparison between Virgil and Ovid, in Ovid, Hercules succeeds in destroying the barrier which is immensely strong but contains no factor in its make up indicative of cunning. Thus Hercules' victory is not merely one of strength over strength, but of strength over cunning.

28 Verg., *Aen.*, 8.228; *ibid.*, 230.
29 *Ibid.*, 8.219–220.
30   prima movet Cacus collata proelia dextra
         remque ferox saxis stipitibusque gerit.

         quis ubi nil agitur, patrias male fortis ad artes
         confugit et flammas ore sonante vomit;

At first Cacus fought hand to hand, and waged battle fierce with rocks and logs. But when these nought availed him, worsted, he had recourse to his sire's tricks, and belched flames from his roaring mouth;

Ov., Fast., 1.569–572

Note that in this passage, too, the belching of flames is portrayed as a trick, an art, something that Cacus can control and manipulate at will, and therefore, equivalent to devious cunning.

31 *Ibid.*, 1.577.
32 Verg., *Aen.*, 8.194.
33 *Ibid.*, 199.
34 *Ibid.*, 252.
35 *Ibid.*, 253.
36 Verg., *Aen.*, 8.251–255.
37 Verg., *Aen.*, 8.249–250.
38 Cf. p. 18.
39 Livy, 1.7.3.
40 See note 9, p. 164, for an alternative to the version to be discussed in this section.
41 Prop., 4.9; Macr., *Sat.*, 1.12.27–28.
42 Prop., 4.9.1–14. For a discussion of the various sources see Winter 1910.
43 *Ibid.*, 22.
44 *Ibid.*, 25–26.
45 *Ibid.*, 62–63.
46 *Ibid.*, 21.
47 See e.g., Cic., *de Or.*, 3.39; Verg., *Aen.*, 8.674.
48 See also pp. 15 *et seq.*
49 Prop. 4.9.32.
50 *Ibid.*, 37–50.
51 Apollod., *Bibl.*, 2.6.3. Propertius is indulging in a bit of poetic licence here. All these episodes that Hercules refers to actually take place later in his career. Stealing the cattle of Geryon, after which he arrived

in Italy, was supposed to have been the tenth of his great labours – see note 16, p. 165. He carried the globe on his shoulders while Atlas went off to steal the apples of the Hesperides for him in the eleventh of the labours. And the journey to the underworld was for the purpose of kidnapping Cerberus in the twelfth and final one – Apollod., *Bibl.*, 2.5. His adventure with Omphale took place later still. He was sold into her service by Hermes so that he could be purified a second time from the crime of murder – this time of Iphitus, son of Eurytus: *ibid.*, 2.6.3.

52 See also Ov., *Fast.*, 2.303 *et seq.*, where in quite a different narrative context Hercules and Omphale exchange clothing.

53 This was just one explanation for the blinding of Tiresias. Apollodorus gives an alternative tradition that Tiresias was blinded for revealing the secrets of the gods to men, *Bibl.*, 3.6.7. Hyginus connects Tiresias' blindness with the story of his sexual inversion, when, having been both man and woman, and being asked to arbitrate in a quarrel between Jupiter and Juno as to which sex derived more pleasure from sexual intercourse, Tiresias took Jupiter's side and said that women derived far more pleasure from sex. Thereupon Juno struck him blind, *Fab.*, 75.

54 Macrob., *Sat.*, 1.12.24. For a different version of the myth see Plut., *Quaest. Rom.*, 20; Arn., *Adv. Nat.*, 5.18; Sex. Clodius *ap.* Lactant., *Div. Inst.*, 1.22.9–11.

55 See pp. 71 *et seq.*

56 Aug., *de Civ. D.*, 6.9; see also Zeitlin 1986.

57 Festus, pp. 364–365 L.

58 This is one explanation suggested by Plutarch for the custom. See *Quaest. Rom.*, 29. Another tradition of the marriage ceremony, the parting of the bride's hair with the point of a bent-headed spear, is also related by Plutarch to the concept of violence, which in this case he connects directly to the violent abduction of the Sabine women, the first Roman wives. See *Quaest. Rom.*, 87.

59 Plut., *Caes.*, 10.

60 Cic., *Mil.*, 27.72.

61 Plut., *Caes.*, 10.

62 Ov., *Ars Am.*, 3.243–244; *ibid.*, 633–638.

63 Juv., 6.320.

64 Macrob., *Sat.*, 1.12.27–28. The main difference in the two versions of the myth is that Macrobius omits the violation by Hercules of the Bona Dea's cultic regulation – a violation made much of by Propertius. Otherwise the myth is essentially the same.

65 Mart., *Epigrams*, 11.1; Cic., *Att.*, 6.5.

66 Tib., 1.6.15; Gell., *N.A.*, 12.1.4 (of a young wife who has just given birth); Ov., *Fast.*, 2.557 (of a woman contemplating a second marriage).

67 Catull., 2; *ibid.*, 35.

68 Juv., 6.127.

69 Prop. 4.9.61.

70 See pp. 18 and 24.

71 See note 9, p. 164.

72 See Platner–Ashby, *s.v. Herculis Invicti Ara Maxima.*
73 See e.g., Plut., *Rom.*, 21 *et seq.*; *ibid.*, *Num.*, 8 *et seq.*; Livy, 1.19–20.
74 Livy, 1.7.3.
75 Dion. Hal., *Ant. Rom.*, 1.31.2.
76 Verg., *Aen.*, 7. 81–106.
77 Ov., *Fast.*, 4.641 *et seq.*
78 Cic., *Nat. D.*, 2.2.6.
79 Macrob., *Sat.*, 1.12.24. Cf. Plut., *Quaest. Rom.*, 20 where Bona Dea is Faunus' wife whom he beats with myrtle for drinking wine.
80 Picus was sometimes called the father of Faunus. See Verg., *Aen.*, 7.48; Aug., *de Civ. D.*, 18.15.
81 Ov., *Fast.*, 3.285 *et seq.*
82 Cic., *Nat. D.*, 3.6.15. For further evidence of the prophetic powers of Faunus see Varro, *Ling.*, 7.3.36; Plut., *Quaest. Rom.*, 20.
83 See Scullard 1981: 72 and 201. Ovid makes Faunus the presiding god of the Lupercalia, *Fast.*, 2.267–268. See also Livy, 1.5.2. with Serv., *Aen.,* 6.775.
84 In terms of space as well as of time Faunus belongs 'outside' Rome. This aspect of the god is not relevant to my analysis, but see Dumézil 1970: 344–350.
85 See also Verg., *Aen.*, 8.314–318.
86 For the horror that this particular form of incest evoked see Ov., *Met.*, 10.298 *et seq.* Another aspect of the inability of Faunus to distinguish sexual boundaries was his willingness to have indiscriminate intercourse with animals. For this reason he was called 'Inuus' *ab ineundo passim cum omnibus animalibus.* Serv., *Aen.*, 6.775.
87 Tac., *Ann.*, 15.41. See Platner–Ashby, *s.v. Herculis Invicti Ara Maxima.*
88 See p. 13.
89 See pp. 5 *et seq.* However this is not a new development in scholarship. For an example of a similar attitude – albeit couched in different terms – of a scholar of an earlier generation see Warde Fowler 1911: 29.
90 F. Cumont 1913: 183; Vermaseren 1963: 162.
91 Gordon 1988: 48.
92 Gordon 1980.
93 Plut., *Pomp.*, 24.
94 Cumont 1913: 36.
95 Gordon 1980.
96 See pp. 96 *et seq.*
97 See note 41, p. 166.
98 Cic., *Att.*, 1.12; *ibid.*, 1.13; *ibid.*, *Dom.*, 29.77; *ibid.*, *Har. Resp.*, 6.12; 17; indeed the Bona Dea's rites were thus described almost by definition.
99 Cic., *Att.*, 1.13.
100 *Ibid.*, 3.
101 Cic., *Att.*, 2.1.5 with Shackleton Bailey's note. Also Quint., *Inst.*, 4.2.88.
102 Cic., *Att.*, 1.16.
103 Livy, 39.13.9; see also Cic., *Leg.*, 2.15.37. See also North 1979: esp. 88–89.
104 Cic., *Leg.*, 2.9.21.

NOTES

105 *Ibid.* with Keyes' note.
106 Ov., *Fast.*, 5.148–158 with Frazer's commentary.
107 Ov., *Fast.*, 5.153
108 Hadrian is said to have built a temple to the Bona Dea. See SHA, *Hadr.*, 19.11. See also Platner–Ashby, *s.v. Bona Dea Subsaxana, Aedes.*
109 Frazer, *op. cit.*; Macrobius also suggests that men were forbidden to enter her temple, *Sat.*, 1.12.26; see also Festus, p. 348 L.
110 Ov., *Ars Am.*, 3.637–638 (my emphasis).
111 See note 4, p. 164, with accompanying text.
112 Macrob., *Sat.*, 1.12.26. See also Brouwer 1989: 346–347.
113 See Piccaluga 1964: 214–215 with notes 76–80.
114 See note 110, p. 169.
115 Ov., *Fast.*, 5.148–158. Ovid does no more than suggest that the ritual took place. Macrobius provides a few details but not many, *Sat.*, 1.12.20–21.
116 Plut., *Caes.*, 9.
117 Plut., *Cic.*, 19.
118 Cic., *Att.*, 1.12; *ibid.*, 1.13; Plut., *Cic.*, 28. The fact that Caesar was also *pontifex maximus* appears to have been irrelevant to the choice of his house as a venue for the rites.
119 A striking example of the derivation of female status from that of the male, and its religious repercussions, is the story of the institution of a cult of Pudicitia Plebeia by a woman called Verginia in 295 BC. Verginia's father was a patrician but she had married a plebeian, the consul, L. Volumnius. She was therefore excluded from participation in the rites of Pudicitia Patricia by patrician women on the grounds that having married out of the patriciate she was no longer one of them. Her response was to set up in her own house a shrine to Pudicitia Plebeia, to be worshipped exclusively by univirate plebeian women. Interestingly the two cults were defined in terms of each other, by a relationship of opposition, which was expressed by the competition of its worshippers for greater matronly chastity (Livy, 10.23.1–9).
120 Plut., *Cic.*, 19; Cic., *Att.*, 1.13.
121 See Plut., *Caes.*, 10.1 and 10.3.
122 Plut., *Cic.*, 20.
123 See e.g., Plut., *Cic.*, 19.4.
124 Juv., 6.340.
125 I cannot resist relating the following story. Long after I first wrote these words, I attended a meeting of the New York City Women's Bar Association. The meeting was held in a big, imposing auditorium. There were at least two hundred women lawyers and law students present and not a single man. But all around the room hung large portraits of dead male lawyers, erstwhile pillars of the profession, gazing sternly down upon us. Our discussion that evening was all about surviving and succeeding as women lawyers in a heavily male dominated profession. The presence of these portraits gave the discussion a peculiarly uncomfortable edge. I was amused to find myself thinking of the festival of Bona Dea, and put down my

sensitivity to the portraits to the comparisons I was making. But I
learned afterwards that my colleagues, who had never heard of Bona
Dea, felt exactly the same way that I had.

126 Cic., *Har. Resp.*, 17.37.
127 Juv., 6.314–345.
128 Plut., *Caes.*, 10.
129 See Versnel: 1993: 229 *et seq.*
130 Juv., 6.335–336.
131 See e.g., Cic., *Att.*, 1.12; Asc., *Mil.*, 46; Sen., *Ep.*, 97.2.
132 Plut., *Quaest. Rom.*, 20.
133 See note 79, p. 168, with accompanying text.
134 Macrob., *Sat.*, 1.12.24–25; cf. Plut., *Quaest. Rom.*, 20.
135 Ov., *Fast.*, 4.721–806.
136 Varro, *Rust.*, 2.1.9; Dion. Hal., *Ant. Rom.*, 1.88.3; see Wissowa 1912:
    199–201; Scullard 1981: 103–105.
137 Cic., *Div.*, 2.47.98; Prop. 4.1.17–20; *ibid.*, 4.73–80; see also Ov., *Fast.*,
    4.807–820.
138 In a stimulating and persuasive discussion of how a rite changes to
    accommodate new social and political needs Beard compares the
    description of the Parilia – now called the Romaia – in Athenaeus,
    8.361e–362a., which tells how the Parilia was apparently celebrated in
    Hadrian's day, with Ovid's description. See Beard 1987.
139 Ov., *Fast.*, 4.784–806.
140 See e.g., Festus, p. 3 L; see also my discussion pp. 15 *et seq.* The
    concept will be discussed further in chapter 4.
141 These were in part the ashes of the foetuses of sacrificed cows,
    burned by the Virgo Vestalis Maxima at the festival of the Fordicidia
    six days earlier. See Ov., *Fast.*, 4.629 *et seq.*
142 *Ibid.*, 771–772.
143 See Prop., 4.4.73–78.
144 See Dumézil 1963: 274; *ibid.* 1970: 39.
145 Tib., 2.5, 87 and 89.
146 Ov., *Fast.*, 4.780. The word translated as wine here is *sapa*. According
    to Pliny it was made by boiling down must to a third of its quantity.
    He also claims that it was devised for adulterating with honey, Pliny,
    H.N., 14.11.80. It is not clear whether there was honey mixed with the
    wine at the Parilia. For an interpretation of the symbolic significance
    of honey see pp. 50 *et seq.*
147 Pliny, *H.N.*, 14.14.
148 *Ibid.*
149 Dion. Hal., *Ant. Rom.*, 2.25.6.
150 Pliny, *H.N.*, 14.14.
151 Val. Max. 6.3.9.
152 Cato *ap.* Gell., *N.A.*, 10.23. Other examples : 'Fabius Pictor has written
    in his *Annales* that a *matrona* was starved to death by her relatives
    for having broken open the casket containing the keys of the wine-
    cellar; . . . Gnaeus Domitius when *iudex* once gave a verdict that a
    certain woman appeared to have drunk more wine than was required
    for the sake of her health without her husband's knowledge, and he
    fined her the amount of her dowry.' Pliny, *H.N.*, 14.14.89–90.

153 Gell., *N.A.*, 10.23; Pliny, *H.N.*, 14.14; see also Plut., *Quaest. Rom.*, 6.; cf. Plut., *Rom.*, 1.4.

154 Ov., *Ars Am.*, 3.765.

155 See Brouwer, *op. cit.*

156 The chapter from which this quote is taken is worth reading in its entirety to appreciate ancient beliefs about the nature of milk.

157 Verg., *Aen.*, 7.807–809; *ibid.*, 11.535 *et seq.* See also the story of Byblis in Ovid, *Met.*, 9.615 *et seq.*

158 Soranus, *Gynaikeia.*, 1.19–20.

159 See also Tib., 1.1.35–36.

160 It was of course not the case that female deities were always offered milk rather than wine. But if one accepts that in this particular case the milk drunk by the shepherd symbolized the female and her special powers of fertility, as opposed to male fertility symbolized by wine, then that symbolism must be extended to other aspects of the rite as well. The deity was not offered wine, nor was she offered the mixture of wine and milk that her worshippers drank. Therefore in the context of this ritual the offering of milk marked the deity out as female.

161 See also Plut., *Coniugalia Praecepta*, 44.

162 Pliny, *H.N.*, 14.6.53.

163 See pp. 84 *et seq.*

2 CERES AND FLORA

1 This is controversial. The speech has also been attributed to Q. Caecilius Metellus Macedonicus, censor in 131 BC. It is believed that it was this very speech that, according to Livy and Suetonius, Augustus once read to the Senate. Livy, *Per.*, 59; Suet., *Aug.*, 89.2. See McDonnell 1987: 81.

2 For the interpretation of satire as misogynistic discourse see e.g., Richlin 1984; Henderson 1989.

3 This, for example, is the reason alleged for the necessity for women *sui iuris*, to be under the guardianship of a *tutor*. G., 1.144. See also Crook 1986b: 85–86.

4 For the participation of young children in ritual see Dion. Hal., *Ant. Rom.*, 2.22.1–2; for the use of virgins in expiatory rituals see e.g., Obsequens, 27a, 34 and 36; for boys and girls performing an expiatory rite together, *ibid.*, 1.

5 The Vestal Virgins are the subject of chapter 4.

6 Livy, 34.

7 According to Cicero only a woman married *cum manu* might be called *materfamilias*. A woman married *sine manu* was *uxor*, Cic., *Top.*, 4.14. See Corbett 1930: 113. These were legal definitions. *Matrona* encompassed both legal categories: both *matresfamiliae* and *uxores* were *matronae*. For the purposes of this analysis I define *matrona* as a wife in a legal Roman marriage, that is, where the partners had *conubium*. For a somewhat different interpretation see Treggiari 1991b: 34–35.

8 The denial of a political identity to women throughout the entire sweep of Roman history from the early Monarchy, through the period of the Republic, to the final collapse of the Empire, was not an inadvertent result of the way the political and social system evolved. That it was perceived as a deliberate and integral part of the system is suggested by a speech made by Hortensia in 42 BC, before the tribunal of the triumvirs in the forum, protesting a tax imposed on the personal wealth of 1400 of the richest women of the city. Hortensia's argument is that women should not be forced to pay taxes since they were not allowed to enjoy any of the rewards of public life. 'Why should we pay taxes when we have no part in the honours, the commands, the statecraft for which you contend against each other . . . ?' Women had in the past made contributions from their personal wealth to the treasury in times of national crisis, but that was an entirely voluntary gesture. It is worth noting that the fact that Hortensia, accompanied by a group of matrons, addressed the triumvirs at a public tribunal was seen, as Cato saw the lobby of 195 BC, as a piece of unmitigated effrontery. None the less, her petition was partially granted. See Appian, *B. Civ.*, 4.32–35. Valerius in his reply to Cato in 195 BC echoes Hortensia's sentiments about women being excluded from public life and its rewards: 'No offices, no priesthoods no triumphs, no decorations, no gifts, no spoils of war can come to them', Livy, 34.7.8. This section may have been directly influenced by Hortensia's speech. Quintilian, who admired the speech, says it was extant and being studied in his own day, Quint., *Inst.*, 1.1.6. For Cicero, a situation where wives had the same rights as husbands was equivalent to the unseemly freedom of slaves or to unfettered domestic animals running amok in the public streets, Cic., *Rep.*, 1.43.67.
9 See also Varro, *ap.* Gell., *N.A.*, 1.17.4.
10 For greater narrative detail see Livy, 1.4; Dion. Hal., *Ant. Rom.*, 1.76–79; Plut., *Rom.*, 3–4.
11 Since the Vestal Virgins will be the subject of the fourth chapter of this book only those features of the priesthood that are important for purposes of the present discussion will be mentioned here. References will be provided in chapter 4.
12 See esp. Dion. Hal., *Ant. Rom.*, 1.77.
13 Ov., *Fast.*, 3.11 *et seq.*; see also, Tib., 2.5.51–54.
14 For various accounts of Rhea Silvia's punishment, see Livy, 1.4.3; Dion. Hal., *Ant. Rom.*, 79.1–3.
15 For example, the moment of Romulus' conception and the moment of his apotheosis were both marked by a total eclipse of the sun, Dion. Hal., *Ant. Rom.*, 2.56.6.
16 The others, Numitor, the grandfather, Amulius, the wicked uncle, Faustulus the shepherd, all feature in the episode where the twins, now grown up, come to claim their birthright. Their mother is conspicuously absent.
17 Ov., *Fast.*, 2.413 *et seq.*; Prop., 4.1.55–56; Dion. Hal., *Ant. Rom.*, 1.79.6.
18 A complementary tradition has it that the twins were nourished by both a woodpecker and a wolf. The woodpecker was also believed

to be sacred to Mars. See Ov., *Fast.*, 3.37–38; Plut., *Quaest. Rom.*, 22. For the value placed on breast feeding see Gell., *N.A.*, 12.1; Tac., *Dial.*, 28.

19 Livy, 1.4.7; Dion. Hal., *Ant. Rom.*, 1.84.
20 See Ov., *Fast.*, 3.55–58; Plut., *Quaest. Rom.*, 34; Aug., *de Civ. D.*, 6.7; Macrob., *Sat.*, 1.10. 11–17; Gell., *N.A.*, 7.7.5 *et seq.*
21 Cic., *ad Brut.* 1.15.8.
22 Gell., *N.A.*, 7.7.5.
23 *Ibid.*
24 Macr., *Sat.*, 1.10.11–17.
25 Plut., *Rom.*, 4–5; see also *ibid.*, *Quaest. Rom.*, 35.
26 Gell., *N.A.*, 7.7.5 *et seq.* See also Dion. Hal., *Ant. Rom.*, 1.87.3.; Pliny, *H.N.* 18.2.6. Note however that Acca Larentia receives no mention in the Acta of the *fratri Arvales*. Also the *fratri* do not appear to have participated in the Larentalia. See Scheid 1990: 590 *et seq.*
27 Varro, *Ling.*, 6.23–24. See also Plut., *Quaest. Rom.*, 34.
28 Actually it may not even have been as formal as this implies. Cornelia, mother of the Gracchi (*ap.* Nepos, frg. 1) uses the term in a way that could just as well suggest an informal prayer offered up to the *manes* of an ancestor.
29 See Scullard 1981: 74–76.
30 Ov., *Fast.*, 2.533 *et seq.*
31 Gell., *N.A.*, 7.7.1.
32 She does not fit, for example, into any of the categories that, according to Cicero, were eligible to be offered cult. See Cic., *Leg.*, 2.8.19.
33 Cic., *Phil.*, 5.14; Pliny, *H.N.* 9.80.170; Suet., *Iul.*, 47–48; Val. Max., 2.2.2; for an invaluable description of all aspects of Roman clothing, see Wilson 1938.
34 Cic., *Rab. Post.*, 9; Livy, 29.19.12; Suet., *Tib.*, 13. Exiles forfeited the right to wear the toga. See Pliny, *Ep.*, 4.11.
35 See pp. 88 *et seq.*
36 Wilson 1938: 60–65; see also Garnsey and Saller 1987: 116–117.
37 Plut., *Quaest. Rom.*, 49.
38 The Salii, for example, wore the *tunica picta* with a bronze breast plate over it. See Livy, 1.20.4. For the Luperci, see Ov., *Fast.*, 2.267 *et seq.*
39 Festus, p. 125 L.
40 Hor., *Sat.*, 1.2.94–95; *ibid.*, 99. The evidence for the dress of the *matrona* has recently been examined in Scholz 1992. See *ibid.*, 140–146 for a convenient compilation of the literary references.
41 Hor., *Sat.*, 1.2.29; Ov., *Ars Am.*, 1.31–32.
42 Wilson 1938: 150–153. Wilson points out that on the *ara pacis* some matrons have their heads veiled while others are bare headed.
43 Val. Max., 6.3.10.
44 Gell., *N.A.*, 6.12.
45 Livy, 34.4.14 *et seq.*
46 See Ov., *Fast.*, 4.134.
47 See Hor., *Sat.*, 1.2.63. For the fact that the *toga* was the recognized badge of the courtesan see Juv., 2.68; Cic., *Phil.*, 2.18.44.
48 Narrative details can be found in Livy, 1.9–13; Dion. Hal., *Ant. Rom.*, 2.30–46; Plut., *Rom.*, 14–19.

49 Plutarch makes the point that the women were all unmarried, except for one who was kidnapped by mistake; proof, he says, that the women were not kidnapped wantonly but for the purpose of lawful marriage, Plut., *Rom.*, 14.6; see also Dion. Hal., *Ant. Rom.*, 2.30.5–6.
50 Livy, 1.9.14.
51 See also Ov., *Fast.*, 3.215 *et seq.*
52 Livy, 1.13.3.
53 See Treggiari 1991b for a comprehensive analysis of the legal and social implications of marriage. My discussion will merely serve to support my analysis of the myth.
54 Crook 1967a: 101. See also Treggiari 1991a: 31–33; Corbett 1930: 92.
55 See Corbett 1930: 68 *et seq.*
56 See Treggiari 1991b: ch. 2, *passim.*
57 Corbett 1930: 24 *et seq.*; Watson 1967: 27; Treggiari 1991b: 43 *et seq.*
58 Watson 1967: 77 *et seq.*; Gardner 1986a: 137 *et seq.* The agnatic relationship was created by statute (legitima cognatio) and was traced through the male line. See G. III. 9.
59 'The most important effect of a valid marriage was that any children would be in the *potestas* of the husband or of his *paterfamilias* if he had one, and be members of his father's gens', Watson 1975: 31. 'A man must marry in order to have legitimate offspring – *sui heredes* – to continue his estate and his cult, and to provide the worship necessary to the peace of the spirit that survived his death', Corbett 1930: 107.
60 See Dixon 1988: esp. 45.
61 It is worth noting also, that in the event of a divorce the children of the marriage belonged to their father. Their mother had no legal rights over them. See Treggiari 1991b: 467. See generally Thomas 1992.
62 Thomas 1992: 90. My parentheses.
63 Livy, 1.13.5.
64 The relative frequency of *cum manu* and *sine manu* marriages is still a matter for debate. Corbett argues that *sine manu* marriage was recognized at Rome as early as the XII Tables and was common practice in the third and second centuries BC; Corbett 1930: 90 *et seq.* Watson believes that the *cum manu* form was very common until just before the time of Cicero. Watson 1967: 19 *et seq.* See also *ibid.,* 1975: 9 *et seq.*; *ibid.,* 1992: 52; Crook 1967: 103; Treggiari 1991b: 32. Marriage according to the ancient ceremony of *confarreatio* was marriage *cum manu*, and the rules for appointing the *flamen Dialis*, for example, which required that he be married by *confarreatio* is further evidence for marriage *cum manu* at a late date, though it was probably extremely rare.
65 Gardner 1986a: 83. For a brief overview of the legal consequences to a woman of a *cum manu* marriage, see Treggiari 1991b: 28 *et seq.*
66 Treggiari 1991b: 443; see also Saller 1984.
67 Plut., *Cat. Min.*, 25.
68 This power of the *paterfamilias* extended to sons as well. Gardner 1986a: 11; Treggiari 1991a: 34.
69 In Dionysius of Halicarnassus' version of the story, the intervention of the Sabine women in the conflict of their father and husbands is much

less dramatic than in Livy. Here the wives are sent – at their own request – as ambassadors to their fathers' camp. The result, of course, was the mingling of the two nations into one. Dion. Hal., *Ant. Rom.*, 2.45. What this incident in the story of the Sabine women – the prototype for Roman marriage – illustrates is the perceived mediatory function of the wife. She was seen as constituting a bridge between two families or even of two powerful men. This is demonstrable in the marriages of, for example, Julia to Pompey, or Octavia to Mark Antony.

70 Treggiari 1991a: 33.
71 See Treggiari 1991a: 41 *et seq.*
72 Treggiari 1991b: 473 *et seq.*
73 See Hopkins 1983: 86 *et seq.*
74 Treggiari 1991b: 33 *et seq.*
75 Corbier argues, quite rightly, that the Roman ideal of marriage was of a lasting, continuous union. Corbier 1991: 49–50. See also Treggiari 1991b: 40 *et seq.* The nostalgia for a time in which divorce did not take place is inherent in the story of Sp. Carvilius Ruga, who was the first, according to tradition, to divorce his wife. It is interesting that the ancient writers give a date for the event. The dates vary widely. Dionysius of Halicarnassus and Gellius give 231 BC, while Valerius Maximus sets it as early as 640 BC. Dion. Hal., *Ant. Rom.*, 2.25.7; Gell., *N.A.*, 17.21.44; Val. Max., 2.1.4. But the establishment of a date serves to mark off 'the good old days' before divorce.
76 Watson 1965, reprinted in Watson 1991.
77 Plut., *Rom.*, 22.3. See Treggiari 1991b: 441 and 459.
78 Val. Max., 2.9.2. See Treggiari 1991b: 442.
79 See M. Humbert 1972. John Crook argues in an unpublished paper, 'Ancient Doublethink', that the Roman attitude towards divorce was paradoxical and that it would be misleading to try to resolve the paradox. Divorce did not bring dishonour to either partner in a marriage; yet women who had been married just once were particularly highly regarded, and life-long marriages idealized. Both of these were features of Roman attitudes towards marriage and divorce. My thanks to Professor Crook for allowing me to use the paper.
80 Festus, p. 82 L. Similarly a woman married more than once could not act as *pronuba* at a wedding. Festus, p. 283 L.
81 For the qualifications of potential Vestals, see pp. 138 *et seq.*
82 Tac., *Ann.*, 2.86.
83 See Treggiari 1991b: 498–499 for legendary and historical examples and the approval with which *univirae* are represented.
84 See Humbert, *op. cit.*, pp. 42 *et seq.*
85 See Corbier 1991.
86 See Hopkins 1983: 237.
87 Treggiari 1991b: 381 and 391; cf. Corbier 1991: 53–54. Women who had become *sui iuris* either through the death of their *paterfamilias*, or through emancipation, could dispose of their property as they wished, although technically they were subject to the supervision of a *tutor*, whose permission was required for any financial transaction. The tutor was usually appointed in the will of the *paterfamilias*. It has

been pointed out that one reason for the *tutor*, who was most commonly a male member of the woman's agnatic family, was to protect her family's interest in her property. However, it appears that as early as 186 BC, women were given the right to choose their own *tutor*, or even subsequently to change him, thus giving a woman almost complete freedom in the management of her financial affairs. See Hopkins 1983: 91.

88 Watson believes that Livy's account of Lucretia's death accurately mirrored the legal realities of her situation. Watson 1975: 35 and 167. Dionysius of Halicarnassus' account differs in detail but leads to the same conclusion. Dion. Hal., *Ant. Rom.*, 4.66 *et seq*. My analysis relies on Livy's account. Livy, 1.57 *et seq*. See also Ov., *Fast.*, 2.784 *et seq*.
89 Livy, 1.57.10. My emphasis.
90 Livy, 1.58.5. My emphasis.
91 Treggiari 1991b: 265 *et seq*.
92 See Treggiari 1991b: 279; cf. Donaldson 1982: 23.
93 See the discussion in Donaldson 1982: 21 *et seq*. See also Bryson 1986.
94 Livy, 1.58.10.
95 Ov., *Fast.*, 1.617 *et seq*.
96 Livy, 2.40.11–12.
97 For a comprehensive account, see Le Bonniec 1958.
98 Verg., *Aen.*, 7.387–388.
99 Ov., *Fast.*, 2.557–560.
100 Prop., 4.11.33.
101 Festus, p. 77 L.
102 Treggiari 1991b: 54.
103 Gardner 1986a: 47. Note that co-habitation by itself was not enough to constitute a valid marriage.
104 Humbert 1972: 5 *et seq*.
105 Catull., 61.76–78; *ibid*., 91–95; *ibid*., 117–119.
106 See Prop., 4.3.13; cf. Plut., *Quaest. Rom.*, 2.
107 Festus, p. 282 L.
108 Pliny, *H.N.*, 16.30.75.
109 See Le Bonniec 1958: 254.
110 Cic., *Nat. D.*, 2.24.62.
111 Cic., 2 *Verr.*, 5.14.36.
112 The most comprehensive account is Bruhl 1953.
113 Aug., *de Civ. D.*, 7.21.
114 *Ibid.*, 4.11.
115 See also *ibid.*, 7.2. Augustine claims Varro as a source, and there is no reason to suspect his characterization of the cult. But see Piganiol's observations on Augustine and Varro. Piganiol 1923: 16–17.
116 Ov., *Fast.*, 3.736 *et seq*.
117 See also Varro, *Ling.*, 6.3.14.
118 Ov., *Fast.*, 3.713 *et seq*.
119 Ov., *Fast.*, 3.771 *et seq*.; see also Cic., *Att.*, 9.6; *ibid.*, 9.17; *ibid.*, 9.19.
120 See e.g., Wiedemann 1989: 113 *et seq*.
121 In 529 AD Justinian abolished physical inspection of boys and fixed upon the end of the fourteenth year as the age at which a boy was

legally considered to possess the capacity to father children, Corbett 1930: 52. However, it is likely that the practice of physical inspection declined much earlier than this. See Gardner 1986: 38. In cases where inspection did not take place, physical capacity for marriage was assumed at around fourteen years of age. See also Eyben (1972).

122 Pliny, *H.N.*, 8.194.

123 Prop., 4.11.33.

124 The ceremony for Q. Cicero's coming of age appears to have taken place in April. See Wiedemann 1989: 86.

125 See App., *B. Civ.*, 4.5.30.

126 See p. 85.

127 See note 77, p. 175, with accompanying text.

128 Dion. Hal., *Ant. Rom.*, 1.33.1; Macrob., *Sat.*, 3.11.1–2. Significantly wine mixed with honey might be offered to Ceres, *ibid.*, 9. According to Cato, Ceres in her capacity as agricultural deity was offered wine, Cato, *Agr.* 134. For the idea that Ceres was especially concerned with the chastity of wives in marriage see also Juv., 6.49–50.

129 Livy, 22.56.4–5; Plut., *Fabius*, 18.1–2; Val. Max., 1.1.15; Festus, p. 86 L.

130 See, conveniently, Le Bonniec 1958: 400 *et seq.*

131 Ov., *Met.*, 10.431–435; *ibid.*, *Ars Am.*, 3.10.

132 In the story of Myrrha as told by Ovid, it was the absence of her mother at the rites of Ceres that gave Myrrha the opportunity of seducing her father, Cinyras. It is clear from this account that sexual intercourse was forbidden to his wife only, not to Cinyras. The fact that he slept with another woman during the rite was not in itself a transgression. It was the fact of incest that evoked horror, Ov., *Met.*, 10.431 *et seq.*

133 Tac., *Ann.*, 2.49. My emphasis. See also Platner–Ashby, *s.v. Ceres, Liber Liberaque Aedes*; *ibid.*, Flora Aedes.

134 These were, in order, the Cerialia, the Fordicidia, the Parilia, the Vinalia, the Robigalia and the Floralia, and were celebrated from 12 April to 3 May. Ov., *Fast.*, 4.393–5.378. The *sacrum anniversarium Cereris* was in August. See Le Bonniec 1958: 403.

135 Most of the detailed evidence for this aspect of the Floralia comes from later writers, although brief corroboration of their views can be found in Ovid. Elaine Fantham's explanation for this is plausible: 'Both the goddess – *sc.* Flora – and her games are ignored by the Augustan writers before Ovid himself. . . . The goddess' mime-festival was a scandal to the more severe and this might explain what seems to be a pattern of studied neglect under Augustus. The Princep's restoration of traditional cult was subordinate to his concern for restored morality.' Fantham 1992.

136 Aug., *Ep.*, 91.5; Sen., *Ep.*, 97; Val. Max., 2.10.8; Minucius Felix refers to the goddess herself as a prostitute – meretrix – and compares her to Acca Larentia. *Oct.*, 25.8.

137 See also Ov., *Fast.*, 5.331 *et seq.*

138 Ov., *Fast.*, 5.355–356; *ibid.*, 4.619–620.

139 For the *sacrum anniversarium Cereris* see Ov., *Met.*, 10.432; Val. Max., 1.1.5.

140 Dio Cass., 58.19; see also, Ov., *Fast.*, 5.361 *et seq.*

3 VENUS

1 Arn., *Adv. Nat.*, 5.18; Sex. Clodius *ap.* Lactant., *Div. Inst.*, 1.22.9–11; Macrob., *Sat.*, 1.12.24–25.

2 See e.g., Verg., *Ecl.*, 7.62; G., 1.28; Verg., *Aen.*, 5.72; Ov., *Fast.*, 4.15. See generally, Maxwell-Stuart 1972.

3 Maxwell-Stuart discusses the ways in which myrtle was used in classical antiquity in symbolic representations of sexuality, *op. cit.*

4 See pp. 48 *et seq.*, with accompanying notes for the prohibition against married women drinking wine.

5 See pp. 48 *et seq.*

6 Gell., *N.A.*, 5.6.

7 See also Pliny, *H.N.*, 15.38.125; Plut., *Marc.*, 22.3–4. Versnel discusses the reasons why an *ovatio* might be granted in place of a triumph. Versnel 1970: 166 *et seq.*

8 Pliny, *H.N.*, 15.36. See also pp. 107 *et seq.* where I discuss this passage further.

9 Val. Max., 8.15.12.

10 Livy, *Epit.*, 63; Dio Cass., 26.87; Plut., *Quaest. Rom.*, 83; Obsequens 37. See generally, Platner–Ashby, *s.v. Venus Verticordia, Aedes.*

11 Ov., *Fast.*, 4.160.

12 I discuss the implications of unchastity among Vestal Virgins in chapter 4.

13 Ov., *Fast.*, 4.291 *et seq.* See also pp. 000 *et seq.*

14 See pp. 80 *et seq.*

15 Hence also the significance of the reason for the dedication of the statue: *quo facilius virginum mulierumque mens a libidine ad pudicitiam converteretur.* So that the hearts of virgins and women would turn more readily from licentiousness to chastity. Val. Max., 8.15.12. Although different categories of women were included in the cult, each had to be true to its own sexual ethics. Thus, although wives and prostitutes, for example, both participated in the rites, Venus Verticordia 'ensured' that wives did not behave like prostitutes.

16 Ov., *Fast.*, 4.133–160.

17 See e.g., Plut., *Num.*, 19.

18 For details of the controversy see Schilling 1982: 389 *et seq.* See also, Pomeroy 1975: 208–209. Kraemer's is probably the most far-fetched account of Ovid's treatment of the festival:

> Can we avoid seeing something ironic in [Ovid's] account of women's worship of Venus Verticordia – Venus who turns the hearts of women towards marital fidelity that contrasted so strongly with Ovid's own life and experiences of Roman society? What do we make of these vastly contradictory accounts of the attitudes and practices of allegedly respectable Roman women? What too do we do with this ancient expression of the sexual double standard? Ovid exemplifies male complicity in the sexual dalliances of elite Roman women, and yet there are no known cults of male chastity and fidelity!

It may not surprise us to find that aristocratic Roman men saw the marital infidelity of Roman women as qualitatively different from their own sexual dalliances. The point here is not only that Roman men considered it acceptable to sleep with a variety of women other than their legal wives, but rather that they were apparently content to place the blame for their liaisons with women legally married to other aristocratic men solely on the women – or perhaps women and the goddess Venus – at least when religion was concerned. Might there not be something subversive and intentional in Ovid's odd conflation of the worship of Fortuna Virilis and Venus Verticordia – a suggestion, perhaps, that the distinctions between chaste married matrons and sexually indiscriminate *humiliores* were not, in fact, nearly as clear as they seemed.

Kraemer 1992: 60–61

19 Mommsen's reconstruction of the entry in the *Fasti Praenestini* reads as follows: *Frequenter mulieres supplicant [honestiores Veneri Verticordiae] fortunae virili, humiliores etiam in balneis, quod in iis ea parte corpor[is] utique viri nudantur, qua feminarum gratia desideratur.* See Scullard 1981: 96. For the original calendar see A. Degrassi 1963: Table 40. Verrius Flaccus' account is most usefully analysed in conjunction with Ovid's exegesis.
20 Macr., *Sat.*, 1.12.15.
21 Plut., *Num.*, 19.2
22 Lydus, *de Mens.*, 4.65.
23 Schilling 1982: 389 *et seq.*
24 Lydus, *op. cit.*
25 See pp. 45 *et seq.*
26 Garnsey 1970: 219 *et seq.*; see also Garnsey and Saller 1987: 109–112.
27 The ritual washing of a cult statue was in itself unexceptional. What is striking about this cult is that the worshippers bathed themselves too, in apparent imitation of the washing of the cult statue.
28 See Schilling 1982: 94. See also Platner–Ashby, *s.v. Venus Obsequens Aedes.*
29 Serv., *Aen.*, 1.720.
30 Livy, 31.8–9.
31 For the antiquity of the cult see Diod. Sic., 4.78.4–5; cf. Strab., 6.2.6; Tac., *Ann.*, 4.43; Suet., *Claud.*, 25.
32 Livy, 22.9.7–11.
33 It was the city of Rome, enclosed within its boundaries, however amorphously defined, that was seen as the special responsibility of the Roman gods. See pp. 153 *et seq.*
34 Livy, 29.10. See also Stehle 1989.
35 In terms of symbolic action in the case of the Magna Mater, Ovid's is the most vivid description. See *Fast.*, 4.247–348. For Juno of Veii see Livy, 5.22.3. I shall rely chiefly on these texts for the following analyses.
36 Livy, 5.21.
37 See also Plut., *Cam.*, 6.
38 See for example, Livy, 29.14; Ov., *Fast.*, 4.291–344. Varro says simply

NOTES

that the goddess was brought from Pergamum, from King Attalus. Varro, *Ling.*, 6.3.15.
39 Ov., *Fast.*, 4.265–272.
40 See Wiseman 1979: 96; Ov., *Fast.*, 4.326: *mira, sed et scaena testificata loquar* – 'My story is a strange one, but it is attested by the stage.'
41 Ov., *Fast.*, 4.321–324.
42 Bremmer 1987b.
43 See Vermaseren 1977: 96. Lucretius gives a description of the ritual procession of the *Galli* escorting the statue. Lucr., *De Rerum Natura*, 2.600 *et seq.* For the exclusion of Roman citizens from the ranks of the *Galli*, see Dion. Hal., *Ant. Rom.*, 2.19. Nearly three centuries earlier when the cult of Ceres, Liber and Libera was introduced into Rome, the Greek priestesses in charge of the cult were made Roman citizens. Cic., *Balb.*, 24.55. Despite the different treatment accorded the religious attendants of Magna Mater and Ceres, Liber and Libera, Festus sees the two cults as parallel. Festus, p. 268 L.
44 But see also Dion. Hal., *Ant. Rom.*, 2.19.
45 Hopkins argues that the distinctions we might be disposed to make between political and religious rituals are not necessarily valid in the Roman context. Hopkins 1991.
46 Note that Minucius Felix, although in an entirely different context, makes no distinction between the *Galli*, the *Salii*, and the *Luperci*. See *Oct.*, 22.8.
47 Ov., *Fast.*, 4.183; see also Catull., 63.
48 See pp. 68 *et seq.*
49 The figure of Claudia Quinta, a symbol not merely of matronly chastity, but of the integrity of the system of sexual categorization, as I have suggested, continued to be important in terms of the cult of the Magna Mater. There was a statue of Claudia Quinta in the goddess' temple. This statue was believed miraculously to have survived, unscathed, two conflagrations of the temple, Val. Max., 1.8.11. I suggest that the presence of the statue be interpreted as an iconic representation of the same sentiments that the story of Claudia Quinta expressed mythically: that the state was, from a ritual perspective, strong and healthy enough to receive unthreatened a cult as 'foreign' as that of Cybele.
50 Livy, 22.9; *ibid.*, 22.10.10; *ibid.*, 23.31.9; cf. Ov., *Fast.*, 4.873–876.
51 Tac., *Ann.*, 4.43; Suet., *Claud.*, 25.
52 Livy, 23.31.9.
53 Livy, 40.34.4; *ibid.*, 30.38.10; Ov., *Fast.*, 4.871. See also Platner–Ashby, *s.v. Venus Erucina, Aedes* (both entries).
54 Strabo, 6.2.6.
55 Varro, *Ling.*, 6.3.16. See also Masurius *ap.* Macrob., *Sat.*, 1.4.6.
56 See e.g., Dumézil 1970: 183 *et seq.*; Schilling 1982: 91 *et seq.*
57 Plut., *Quaest. Rom.*, 45.
58 See Schilling 1982: 100.
59 See e.g., the story of Myrrha as related by Ovid, *Met.*, 10.312 *et seq.*

4 THE USES OF VIRGINITY: THE VESTALS AND ROME

1 Without ceremony, that is, in comparison to the elaborate ritual of the punishment of the Vestal. Execution by public flogging can otherwise hardly be called unceremonious.
2 Cf. Fraschetti 1981, for an alternative interpretation of the ritual.
3 See Nock 1972: vol. 1, p. 254 with notes.
4 See Cornell 1981.
5 See MacBain 1982: esp. ch. 4. There appears to have been a formal procedure involved in the recognition and expiation of prodigies in which the senate played the central role. It was this body that decided which of the phenomena reported to them were to be recognized as prodigies. Having made the decision they then referred the matter to one of the priestly colleges. See Bloch 1963: 120–122. There is no evidence that the senate was involved in the trial and punishment of an unchaste Vestal.
6 MacBain 1982: 43. McBain assumes that all *haruspices* at Rome were Etruscans. North, however, observes that this need not have been the case, although *haruspices* appear generally to have been regarded as outsiders, whether this status was real or fictional. North 1989: 609. For my purpose this distinction does not much matter.
7 See e.g., Obsequens, 22; 32; 34; 36; 48. See also MacBain 1982: Appendix E. MacBain points out that apart from one instance (Obsequens, 27) of an androgyne cast into the river, they were all cast into the sea.
8 *Hominem mortum in urbe ne sepelito neve urito* – 'No corpse must be buried or burned within the City.' Cic., *Leg.*, 2.23.58. See also, Serv., *Aen.*, 11.143. There were individual exceptions. Plutarch writes that one of the honours granted to P. Valerius Publicola was that by the citizens' vote he was buried within the city walls in recognition of his services to the Roman people. This privilege was also granted to his descendants, but they availed themselves of it only symbolically. The body was carried into the city, a lighted torch placed for an instant underneath it, and then removed. Plut., *Publiocola*, 23. Generals who had celebrated a triumph also had a symbolic rite of burial within the city. After the body was cremated a single bone was taken into the city and buried there. See Plut., *Quaest. Rom.*, 79. See, generally, Robinson 1975.
9 Plut., *Quaest. Rom.*, 96. It is a pity that Plutarch is not more specific about which priests in particular made these offerings. It is tempting to assume that they were in fact members of the pontifical college who bore the responsibility of convicting the women. But we do not, unfortunately, have enough evidence to make such an argument possible.
10 Cornell 1981: 27–28.
11 For a discussion of the problem of human sacrifice in Rome, see MacBain 1982: 60–64 with references. The evidence suggests that human sacrifice could have taken place more often than the recorded instances might lead us to assume. The practice was outlawed as late as 97 BC. See also Fraschetti 1981.

12 Livy, 22.57.2; see also Plut., *Quaest. Rom.*, 83.
13 Modern scholarship has tended to lose sight of the fundamental importance of the notion of virginity to the institution of the Vestal Virgins.
Largely responsible for this trend has been Mary Beard's suggestion
that the Vestals were best seen as representing simultaneously the
characteristics of virgins, matrons and men, Beard 1980. For a direct
challenge to this theory and a deconstruction of its supporting argu-
ments see Staples 1993: 131 *et seq.* Beard appears now to have
retreated from her former position in an 'affectionate critique' of
herself. See Beard 1995.
14 In some societies to this day – orthodox Hindus in modern India are
a good example – a bride may be repudiated by her new husband if
he suspects on their wedding night that she did not come to him as a
virgin. The Romans never put a similar value on virginity. Though
adulterous wives could by law be killed by either father or husband,
and were on occasion, we have no examples of an unmarried girl
punished for losing her virginity.
15 For an analysis of the distinction between physiological and seman-
tically loaded virginity see Hastrup 1978.
16 Dio Cass., 47.19.4.
17 See e.g., Dion. Hal., *Ant. Rom.*, 8.89.3 *et seq.*; *ibid.*, 9.40.
18 Pliny, *Ep.*, 4.11.
19 See p. 134.
20 Livy, 22.57; Plut., *Fabius*, 18.4. North relates the trial of the Vestals
to the threat of invasion by the Cimbri and the Teutones. See North
1968. See also Cornell 1981.
21 Livy, *Epit.* 63; Dio Cass., 26.88.
22 For an evocative description of the emotions engulfing Rome in 216
and the desperate attempts by the authorities to quell the panic that
was caused by news of the defeat of the army, see Livy 22.54–56. The
loss of men was so great according to this account that the *sacrum
anniversarium Cereris* had to be omitted that year because all the
women were in mourning and mourners were not allowed to participate in the rites. The senate was forced to limit the usual ten-month
period of mourning to thirty days. Livy, 34.6.15. Plutarch, in a slightly
variant account, says that it was considered more prudent to omit the
festival because the small number and dejected mien of the participants would serve to emphasize the calamity that Rome had suffered.
Plut., *Fabius*, 18.2. In other words the omission of the festival was not
forced on the state as Livy suggests, but was a deliberate decision
taken to prevent aggravating the hysteria of the moment.
    For a discussion of the religious turmoil in the last 15 years of the
second century BC in the context of which the trials of 114 took place,
see Rawson 1974.
23 See p. 105.
24 See Rawson 1974: 207. She interprets this as a plebeian challenge to
the religious authority of the patricians.
25 Dion. Hal., *Ant. Rom.*, 3.67.2.
26 Scheid 1981: 146.
27 Pliny, *Ep.* 4.11.

NOTES

28 Plut., *Crass.*, 1.2.
29 Livy, 4.44.11.
30 Further examples are Dion. Hal., *Ant. Rom.*, 8.89; *ibid.*, 9.40.
31 The most comprehensive ancient account of the rules governing the Vestals is Gellius, *N.A.*, 1.12.
32 See p. 74.
33 Default rules are legislatively or judicially imposed rules that govern contracts unless the parties contract around the rules. Similarly a Roman citizen male could have children with any category of woman he pleased. But if he wanted children that were legally his, he had to possess the right of *conubium* with their mother and had to be in a relationship of *iustum matrimonium* with her. Otherwise the children would belong to her.
34 Gell., *N.A.*, 1.12.9, my emphasis.
35 'Three elements may be seen in a [person's] status in Roman law – liberty, citizenship, and family rights – and changes of status may be analysed accordingly. The Romans speak in this connection of *capitis deminutio*, or deterioration of status. *Capitis deminutio maxima* is the loss of all three elements, i.e. enslavement; *capitis deminutio media* is the loss of citizenship and family rights, usually as a punishment; and *capitis deminutio minima*, the most common, is the loss merely of family rights by either adoption, adrogation, marriage with *manus*, or emancipation.' Nicholas 1962: 96.
36 Nicholas 1962: 80.
37 See note 13, p. 182.
38 It is important to note that the new Vestal's status would also not correspond to her grandfather's status if he was still alive. Although neither would be subject to *patria potestas*, a *paterfamilias* exercised *potestas*, while a Vestal did not. This is a critical difference.
39 Some scholars have suggested that the Vestals were in the *potestas* of the *pontifex maximus*. See Lacey 1986: 126. The *pontifex* had disciplinary powers over the Vestals if they transgressed in their ritual duties, such as, for example, allowing the sacred fire in the temple to go out. He had absolutely no control over their property, which was a cornerstone of the institution of *patria potestas*. Cf. Gardner 1986a: 23. The controversy as to whether the *pontifex* stood in the position of father or husband to the Vestals is thus gratuitous.
40 Religious functionaries in Rome were as a rule not confined to their ritual duties. Men were by and large free to pursue other interests. Sometimes a rule governing a priesthood would clash with a rule governing some other area of activity and this could keep a man from pursuing some particular ambition. So, for example, the *flamen Dialis* appeared to be excluded from political office because the rule forbidding the *flamen* to swear an oath prevented him from taking the oath of office. Plut., *Quaest. Rom.*, 96; Dion. Hal., *Ant. Rom.*, 2.67.4–5. But these rules were circumvented, often ingeniously, when occasion demanded. In 209 BC, for example, the Senate allowed the *flamen Dialis*, G. Valerius Flaccus to take up the office of curule aedile by taking the oath of office

183

by proxy. Livy, 31.50. In the case of a Vestal it was never possible to bend the rules.

41 Plut., *Num.*, 10. A Vestal could in theory own considerable wealth. She was paid a sum of money when entering the priesthood by the state, and was thereafter supported by a stipend from the treasury. And although she had, of course, no intestate claim on anybody she was allowed to receive gifts and bequests. See Livy 1.20; Tac., *Ann.*, 4.16.

42 Pliny, *Ep.*, 7.19.

43 Scullard 1981: 75, with note 79.

44 Cic., *Cael.*, 14.34; Val. Max., 5.4.6; Suet., *Tib.*, 2.4. See also Cic., *Mur.*, 73.

45 See for example CIL 6.32414–32419. These all appear to be dedications to the same woman, Flavia Publicia, the *Virgo Vestalis Maxima*. Of these inscriptions, 32414 and 32415 record filiation, the others do not.

46 See Gardner 1986a: 5 and 24.

47 Dio Cass., 56.10.2.

48 For a discussion of the function of dress in maintaining ritual categories see pp. 68 *et seq.*

49 Plut., *Num.*, 10.3; Dio Cass., 47.19.4.

50 Plut., *Quaest. Rom.*, 81.

51 Festus, p. 82 L. See also Plut., *Quaest. Rom.*, 113.

52 In AD 14 a sycophantic senate proposed that Livia, who on Augustus' death became the *flaminica Divi Augusti*, should be granted the privilege of a *lictor*. Tiberius refused to allow this except when Livia was functioning as *flaminica*. Tac., *Ann.*, 1.14.3; Dio Cass. 56.46.2. According to Tacitus, Tiberius saw Livia as a threat to his own authority. To have allowed her the privilege of a *lictor* at all times would have marked her out as powerful, dangerously powerful as far as Tiberius was concerned. Granting a *lictor* to the *flaminica Divi Augusti*, however, was an indication of the importance given to the cult of Augustus. The *flaminica*, in this case Livia, derived her power from that of the cult. There was no political dimension to that power and hence no threat to Tiberius.

53 Festus, p. 454 L.

54 Pliny, *H.N.*, 8.7.194.

55 Festus, p. 55 L.

56 Festus p. 82 L; Pliny, *H.N.*, 21.22.46.

57 Festus, p. 79 L.

58 Beard 1980: 16.

59 For a discussion of the evidence for the nature of the *stola* see Wilson 1938: 155 *et seq.* See also Hor., *Sat.*, 1.2.94–95; Ov., *Ars Am.*, 1.31–32.

60 Wilson 1938: 159. See also Scholz 1992: esp. 88 *et seq.*

61 Livy, 1.20.3.

62 Dion. Hal., *Ant. Rom.*, 2.67.2–3; Plut., *Num.*, 10.2.

63 Beard 1980.

64 Pliny, *H.N.*, 28.3.13.

65 Dion. Hal., *Ant. Rom.*, 2.68–69.

66 Plut., *Num.*, 9.5. See also Dion. Hal., *Ant. Rom.*, 2.64.5. Cicero, in

NOTES

enumerating the religious laws of his ideal state, sees the tending of the public hearth fire as the Vestals' sole duty. Cic., *Leg.*, 2.8.20.
67 Cic., *Leg.*, 2.12.29; Ov., *Fast.*, 6.283 *et seq.*; Plut., *Num.*, 9.5; Dion. Hal., *Ant. Rom.*, 2.66
68 Cic., *Font.*, 21; Dionysius of Halicarnassus says it was potentially the most powerful signifier of the possibility that a Vestal might have been unchaste. Dion. Hal., *Ant. Rom.*, 2.67. However, the story of Aemilia indicates that it did not necessarily signify such an event.
69 Livy, 28.11.6–7; Plut., *Num.*, 10.4. Festus, p. 94. L.
70 Ov., *Fast.*, 6.295–298.
71 See the discussion on pp. 15 *et seq.*
72 The stories are very similar. For Romulus see Plut., *Rom.*, 2.3 *et seq.*; for Servius, Plut., *de Fort. Rom.*, 10; Ov., *Fast.*, 6.629 *et seq.*
73 Paul., *Dig.*, 48.1.2; see also Livy , 25.4; Cic., *Caecin.*, 100; Sall., *Cat.*, 51.
74 Plut., *Num.*, 13.2; see also Prop., 4.4, where the duties of a Vestal are poetically represented in terms of fetching water. Dumézil 1970: 319.
75 Ov., *Fast.*, 3.259 *et seq.*
76 Ov., *Fast.*, 3.143–144; Macrob., *Sat.*, 1.12.6.
77 See p. 148.
78 See Dion. Hal., *Ant. Rom.*, 2.67.5.
79 See Cornell 1981: 29 *et seq.* with references.
80 See Cic., *Rep.*, 2.31.53: *ne quis magistratus civem Romanum adversus provocationem necaret neve verberaret.* Cf. *ibid.*, 54, which suggests that the *ius provocationis* was, in fact, older than the Valerian Law. See also Dion. Hal., *Ant. Rom.*, 5.19.4, which suggests that the *ius* could be invoked in the case of lesser penalties as well. Note that Mommsen believed that women had no right to *provocatio*. Mommsen 1899: 143, 475. But there is no direct evidence as to this.
81 See p. 131.
82 It appears that the powers the *pontifices* had over the Vestals, in the matter of both trial and execution, were unique. Alan Watson writes of the usual powers of the college, 'No action was taken by the pontiffs on their responsum. It was declaratory only, to set out the proper conduct of men and gods, and it was not followed by execution of judgement. Nor could it be. It was not normally part of the college of Pontiffs' function to examine the facts. They responded only to the terms of the facts proposed to them.' Watson 1992: 6.
83 See note 39, p. 183.
84 Livy, 26.27.14; *ibid.*, 5.52.7. See also Cic., *Phil.*, 11.10.24.
85 See Plut., *Num.*, 9.8; Ov., *Fast.*, 6.417 *et seq.*; Dionysius of Halicarnassus says that both the Vestals and the *pontifex maximus* had access to the palladium. Dion. Hal., *Ant. Rom.*, 2.66. Ovid seems to suggest that it was only men, including the *pontifex maximus*, that were forbidden to see or touch the object. Ov., *op. cit.*, 6.4.17 *et seq.* There was a tradition that in 241 BC L. Caecilius Metellus, the *pontifex maximus*, was struck blind when he rescued the holy objects from a fire that engulfed the *aedes Vestae*. Pliny, *H.N.*, 7.43.139 *et seq.* Ovid mentions the rescue but not the blinding, Ov., *op. cit.*, 6.4.17 *et seq.* Dumézil points out that the story of Metellus' blinding must be apocryphal because he was elected

NOTES

dictator in 224. Dumézil 1970: 325.
86 Dion. Hal., *Ant. Rom.*, 2.66; Plut., *Num.*, 9.8; *ibid.*, *Cam.*, 20.3.
87 Dion. Hal., *Ant. Rom.*, 2.66; *ibid.*, 1.69; Plut., *Cam.*, 20.5.
88 Livy, 5.52.
89 Dion. Hal., *Ant. Rom.*, 24.2.; Festus, p. 124 L; Tib., 1.5.14.
90 *Immolare est mola, id est farre molito et sale hostiam perspersam sacrare.* Festus, p. 97 L.
91 Pliny, *H.N.*, 31.41.89.
92 Pliny, *H.N.*, 18.2.7; Plut., *Num.*, 14.
93 Cazanove 1987. Cazanove cites three factors as evidence for what he calls 'the ritual incapacity of Roman women'. These are the ancient prohibition against Roman matrons drinking undiluted wine (*temetum*); the belief that they were not allowed to grind corn; and the fact that they were not allowed to butcher meat. Since wine, ground corn in the form of *mola salsa* and animal sacrifice were essential elements in sacrifice, he concludes that women were excluded from sacrifice. There is no direct evidence that women could not sacrifice. On the contrary, we have many references to women sacrificing. An important one comes from Varro: *Romam ritu sacrificium feminae cum faciunt, capita velant* – 'According to Roman rites, when women perform sacrifice, they veil their heads', Varro, *Ling.*, 5.29.130. Prostitutes who touched the altar of Juno sacrificed to her a lamb, and widows who remarried before the required ten-month period of mourning was over sacrificed a pregnant cow. Cazanove's explanation is that neither prostitute nor widow were in *patria potestas* and they were therefore exempt from the prohibition. But a prostitute could well be in *patria potestas*, as could a widow who had married *sine manu* and whose father was still alive. Likewise, a wife married *sine manu* was free of *patria potestas* if her father had died. The *flaminica Dialis* and the *Regina Sacrorum* also offered animal sacrifice. Also, the prohibition against drinking wine applied only to matrons who comprised only one ritual category of women. Note also that consumption of wine was not a part of sacrifice. Wine was used in libation and there is no evidence that women were not allowed to pour libations. Also, wine is used in all female festivals, for example that of Bona Dea. As for butchering meat, the sacrificial animal was killed by a special functionary, the *popa*, and never by the sacrificer himself. So women would have been at no disadvantage in this regard. Finally, sacrifice was not limited to blood sacrifice. In sum, there is no evidence to support an argument that women were excluded from Roman sacrifice.
94 *Exesto, extra esto. Sic enim lictor in quibusdam sacris clamitabat: hostis, vinctus, mulier, virgo exesto.* Festus, p. 72 L. This passage of Festus has also been taken as evidence – by Scheid following Cazanove – suggestive of the fact that women in general were excluded from all sacrifice. However, this would make women the ritual equivalents of foreigners and prisoners in chains; again an absurd proposition given the evidence for the wide participation of women in state ritual. Also Festus is explicit on the point that the formula was not a general one: – *lictor* in quibusdam sacris *clamitabat* – If women were

186

excluded from *certain sacrifices* the implication must surely be that there were others in which women could participate.

95 The preparation of *mola salsa* also involved the ritual use of fire and water. Numa, who instituted the use of *mola salsa* in sacrifice, also decreed that the spelt – *far* – had to be toasted before it was ground to make the *mola*. Otherwise it would not be fit to offer the gods. Pliny, *H.N.*, 18.2.7. Thus preparation of the grain required the use of fire. The preparation of the brine formalized the use of water in that only water from a natural source might be used: *aquam . . . praeterquam per fistulas venit, addunt*. Festus, p. 152 L.

96 See p. 46, with note 141.

97 Ov., *Fast.*, 4.637–640; *ibid.*, 4.731–734.

98 See pp. 40 *et seq.*

99 Varro, *ap.* Gell., *N.A.*, 14.7.7; Serv., *Aen.*, 7.153. For the antiquity of the temple see Ov., *Fast.*, 6.257 *et seq.*; Dion. Hal., *Ant. Rom.*, 2.65–66; Plut., *Num.*, 11. See also Platner–Ashby, *s.v.* '*Vesta Aedes*'.

BIBLIOGRAPHY

PRIMARY SOURCES WITH ABBREVIATIONS USED IN THE TEXT

Apollod., *Bibl.*	Apollodorus, *Bibliotheca*
App., *B. Civ.*	Appian, *Bella Civilia*
Arn., *Adv. Nat.*	Arnobius, *Adversus Nationes*
Asc., *Mil.*	Asconius, *Commentary on Cicero, Pro Milone*
Aug.	Augustine
de Civ. D.	*De Civitate Dei*
Ep.	*Epistulae*
Cato, *Agr.*	Cato, *Agricultura*
Catull.	Catullus
Cic.	Cicero
ad Brut.	*Epistulae ad Brutum*
Att.	*Epistulae ad Atticum*
Balb.	*Pro Balbo*
Brut.	*Brutus*
Caecin.	*Pro Caecina*
Cael.	*Pro Caelio*
de Or.	*De Oratore*
Div.	*De Divinatione*
Dom.	*De Domo Sua*
Font.	*Pro Fonteio*
Har. Resp.	*De Haruspicium Responso*
Leg.	*De Legibus*
Mil.	*Pro Milone*
Mur.	*Pro Murena*
Nat. D.	*De Natura Deorum*
Phil.	*Oratores Philippicae*
Rab. Post.	*Pro Rabirio Postumo*
Rep.	*De Republica*
Top.	*Topica*
Verr.	*In Verrem*
CIL	Corpus Inscriptionum Latinarum

Dio Cass.	Dio Cassius, *Roman History*
Diod. Sic.	Diodorus Siculus, *Bibliotheke*
Dion. Hal., *Ant. Rom.*	Dionysius of Halicarnassus, *Antiquitates Romanae*
Festus	Festus [ed. W.M. Lindsay, Leipzig: Teubner, 1913]
G.	Gaius, *Institutiones*
Gell., *N.A.*	Aulus Gellius, *Noctes Atticae*
Hor., *Sat.*	Horace, *Saturae*
Hyginus, *Fab.*	Hyginus, *Fabulae*
Inst.	Justinian, *Institutiones*
Juv.	Juvenal, *Saturae*
Lactant., *Div. Inst.*	Lactantius, *Divinae Institutiones*
Livy	Livy, *Ab Urbe Condita*
Epit.	*Epitomae*
Per.	*Periochae*
Lucr., *De Rerum Natura*	Lucretius, *De Rerum Natura*
Lydus, *de Mens.*	Lydus, *De Mensibus*
Macr., *Sat.*	Macrobius, *Saturnalia*
Mart., *Epigrams*	Martial, *Epigrams*
Minucius Felix, *Oct.*	Minucius Felix, *Octavius*
Nepos, frg.	Cornelius Nepos, *Vitae Cum Fragmentis*
Obsequens	Obsequens
Ov.	Ovid
Ars Am.	*Ars Amatoria*
Fast.	*Fasti*
Met.	*Metamorphoses*
Paul., *Dig.*	Paulus, *Digest* (Justinian)
Pliny, *Ep.*	Pliny (the Younger), *Epistulae*
Pliny, *H.N.*	Pliny (the Elder), *Naturalis Historia*
Plut.	Plutarch
C. Gracch.	*Gaius Gracchus*
Caes.	*Caesar*
Cam.	*Camillus*
Cat. Min.	*Cato Minor*
Cic.	*Cicero*
Coniugalia Praecepta	*Coniugalia Praecepta*
Crass.	*Crassus*
de Fort. Rom.	*De Fortuna Romanorum*
Fabius	*Fabius*
Marc.	*Marcellus*
Num.	*Numa*
Pomp.	*Pompeius*
Publicola	*Publicola*
Quaest. Rom.	*Quaestiones Romanae*
Rom.	*Romulus*
Sull.	*Sulla*

Prop.	Propertius, *Elegia*
Quint., *Inst.*	Quintilian, *Institutio Oratoria*
Sall., *Cat.*	Sallust, *Bellum Catilinae*
Sen., *Ep.*	Seneca, *Epistulae*
Serv., *Aen.*	Servius, *Commentary on the Aeneid*
SHA, *Hadr.*	*Scriptores Historiae Augustae, Hadrian*
Soranus, *Gynaikeia*	Soranus, *Gynaikeia*
Strab.	Strabo, *Geographia*
Suet.	Suetonius
Aug.	*Divus Augustus*
Claud.	*Divus Claudius*
Iul.	*Divus Iulius*
Tib.	*Tiberius*
Tac.	Tacitus
Ann.	*Annales*
Dial.	*Dialogus de Oratoribus*
Tert., *De Spect.*	Tertullian, *De Spectaculis*
Tib.	Tibullus, *Carmina*
Val. Max.	Valerius Maximus, *Facta et Dicta Memorabilia*
Varro	Varro
Ling.	*De Lingua Latina*
Rust.	*Res Rustica*
Verg.	Virgil
Aen.	*Aeneid*
Ecl.	*Eclogues*

SECONDARY SOURCES

Altheim, F. (1938) *A History of Roman Religion*, London.

Ardener, Anderson, W. S. (1964) 'Hercules exclusus: Propertius 4.9', *American Journal of Philology* 85: 3 *et seq.*

S. (ed.) (1981) *Women and Space*, Oxford.

—— (ed.) (1982) *Perceiving Women*, London.

Azmon, Y. (1981) 'Sex, power and authority', *British Journal of Sociology* 32.4: 547 *et seq.*

Bailey, D. R. Shackleton (1965–1970) *Cicero's Letters to Atticus*, 7 vols, Cambridge.

Balsdon, J. P. V. D. (1962) *Roman Women: Their History and Habits*, London.

—— (1969) *Life and Leisure in Ancient Rome*, New York.

Banton, M. (ed.) (1966) *Anthropological Approaches to the Study of Religion*, New York.

Bauman, R. (1992) *Women and Politics in Ancient Rome*, London.

Bayet, J. (1926) *Les Origines de l'Hercule Romaine*, Paris.

—— (1957) *Histoire Politique et Psychologique de Religion Romaine*, Paris.

—— (1971) *Croyances et Rites dans la Rome Antique*, Paris.

Beard, M. (1980) 'The sexual status of the Vestal Virgins', *Journal of Roman Studies* 70: 12 *et seq.*

—— (1987) 'A complex of times: no more sheep on Romulus' birthday', *Proceedings of the Cambridge Philological Society* 213 (n.s.33): 1 *et seq.*

—— (1989) 'Acca Larentia gains a son: myths and priesthood at Rome', in M. M. Mackenzie and C. Roueché (eds), *Images of Authority. Papers Presented to Joyce Reynolds on the Occasion of her 70th Birthday*, Cambridge Philological Society, supplementary volume, 16.

—— (1995) 'Re-reading (Vestal) virginity', in R. Hawley and B. Levick (eds) *Women in Antiquity: New Assessments*, London and New York.

Beard, M. and Crawford, M. (1985) *Rome in the Late Republic*, Ithaca, NY.

Beard, M. and North, J. (eds) (1990) *Pagan Priests: Religion and Power in the Ancient World*, Ithaca, NY.

Bloch, R. (1963) *Les Prodiges dans l'Antiquité*, Paris.

Bömer, F. (1958) *P. Ovidius Naso. Die Fasten*, Heidelberg.

Bradley, K. R. (1986) 'Wet nursing at Rome: a study in social relations', in B. Rawson (ed.) *The Family in Ancient Rome: New Perspectives*, Ithaca, NY.

—— (1991) *Discovering the Roman Family: Studies in Roman Social History*, New York.

Braund, S. H. (1992) 'Juvenal – misogynist or misogamist?,' *Journal of Roman Studies* 82: 71 *et seq.*

Bremmer, J. (ed.) (1987a) *Interpretations of Greek Mythology*, London.

—— (1987b) 'Slow Cybele's Arrival', in J. Bremmer and N. Horsfall (eds) *Roman Myth and Mythography*, Institute of Classical Studies, Bulletin Supplement 52, London.

Bremmer, J. and Horsfall, N. (1987) *Roman Myth and Mythography*, Institute of Classical Studies, Bulletin Supplement 52, London.

Brouwer, H. H. J. (1989) *Bona Dea: The Sources and a Description of the Cult*, Leiden.

Bruhl, A. (1953) *Liber Pater*, Paris.

Bryson, N. (1986) 'Two narratives of rape in the visual arts: Lucretia and the Sabine women', in S. Tomaselli and R. Porter (eds) *Rape*, Oxford.

Burkert, W. (1979) *Structure and History in Greek Mythology and Ritual*, Berkeley, CA.

Cameron, A. and Kuhrt, E. (eds) (1983) *Images of Women in Antiquity*, London.

Cantarella, E. (1987) *Pandora's Daughters*, trans. M. Fant, Baltimore.

Cazanove, O. de (1987) 'Exesto. L'incapacité sacrificielle des femmes à Rome', *Phoenix* 41: 159 *et seq.*

Clark, G. (1981) 'Roman women', *Greece & Rome* 28: 193 *et seq.*

Cole, S. G. (1984) 'The social function of rituals of maturation: the Koureion and the Arkteia', *Zeitschrift für Papyrologie und Epigraphik* 55: 233 *et seq.*

Corbett, P. E. (1930) *The Roman Law of Marriage*, Oxford.

Corbier, M. (1991) 'Divorce and adoption as Roman familial strategies', in B. Rawson (ed.) *Marriage, Divorce and Children in Ancient Rome*, Oxford.

Cornell, T. (1975) 'Aeneas and the twins', *Proceedings of the Cambridge Philological Society* 21: 1 *et seq.*

—— (1981) 'Some observations on the "crimen incesti"' in *Le Délit Religieux dans la Cité Antique*, Collection de l'École Française de Rome, 48: 27 *et seq.*

Crook J. A. (1967a) *Law and Life of Rome*, Ithaca, NY.

—— (1967b) 'Patria Potestas', *Classical Quarterly* 17: 113 *et seq.*

—— (1986a) 'Women in Roman succession', in B. Rawson (ed.) *The Family in Ancient Rome: New Perspectives*, Ithaca, NY.

—— (1986b) 'Feminine inadequacy and the senatusconsultum Velleianum', in B. Rawson (ed.) *The Family in Ancient Rome: New Perspectives*, Ithaca, NY.

Culham, P. (1987) 'Ten years after Pomeroy: studies of the image and reality of women in antiquity', *Helios* 9: 30 *et seq.*

Cumont, F. (1913) *Les Mystères de Mithras*, Brussels.

Daremberg, C. and Saglio, E. (eds) (1877 on) *Dictionnaire des Antiquités Grecques et Romains*, Paris.

Degrassi, A. (1963) *Inscriptiones Italiae*, Rome.

Delaney, C. (1986) 'The meaning of paternity and the virgin birth debate', *Man* 21: 494 *et seq.*

Delcourt, M. (1961) *Hermaphrodite: Myths and Rites of the Bisexual Figure in Classical Antiquity*, London.

Detienne, M. (1977) *The Gardens of Adonis: Spices in Greek Mythology*, trans. J. Lloyd, Hassocks.

—— (1981a) *L'Invention de la Mythologie*, Paris.

—— (1981b) 'The myth of honeyed Orpheus', in R. L. Gordon (ed.) *Myth, Religion and Society*, Cambridge.

—— (1989) *L'Écriture d'Orphée*, Paris.

Dixon, S. (1984) 'Infirmitas sexus: womanly weakness in Roman law', *Tijdschrift voor Rechtsgeschiedenis* 52: 343 *et seq.*

—— (1985) 'The marriage alliance in the Roman elite', *Journal of Family History* 10: 353 *et seq.*

—— (1988) *The Roman Mother*, Norman, OK.

—— (1992) *The Roman Family*, Baltimore.

Donaldson, I. (1982) *The Rapes of Lucretia: A Myth and its Transformation*, Oxford.

Douglas, M. (1966) *Purity and Danger: An Analysis of Concepts of Pollution and Taboo*, London.

—— (1967) 'The meaning of myth', in E. R. Leach (ed.) *The Structural Study of Myth and Totemism*, London.

—— (1975) *Implicit Meanings: Essays in Anthropology*, London.

Dumézil, G. (1963) 'Te, amata capio', *Revue des Études Latines* 41: 89 *et seq.*

—— (1970) *Archaic Roman Religion*, trans. P. Krapp, Chicago.

—— (1975) *Fêtes Romaines d'Été et d'Automne*, Paris.

—— (1979) *Ideés Romaines*, Paris.

—— (1988) *Mitra-Varuna*, trans. D. Coltman, New York.

Dupont, F. (1992) *Daily Life in Ancient Rome*, trans. C. Woodall, Oxford.

Durkheim, E. (1965) *The Elementary Forms of the Religious Life*, trans. J. W. Swain, New York.

Evans-Pritchard, E. E. (1965a) *Theories of Primitive Religion*, Oxford.

—— (1965b) *The Position of Women in Primitive Societies and Other Essays in Social Anthropology*, New York.

Eyben, E. (1972) 'Antiquity's view of puberty', *Latomus* 31: 678 *et seq.*

Fantham, E. (1992) 'Ceres, Liber and Flora: Georgic and anti-Georgic elements in Ovid's *Fasti* ', *Proceedings of the Cambridge Philological Society* 38: 391 *et seq.*

Fau, G. (1978) *L'Émancipation Féminine à Rome*, Paris.

Feeney, D. C. (1991) *The Gods in Epic: Poets and Critics of the Classical Tradition*, Oxford.

Finley, M. I. (1968) *Aspects of Antiquity*, New York.

—— (ed.) (1974) *Studies in Ancient Society*, London.

Floratos, C. (1960) 'Veneralia', *Hermes* 88: 197 *et seq.*

Foley, H. P. (ed.) (1982) *Reflections of Women in Antiquity*, New York.

Fordyce, C. J. (1977) *Aeneid Books 7–8 with a Commentary*, Oxford.

Foucault, M. (1977) *Discipline and Punish: The Birth of the Prison*, trans. A. Sheridan, New York.

—— (1978; 1985; 1986) 1. *The History of Sexuality* 2. *The Use of Pleasure* 3. *The Care of the Self*, trans. R. Hurley, New York.

Fraschetti, A. (1981) 'Le sepolture rituali del Foro Boario', in *Le Délit Religieux dans la Cité Antique*, Collection de l'École Française de Rome 48: 50 *et seq.*

Frazer, J. G. (1929) *Publii Ovidii Nasonis Fastorum Libri Sex*, 5 vols, London.

Friedländer (1922) *Darstellung aus der Sittengeschichte Roms*, 10th edn, Leipzig.

Gagé, J. (1963) *Matronalia*, Brussels.

Galinsky, G. K. (1966) 'The Hercules–Cacus Episode in Aeneid VIII', *American Journal of Philology* 87: 18 *et seq.*

—— (1969) *Aeneas, Sicily and Rome*, Princeton, NJ.

—— (1972) *The Herakles Theme*, Totowa, NJ.

Gardner, J. F. (1986a) *Women in Roman Law and Society*, London.

—— (1986b) *Proofs of Status in the Roman World*, Bulletin of the Institute of Classical Studies 33, London.

Garnsey, P. (1970) *Social Status and Legal Privilege in the Roman Empire*, Oxford.

Garnsey, P. and Saller, R. (1987) *The Roman Empire: Economy, Society and Culture*, Berkeley, CA.

Geertz, C. (1973) *Interpretations of Culture*, New York.

Gellner, E. (1985) *Relativism and the Social Sciences*, Cambridge.

Gilmartin, K. (1968) 'Hercules in the Aeneid', *Vergilius* 14: 41 *et seq.*

Gordon, A. D., Buhle, M. J. and Dye, N. S. (1976) 'The problem of women's history', in B. A. Carrol (ed.) *Liberating Women's History*, Urbana, IL.

Gordon, R. L. (1980) 'Reality, evocation and boundary in the mysteries of Mithras', *Journal of Mithraic Studies* 3:19 *et seq.*

—— (ed.) (1981) *Myth, Religion and Society: Structuralist Essays by M. Detienne, L. Gernet, J.-P. Vernant and P. Vidal-Naquet*, Cambridge and Paris.

—— (1988) 'Authority, salvation and mystery in the mysteries of Mithras', in M. Beard, J. Huskinson and J. Reynolds (eds) *Image and Mystery in the Roman World: Papers given in Memory of Joscelyn Toynbee*, Cambridge.

Gould, J. (1980) 'Law, custom and myth: aspects of the social position of women in classical antiquity', *Journal of Hellenic Studies* 100: 38 *et seq.*

Grant, M. (1971) *Roman Myths*, New York.

—— (1992) *Greeks and Romans: A Social History*, London.

Greenidge, A. H. J. (1901) *The Legal Procedure of Cicero's Time*, Oxford.

Grimal, P. (ed.) (1965–1974) *Histoire Mondiale de la Femme*, 4 vols, Paris.

Gruen, E. S. (1990) *Studies in Greek Culture and Roman Policy*, Leiden.

Guizzi, F. (1962) *Il Sacerdozio di Vesta. Aspetti Giuridici dei Culti Romani*, Naples.

Hallett, J. P. (1984) *Fathers and Daughters in Roman Society: Women and the Elite Family*, Princeton.

—— (1989) 'Women as same and other in classical Roman elite', *Helios* 16.1: 59 *et seq.*

Hastrup, K. (1978) 'The semantics of biology: virginity', in S. Ardener (ed.) *Defining Females*, New York.

Hawley, R. and Levick, B. (eds) (1995) *Women in Antiquity: New Assessments*, London and New York.

Henderson, J. (1989) 'Satire writes "Woman": Gendersong', *Proceedings of the Cambridge Philological Society* 35: 50 *et seq.*

Hillard, T. (1989) 'Republican politics, women and the evidence', *Helios* 16.2: 165 *et seq.*

Hopkins, K. (1965) 'The age of Roman girls at marriage', *Population Studies* 18: 309 *et seq.*

—— (1983) *Death and Renewal*, Cambridge.

—— (1991) 'From violence to blessing: symbols and rituals in ancient Rome', in A. Molho, K. Raaflaub and J. Emlen (eds) *City States in Classical Antiquity and Medieval Italy*, Stuttgart.

Humbert, M. (1972) *Le Remariage à Rome: Étude d'Histoire Juridique et Sociale*, Milan.

Humphreys, S. (1978) *Anthropology and the Greeks*, London.

Jocelyn, H. D. (1966) 'The Roman nobility and the religion of the Republican state', *Journal of Religious History* 4: 89 *et seq.*

Jolowicz, H. F. and Nicholas, B. (1972) *Historical Introduction to the Study of Roman Law*, 3rd edn, Cambridge.

Kertzer, D. I. and Saller, R. P. (ed.) (1991) *The Family in Italy from Antiquity to the Present*, New Haven and London.

Keyes, C. W. (1928) *Cicero: De Re Publica; De Legibus*, Loeb Classical Library, Cambridge.

Kirk, G. S. (1970) *Myth, its Meanings and Functions in Ancient and Other Cultures*, Cambridge.

Kraemer, R. S. (ed.) (1988) *Maenads, Martyrs, Matrons, Monastics: A Source Book on Women's Religions in the Greco-Roman World*, Philadelphia.

—— (1992) *Her Share of the Blessings: Women's Religions among Pagans, Jews, and Christians in the Greco-Roman World*, New York and Oxford.

Krenkel, W. (1988) 'Prostitution', in M. Grant and R. Kitzinger (eds) *Civilization of the Ancient Mediterranean*, New York.

Lacey, W. K. (1986) 'Patria Potestas', in B. Rawson (ed.) *The Family in Ancient Rome*, Ithaca, NY.

Latte, K. (1960) *Römische Religionsgeschichte*, Munich.

—— (1967) *The Structural Study of Myth and Totemism*, London.
—— (1969) *Genesis as Myth and Other Essays*, London.
—— (1976) *Culture and Communication: The Logic by which Symbols are Connected*, Cambridge.
Leach, E. R. and Aycock, D. A. (1983) *Structuralist Interpretations of Biblical Myth*, Cambridge.
Le Bonniec, H. (1958) *Le Culte de Cérès à Rome. Des Origines à la Fin de la République*, Paris.
Lefkowitz, M. R. (1983) 'Wives and husbands', *Greece & Rome* 30.1: 31 *et seq.*
Lefkowitz, M. R. and Fant, M. B. (1982) *Women's Life in Greece and Rome: A Sourcebook*, London.
Lévi-Strauss, C. (1963) *Structural Anthropology*, trans. C. Jacobson and B. Grundfest, New York.
Liebeschuetz, J. H. W. G. (1979) *Continuity and Change in Roman Religion*, Oxford.
Littleton, C. S. (1982) *The New Comparative Mythology: An Anthropological Assessment of the Theories of Georges Dumézil*, Berkeley and Los Angeles.
MacBain, B. (1982) *Prodigy and Expiation: A Study in Religion and Politics in Republican Rome*, Brussels.
MacCormack, G. (1975) 'Wine drinking and the Romulan law of divorce', *Irish Jurist*, n.s. 10: 170 *et seq.*
McDonnell, M. (1987) 'The speech of Numidicus at Gellius *N.A.* 1.6', *American Journal of Philology* 108.1: 81 *et seq.*
McGinn, T. A. J. (1989) 'The taxation of Roman prostitutes', *Helios* 16.1: 79 *et seq.*
Maxwell-Stuart, P. G. (1972) 'Myrtle and the Eleusinian mysteries', *Wiener Studien* 85: 10 *et seq.*
Merlin, A. (1906) *L'Aventin dans l'Antiquité*, Paris.
Mernissi, F. (1977) 'Women, saints, and sanctuaries', *Signs* 3.1: 101 *et seq.*
Michels, A. K. (1967) *The Calendar of the Roman Republic*, Princeton.
Momigliano, A. (1955–1984) *Contributi alla Storia degli Studi Classici*, Rome.
—— (1984) 'The theological efforts of the Roman upper classes in the first century BC', *Classical Philology* 79: 199 *et seq.*
Mommsen, T. (1899) *Römisches Strafrecht*, Leipzig.
Moreau, P. (1982) *Clodiana Religio: Un Procès Politique en 61 Av. J.C.*, Paris.
Nicholas, B. (1962) *An Introduction to Roman Law*, Oxford.
Nicolet, C. (ed.) (1970) *Recherches sur les Structures Sociales dans l'Antiquité Classique*, Paris.
Nock, A. D. (ed.) Z. Stewart (1972) *Essays on Religion and the Ancient World*, 2 vols, Oxford.
North, J. A. (1968) 'The inter-relation of state religion and politics from the second Punic War to the time of Sulla', Oxford: unpublished D.Phil. dissertation.
—— (1976) 'Conservatism and change in Roman religion', *Papers of the British School at Rome* 44: 1 *et seq.*
—— (1979) 'Religious toleration in Republican Rome', *Proceedings of the Cambridge Philological Society* 205, n.s. 25: 85 *et seq.*
—— (1983) 'These he cannot take', *Journal of Roman Studies* 73: 169 *et seq.*

—— (1986) 'Religion and politics from republic to principate', *Journal of Roman Studies* 76: 251 *et seq.*

—— (1989) 'Religion in Republican Rome', *Cambridge Ancient History* 7.2: 573 *et seq.*

O'Flaherty, W. D. (1973) *Asceticism and Eroticism in the Myth of Siva*, New York.

—— (1980) *Women, Androgynes and Other Mythical Beasts*, Chicago.

Ogilvie, R. M. (1965) *A Commentary on Livy, Books 1–5*, Oxford.

Peradotto, J. and Sullivan, J. P. (eds) (1984) *Women in the Ancient World: The Arethusa Papers*, Albany, NY.

Piccaluga, G. (1964) 'Bona Dea, due contributi all' interpretazione del suo culto', *Studie Materiali de Storia delle Religioni* 35: 195 *et seq.*

Piganiol, A. (1923) *Recherches sur les Jeux Romains*, Strasbourg.

Platner, S. B. and Ashby, T. (1929) *A Topographical Dictionary of Ancient Rome*, Oxford.

Pomeroy, S. B. (1975) *Goddesses, Whores, Wives and Slaves*, New York.

—— (1976) 'The relationship of the married woman to her blood relatives in Rome', *Ancient Society* 7: 215 *et seq.*

—— (ed.) (1991) *Women's History and Ancient History*, Chapel Hill & London.

Purcell, N. (1986) 'Livia and the womanhood of Rome', *Proceedings of the Cambridge Philological Society* 212 n.s. 32: 78 *et seq.*

Raditsa, L. F. (1980) 'Augustus' legislation concerning marriage, procreation, love affairs and adultery', *Aufstieg und Niedergang der Römischen Welt* 2.13: 278 *et seq.*

Rawson, B. (1974) 'Roman concubinage and other "de facto" marriages', *Transactions of the American Philological Association* 104: 279 *et seq.*

—— (ed.) (1986) *The Family in Ancient Rome: New Perspectives*, Ithaca, NY.

—— (1989) 'Spurii and the Roman view of illegitimacy', *Antichthon* 23: 10 *et seq.*

—— (ed.) (1991) *Marriage, Divorce, and Children in Ancient Rome*, Oxford.

Rawson, E. (1974) 'Religion and politics in the late second century BC at Rome', *Phoenix* 28: 193 *et seq.*

Riccobono, S. *et al.* (eds) (1940–1943) *Fontes Iuris Romani Anteiustiniani*, 3 vols, Florence.

Richlin, A. (1983) *The Garden of Priapus: Sexuality and Aggression in Roman Humour*, New Haven and London.

—— (1984) 'Invective against women in Roman Satire', *Arethusa* 17.1: 67 *et seq.*

—— (1992) *Pornography and Representation in Greece and Rome*, New York.

Robinson, O. (1975) 'The Roman law on burials and burial grounds', *Irish Jurist*, n.s. 10: 175 *et seq.*

Roscher, W. H. (ed.) (1884 on.) *Ausführliches Lexikon der Griechischen und Römischen Mythologie*, Leipzig.

Rose, H. J. (1926) 'De Virginibus Vestalibus', *Mnemosyne*, n.s. 54: 440 *et seq.*

Rosenblum, K. E. (1975) 'Female deviance and the female sex role: a preliminary investigation', *British Journal of Sociology* 26.2: 169 *et seq.*

Rouselle, A. (1983) *Porneia: On Desire and the Body in Antiquity*, trans. F. Pheasant, Oxford.

Ryberg, I. S. (1955) 'Rites of the state religion in Roman art', *Memoirs of the American Academy at Rome* 22.

Saller, R. P. (1980) 'Anecdotes as historical evidence for the principate', *Greece & Rome* 27: 69 *et seq.*

—— (1984) 'Familia, Domus and the Roman conception of the family', *Phoenix* 38: 336 *et seq.*

—— (1986) 'Patria Potestas and the stereotype of the Roman family', *Continuity and Change* 1: 7 *et seq.*

—— (1987) 'Men's age at marriage and its consequences in the Roman family', *Classical Philology* 82: 21 *et seq.*

—— (1991) 'Roman heirship strategies', in D. I. Kertzer and R. P. Saller (eds) *The Family in Italy from Antiquity to the Present*, New Haven and London.

Sanders, H. A. (1938) 'A Latin marriage contract', *Transactions of the American Philological Association* 69: 104 *et seq.*

Scheid, J. (1981) 'Le délit religieux dans la Rome tardo-républicaine', in *Le Délit Religieux dans la Cité Antique*, Collection de l'École Française de Rome 48.

—— (1985a) *Religion et Piété à Rome*, Paris.

—— (1985b) 'Numa et Jupiter ou les dieux citoyens de Rome', *Archives de Sciences Sociales des Religions* 59.1: 41 *et seq.*

—— (1986) 'Le flamine de Jupiter, les Vestales et le général triomphant: variations romaines sur le thème de la figuration des dieux', *Le Temps de la Reflexion* 7: 213 *et seq.*

—— (1990) *Romulus et ses Frères: Le Collège des Frères Arvales: Modèle du Culte Public dans la Rome des Empereurs*, Rome.

—— (1992a) 'The religious roles of Roman women', in P. S. Pantel (ed.) *From Ancient Goddesses to Christian Saints*, trans. A. Goldhammer, Cambridge and London.

—— (1992b) 'Myth, cult and reality in Ovid's *Fasti* ', *Proceedings of the Cambridge Philological Society* 38: 118 *et seq.*

Schilling, R. (1979) *Rites, Cultes, Dieux de Rome*, Paris.

—— (1982) *La Religion Romaine de Venus*, 2nd edn, Paris.

Schneider, J. (1971) 'Of vigilance and virgins', *Ethnology* 9: 1 *et seq.*

Scholz, B. I. (1992) *Untersuchungen zur Tracht der Römischen Matrona*, Cologne.

Scullard, H. H. (1980) *History of the Roman World from 753 to 146 BC*, 4th edn, London.

—— (1981) *Festivals and Ceremonies of the Roman Republic*, London.

Seltman, C. (1956) *Women in Antiquity*, London.

Skinner, M. (ed.) (1987) 'Rescuing Creusa: new methodological approaches to women in antiquity', *Helios*, n.s. 13.2.

Small, J. P. (1982) *Cacus and Marsyas in Etrusco-Roman Legend*, Princeton.

Sperber, D. (1975) *Rethinking Symbolism*, trans. A. Morton, Cambridge.

—— (1985) 'Anthropology and psychology: towards an epidemiology of representations', *Man*, n.s. 20.1: 73 *et seq.*

Stambaugh, J. E. (1978) 'The functions of Roman temples', *Aufstieg und Niedergang der Römischen Welt* 16.1: 584 *et seq.*

Staples, A. (1993) *Gender and Boundary in Roman Religion*, Cambridge: unpublished Ph.D dissertation.

Stehle, E. (1989) 'Venus, Cybele and the Sabine women: the Roman construction of female sexuality', *Helios* 16.2: 143 *et seq.*

Sutton, D. (1977) 'The Greek origins of the Cacus myth', *Classical Quarterly*, n.s. 27: 391 *et seq.*

Szemler, G. J. (1972) *The Priests of the Roman Republic*, Brussels.

Tanner, R. G. (1970–1971) 'Some problems in Aeneid 7–12', *Proceedings of the Vergil Society* 10: 37 *et seq.*

Taylor, L. R. (1949) *Party Politics in the Age of Caesar*, Berkeley, CA.

Thomas, Y. (1992) 'The division of the sexes in Roman law', in P. S. Pantel (ed.) *From Ancient Goddesses to Christian Saints*, trans. A. Goldhammer, Cambridge and London.

Treggiari, S. (1982) 'Consent to Roman marriage: some aspects of law and reality', *Échos du Monde Classique/Classical Views*, n.s. 1: 34 *et seq.*

—— (1991a) 'Divorce Roman style: how easy and how frequent was it?', in B. Rawson (ed.) *Marriage, Divorce and Children in Ancient Rome*, Oxford.

—— (1991b) *Roman Marriage: iusti coniuges from the Time of Cicero to the Time of Ulpian*, Oxford.

Turner, T. S. (1977) 'Narrative structure and mythopoesis: a critique and reformulation of structuralist concepts of myth, narrative and poetics', *Arethusa* 10.1: 103 *et seq.*

Van Gennep, A. (1960) *The Rites of Passage*, trans. M. Vizedom and G. Caffee, Chicago.

Vermaseren, M. J. (1963) *Mithras, the Secret God*, trans. T. and V. Megaw, London.

—— (1977) *Cybele and Attis*, trans. A. M. H. Lemmers, London.

Vernant, J. P. (1965) *Mythe et Pensée chez les Grecs*, Paris.

Versnel, H. S. (1970) *Triumphus*, Leiden.

—— (1993) *Transition and Reversal in Myth and Ritual*, Leiden.

Veyne, P. (1983) 'Le folklore à Rome et les droits de la conscience publique sur la conduite individuelle', *Latomus* 42.1: 3 *et seq.*

Wadley, S. S. (1977) 'Women and the Hindu tradition', *Signs* 3.1: 113 *et seq.*

Wallace-Hadrill, A. (1981) 'Family and inheritance in the Augustan marriage laws', *Proceedings of the Cambridge Philological Society* 207: 58 *et seq.*

—— (1987) 'Time for Augustus: Ovid, Augustus and the *Fasti* ', in M. Whitby, P. Hardie and M. Whitby (eds) *Homo Viator: Classical Essays for John Bramble*, Bristol.

—— (1988) 'The social structure of the Roman house', *Papers of the British School at Rome* 56: 43 *et seq.*

Warde Fowler, W. (1899) *The Roman Festivals of the Period of the Republic*, London.

—— (1911) *The Religious Experience of the Roman People from the Earliest Times to the Age of Augustus*, London.

—— (1914) *Roman Ideas of Deity in the Last Century before the Christian Era*, London.

Wardman, A. (1982) *Religion and Statecraft among the Romans*, Baltimore.

Warner, M. (1976) *Alone of All her Sex: The Myth and Cult of the Virgin Mary*, London.

Watson, A. (1961) '"Captivitas" and "matrimonium"', *Tijdschrift voor Rechtsgeschiedenis* 29: 243 *et seq.*

—— (1965) 'The divorce of Carvilius Ruga', *Tijdschrift voor Rechtsgeschiedenis* 33: 38 *et seq.*

—— (1967) *The Law of Persons in the Later Roman Republic*, Oxford.

—— (1970a) *The Law of the Ancient Romans*, Dallas.

—— (1970b) 'The development of the praetor's edict', *Journal of Roman Studies* 60: 105 *et seq.*

—— (1974) *Law Making in the Later Roman Republic*, Oxford.

—— (1975) *Rome of the XII Tables: Persons and Property*, Princeton.

—— (1991) *Studies in Roman Private Law*, London and Rio Grande.

—— (1992) *The State, Law and Religion: Pagan Rome*, Athens, GA.

Wiedemann, T. E. J. (1989) *Adults and Children in the Roman Empire*, London.

Williams, G. (1958) 'Some aspects of Roman marriage ceremonies and ideals', *Journal of Roman Studies* 48: 16 *et seq.*

Wilson, L. M. (1924) *The Roman Toga*, Baltimore.

—— (1938) *The Clothing of the Ancient Romans*, Baltimore.

Winter, J. G. (1910) 'The myth of Hercules at Rome', in H. A. Sanders (ed.) *Roman History and Mythology*, Ann Arbor, MI.

Wiseman, T. P. (1974) *Cinna the Poet and Other Roman Essays*, Leicester.

—— (1979) *Clio's Cosmetics*, Leicester.

—— (1983) 'The wife and children of Romulus', *Classical Quarterly* 33: 445 *et seq.*

Wissowa, G. (1912) *Religion und Kultus der Romer*, 2nd edn, Munich.

Zarker, J. W. (1972) 'The Hercules theme in the Aeneid', *Vergilius* 18: 34 *et seq.*

Zeitlin, F. I. (1982) 'Cultic models of the female: rites of Dionysus and Demeter', *Arethusa* 15: 129 *et seq.*

—— (1986) 'Configurations of rape in Greek myth', in S. Tomaselli and R. Porter (eds) *Rape*, Oxford.

INDEX

Le Bonniec, H. 157
lectisternium 115
Liber 12, 49, 87–8, 157; temple of,
    86, 89, 90; *see also* Liberalia
Libera, 12, 49, 87; temple of, 86, 89
Liberalia 88–9
Licinia 138; *see also* Vestal Virgins
Licinius, L. Porcius 121
lictor 145–7
Livy 59–62, 70, 71–2, 74–5, 80–2,
    83, 113, 115–16, 134, 138, 147,
    153, 160
Lucretia 56, 62, 71, 80–2, 104
Lupa 63, 64; *see also* Acca Larentia;
    wolf
Luperci 69, 118
Lydus 109, 110
lyric 4

MacBain, B. 133
Macrobius 17, 24, 29, 31, 65, 99,
    109, 125
Magna Mater 62, 104, 115, 116–20
male and female, opposition of 16,
    17, 27, 28; *see also* fire and
    water, opposition of; myth:
    aetiological (*Ara Maxima*)
manus 75
Marcia 76
Marcus Aurelius 76
maritalis affectio 72, 85–6
Mark Antony 69
marriage 12, 17, 29, 57, 59, 72–3,
    76, 77, 83, 85, 87, 88–90; *cum
    manu* 75, 141, 142; *sine manu*
    75, 76, 142; *see also* Ceres, in
    marriage, function of; *iustum
    matrimonium*
Mars 63, 64, 74, 115
Mars Gradivus 6
Masurius Sabinus 66, 86
Mater Matuta 5
matronae 6, 7, 30, 31, 42, 46, 48,
    50, 56, 62–3, 71, 72, 76, 80–3,
    84, 86, 103–4, 113, 117, 139–40,
    146 (*see also stola; univira*); as
    ritual category 58, 67–8, 70,
    89–92, 97, 106, 111 (*see also*
    categorization); chastity of 104,

119–20 (*see also* Lucretia); *see
    also* misogynistic discourse
    concerning 55–6, 59–62
Medea 41; *see also* Bona Dea
men, political dominance of 2, 55,
    60–1; religious roles of, 5, 6, 11,
    13, 14, 42–3, 92–3, 110
meretrix 70; *see also* prostitutes
Mezentius 122–3
milk 12, 44, 45, 46, 47, 49–50, 100
misogyny 55–8, 59–62, 77
mistress 31; *see also* concubine
Mithras, rites of 36–8, 40
mola salsa see Vestal Virgins: ritual
    duties of
Mommsen, T. 109–10, 111
mother 73, 79, 140; of Coriolanus
    62; of Romulus 62–5; *see also*
    Acca Larentia; Rhea Silvia
myrtle 28, 44, 47, 99–107, 110, 112,
    122, 125, 157
myth 4, 28, 56, 71, 149;
    aetiological (*Ara Maxima*) 12,
    15, 17–24, 24–30, 31, 35–6,
    164n.9; aetiological (Bona Dea)
    12, 15, 28, 29, 35–6, 41, 47, 49,
    82, 99–100, 125–6; aetiological
    (Faunus), 12, 34; aetiological
    (Venus Verticordia), 103–4; of
    Romulus' birth 62–3; of the
    Sabine women 28–9, 67, 71–2,
    76; *see also* Acca Larentia;
    Carmenta; Lucretia

Numa 6, 33–4, 35, 71, 80, 148, 150,
    154
Numidicus, Q. Metellus 57

Obsequens 134
Omphale 27–8, 34, 35
ovatio 101
Ovid 11, 17–18, 20–2, 30, 33–4, 41,
    45–6, 48, 66–7, 85, 87, 93, 104,
    107, 109–12, 117, 118, 121–4

Pales 47, 50
palla 69
Parentalia 66–7, 143–4

Tarentum 14
Tarquinius Collatinus 80–1
Tarquinius Priscus 137
Tarutilus 65, 66
Terentia 42, 160
Tertullian 92
Tiberius 120
Tibullus 46, 47, 50
Tiresias 28,
Titus Tatius 75
toga: worn by children 89; worn
  by men 68–9, 70, 88; worn by
  prostitutes 70
togata see toga: worn by
  prostitutes
togatus see toga: worn by men
torches: at the Floralia, 93; at
  weddings, 84–6, 90
Treggiari, S. 77
Turnus 122
tunic: worn by men, 68–9, 70;
  worn by women, 69; *see also*
  stola; tunica recta
tunica recta 89, 146
tutor 143, 160

univira 79
uxor see matronae

Valerius 59, 61, 62, 160
Valerius Maximus 48, 70, 104, 119
Van Gennep, A. 146
Varro 16, 66, 121, 123, 149, 155
Veii 153; *see also* Juno Regina
Venus 8, 12, 16, 97, 99–102, 115,
  120, 121
Venus Erycina 98, 103, 114, 120;
  temple of, 121–3
Venus Obsequens 98, 103, 113
Venus Verticordia 5, 98, 102–13;
  see also Fortuna Virilis
Vermaseren 119
Verrius Flaccus 109, 111
Versnel, H.S. 12, 43
Vesta 8, 12, 106
Vestal Virgins 4, 6, 13, 39, 41, 42,
  44, 46, 63, 79, 104–6, 117;
  isolation of 140, 143– 4, 152;
  legal status of 141–3, 145; live

interment of 129, 132–3, 137;
  miraculous powers of 148;
  natural relationships of 144;
  and the palladium 152– 3;
  personal appearance of 145–7;
  and the political stability of
  Rome 135–7; and the *pontifex*
  maximus 137, 143, 148;
  punishment of the lovers of
  137; qualifications of 129,
  138–40; ritual duties of 148,
  150, 154–5; ritual status of 143,
  147; social life of 136, 145, 161;
  unchaste, trial of 136; *see also*
  crimen incesti; lictor; Rhea
  Silvia
Vinalia Priora 122–5
Vinalia Rustica 113
violence 12, 27, 28–30, 81–2, 90,
  99
Virgil 17, 18, 19, 20, 21, 22, 26, 27,
  33, 51, 84
virgins 29, 58, 62, 78, 104, 111, 117
vis see violence
Vulcan 18, 20

Wardman, A. 8
water 12, 16, 25, 27, 28; as
  representation of the female
  principle 16, 17, 149; *see also*
  fire and water, opposition of
Watson, A. 78
weddings, rituals connected with
  29, 85, 89, 149; torch of white
  pine used at 84–5, 90
Wilson, L.M. 69, 70
wine 12, 17, 33, 44, 45, 46, 47, 90,
  93, 99–100, 121; as representing
  maleness, 48–9, 51, 87, 100,
  126; and women, 48–9; *see also*
  Liber
Wissowa, G. 133
wives 78; *see also matronae*
wolf 63, 64
women: in antiquity, scholarship
  on 1; elite 30; goddess of 31
  (*see also* Bona Dea); old *see*
  anus; Roman, absence of
  constitutional role of 2, 3, 7, 8,